Two Left Feet

Tomasina Decrescenzo

Copyright © 2022 Tomasina Decrescenzo
All rights reserved
First Edition

PAGE PUBLISHING
Conneaut Lake, PA

First originally published by Page Publishing 2022

ISBN 978-1-6624-2410-6 (pbk)
ISBN 978-1-6624-2411-3 (digital)

Printed in the United States of America

DEDICATION

To the melting pot of characters
On the block where I grew up—
Thank you for molding and shaping me
Into the person I was destined to become.
And to Fannie—
Who always added heat to the pot
With a twinkle of her eye and a
Sprinkle of her hot Sicilian pepper flakes.

CHILDHOOD FRIENDS

Childhood friends are the comfort of home
Without the fight.
Siblings once removed,
Relaxed as worn-out shoes,
They see through your skin,
Know where you've been.
No need to compete,
Nothing to prove.
You knew each other when
You had nothing to lose.

INTRODUCTION

In a way, it seems as though it were a million years ago, and at the same time, I can remember it as though it were yesterday. I suppose that it's because the experience occupies that very special place in human memory, the place where only childhood experiences reside. Untouched and unharmed by the wounds of time and the scars of adulthood, they lie fresh and sweet in their own private alcove, never gathering moss, never stale, never stagnant. They are easily accessible and readily available. You can draw on their fragrant aroma whenever you are in need of a pleasant thought, a happy feeling, a lighthearted childlike sensation. You just reach into the back of your head, on the far left corner, and it will be there among all the other neighboring childhood fancies, memories, and dreams. Light is always pouring through the little white window, and it is always kept slightly open. You just reach in and grab a memory. A little bit of heaven that can put a smile on your face and fill you with a warm sweet feeling that can match no other.

CHAPTER 1

Michelina
The Good Witch

I was ten years old when I realized that I inherited my mother's crazy sense of humor. She never told jokes or made anybody laugh and really wasn't very funny at all, come to think of it. As a matter of fact, my mother was stone-cold serious and ruled us with an iron fist.

So where was her crazy sense of humor? Any woman who named her kids after pastry, legumes, and a tire company had'da have a very weird sense of humor or a deep-seated hatred for her kids. Now I'd rather believe that the prior was true because there's no way in hell (I mean heck) that my own mother would'a wanted to see me suffer a childhood of such shame and embarrassment.

Let me explain. My name is Mikey (pronounced as My-Key), which is really short for Michelina. Now Michelina might not seem like such a bad name, especially these days when retro names are in and all the Hollywood stars have four-syllable names. But the old adage of everything old is new again doesn't mean much to a ten-year-old kid living in Brooklyn during the fifties and sixties when being called Patty or Cathy were the norm.

Every time my mother came out on the stoop to call me in to eat, I wanted to duck behind a bush. Try finding a bush when you need one, especially on a city street in Brooklyn. You'd think that I woulda gotten used'ta all the wisecracks from the kids and grew a tough skin, but it never got easier when one of the kids, usually a nasty boy, would yell out, "Help! I can't find my key!" This came in especially handy when we were roller-skating and somebody lost their skate key. In those days, you wore a key tied to a rope around your neck that opened and closed the skates, adjusting them to fit your foot. That way, we were able to borrow each other's skates as long as you had an average kid-size foot. Of course, if you were bigfoot or the girl who lived around the corner in the apartment house, it would'a never worked. There was a girl who lived around the corner that nobody ever played with. We didn't even know her name or what school she went to. When I think about it now, I guess we were mean to her, calling her monster and then running away whenever she passed us. She was so big, not just tall, but big like a grown man with wild bushy hair and kinda hunchbacked. She was really scary to look at, especially the first time you saw her. Now I feel really bad that none of us kids ever talked to her, and guilty that I was so upset everybody teased me about my name. Wonder what I would'a done if they called me monster?

Life would be so nice if you could go back in time to correct the mistakes you made when you were a stupid kid. Unfortunately, we don't realize these things until we're too old to change them.

Anyway, getting back to my name problems, there was always one idiot boy, mostly it was Charlie Desanto, who'd yell out, "Help, I can't find my key!" Then he'd stop and point to me and yell, "Oh, there it is!" Hahaha! Big joke! Then of course, all the stupid boys would laugh like hyenas. This was a standard on our block for a couple'a years now, and I was getting pretty sick of it. I think they even started getting sick of it and started a new joke to make fun'a my name.

There was a famous tire company named *Michelin*, and one day, Charlie Desanto got an idea in that numb-skulled head'a his. He noticed that some of the tires on cars said *Michelin*, so he yelled out, "Hey, look, everybody, Michelina has her own tire company!" "You must be really rich!" "Whadd'ya livin' in this neighborhood for?" "Can you give us a ride around the block?" Hahaha! I wanted'a barf! Well, this caught on pretty fast with the neighborhood juvenile delinquents, and before long, I was wishing they'd go back to the My-key thing again. Either way, my life was no picnic!

Now maybe you think that I had'da be named Michelina after my dead grandmother, or my aunt, the nun, who saved sick kids in India, but no! Nothin' that exotic. It musta been a law that kids had'da be named after their grandparents in Italian families, or you went to jail because every Italian kid was named after their grandmother or grandfather. Now this only worked if you had four kids or less. After that, you had'da start namin' after crazy aunts and uncles. This was never really a problem in an Italian household because, for some reason, we never had more than three kids. Unlike the Irish, whose lucky number musta been seven because they always had seven kids, the Italians' lucky number was three.

Michelina wasn't my grandma or a long-lost relative or even the lady who started the tire company but some weird old lady that I never even met. Rumor has it, that in the old days, when my grandpa Mike had a farm in New Jersey with cows, chickens, and goats, Michelina saved him from ruin. Let me explain. Grandpa wasn't only a farmer but a bigshot businessman in their town. Apparently, he owned more livestock than any farmer in the state of New Jersey and was very well-respected. He sold eggs and milk to his neighbors, as well as homemade goat cheese strained by his own two hands. I remember my grandmother saying that he had hands of gold, and taking it literally, imagined him as King Midas or something. I later realized what she meant because he was a rare breed in a man. He was a farmer, a winemaker, a carpenter, a landowner, and a shrewd businessman.

Anyway, there was an evil old woman named Rosalina, who lived down the road from grandpa and she was jealous of his prosperity and angry at the fact that she needed to buy from him because she didn't have a farm of her own. She complained that Grandpa sold her rotten eggs and got her sick, so she put a curse on him. They called it the evil eye. In Italian, it was known as *malocchio*. Maybe you don't believe in witches, but according to family legend, it happened. So Rosalina puts a *malocchio* on Grandpa's farm that all his chickens shouldn't lay eggs and all his cows and goats stop making milk. It wasn't long before Grandpa started'a go bankrupt, losing customers, and havin'ta buy his own milk and eggs from other farmers. Well, if you knew Grandpa, you'd know that seeing him explode was not a pretty sight, and Vesuvius had nothin' on him when he lost his temper. But he couldn't prove what Rosalina did, and he couldn't take her to court, so what did he do? This is where my namesake Michelina comes in. Michelina was also a neighbor of Grandpa and a *gumada* of Grandma. *Gumada* was the Italian translation of godmother but was also used as a term for a close family friend besides another meaning, I'd later find out about.

Well, it turns out that Michelina was a pretty good witch in her own right and was Glenda the Good Witch to Rosalina's evil witch of the west. I'm not exactly sure what Michelina did, but she was able to reverse Rosalina's curse and save Grandpa's farm. As a matter of fact, Grandpa's chickens started laying bigger, fresher-tasting eggs, and his milk and cheese were so tasty that people started coming over from New York to buy them. He became very wealthy, or what was considered wealthy in those days, and he never forgot what Michelina did for him. He lent her one thousand dollars, which was a lotta money back then so that she could fulfill her lifelong dream of opening her own Italian restaurant. She named it Michelina's of course and became very successful.

Unfortunately, she died a sudden and mysterious death about ten years later. She never married or had children of her own, so she left the restaurant to my grandma Fannie. They continued to call it Michelina's, but it didn't stay open too long. My grandma Fannie was a good cook, but nobody could get the sauce to taste like Michelina's. Many cooks tried to no avail. Even though she left her recipes, her secret ingredient was missing. Who knew how she stirred her pot, or what she put in it, but then they all knew that Michelina really was a witch.

On her deathbed, she asked Fannie to please name her first daughter after her, and Fannie promised, or she'd never eat another meatball again.

But we all know that my mother's name is Lucy. It seemed that Grandpa was more scared'a the Sicilian curse for not namin' your first daughter after your dead mother than he was of any curse Michelina could spin. After all, she was a good witch, right? An oversight on his part if you ask me. After Lucy was named, it was all downhill after that. Lucy was okay, but Fannie never ate another meatball. She gagged every time she tried to put one in her mouth. And Grandpa's farm went to the dogs. His chickens started layin' rotten eggs, that smelled so foul, neighbors from miles around were wearin' kerchiefs over their noses to block the stench that reeked throughout the land. They had'da get rid'a the farm, which ended up more like a toxic waste dump, and escape to Brooklyn.

Lucy grew up shielded from the truth about what her name should'a been until she gave birth to me. That's when Grandma and Grandpa spilled the ugly truth and guilted my mother into namin' me Michelina so that another generation wouldn't have'ta live in the shadow of her wrath. So ended the curse of Michelina. It ended with me the day I took her name, and I'll take it to my grave. Although Grandpa never got his farm back and Fannie never ate another meatball, I thought it was so strange that Lucy of all people would grow up to make the best meatballs in all the land. People traveled from New Jersey to come and taste them. Michelina? Maybe. I don't know, but thanks to me, the curse is broken. I hope.

CHAPTER 2

Father Sambino

I grew up being called Mikey, short for Michelina, and hadda endure all the humiliation that went with it. Well, my mother's flair for the absurd didn't end with me when it came'ta namin' her children. Being an adult, I can now appreciate unique and interesting names, but it seems as though they can't truly fit you until you have matured and grown into them.

So I came up with a brilliant idea! Children should be given their childhood names like Billy and Tommy and Suzie, and then when they grow up, they can start using their adult names like Sebastian, Maximillian, and oh yeah, Michelina.

It's like wearing clothes that are too loose and baggy on you. They'll just slide off and you'll be left standing there in the middle'a the street with only your bloomers on! Or worse, naked (God forbid) if it was one'a those days when you didn't listen to your mother and went out without any on. The only time I could ever imagine that happening would be if it was laundry day, which was always on Saturday, and the only clean pair of underwear you had left were the ones that said Sunday on them. I remember having underwear with the days of the week on them and would never wear a Sunday on a Saturday, but that's just me.

Anyway, getting back to the names, my brother's name was Sammy. Pretty normal, you would think, right? Wrong! Of course, it was short for something—Sambino (pronounced as Sam-bean-o). Lucky for Sammy, though, that he got away with just being called

Sammy—even in school! The only place that he was known as Sambino was on his birth certificate, and I guess his baptism certificate too. But otherwise, it was a deep dark secret that nobody knew except my mother and father, not even me until I was too old to have fun teasing him about it. Not fair! I got gypped! Thinking about it now, it seems pretty strange that they called him Sammy in school because we went to Catholic school, and they always called you by your real name, like the kid in my class whose real name was Salonzo. Everybody in the neighborhood called him Sally boy, but I guess I couldn't have pictured Sister Margaret Angela calling him that. It would'a been so funny, and we would'a all laughed, and then she would'a hit us with the ruler, her true evil colors flying around the classroom like a runaway rainbow. Then the laughter would'a ended—for good!

So I keep coming back'ta the question of how Sammy was spared a lifetime of shame, and the only thing I can come up with is that my mother and father sold his soul to the church in exchange for their silence. Now this might sound far-fetched, but not if you knew Sammy. When we were kids and everybody else played cowboys and Indians or cops and robbers, Sammy played priest and sinners. I'll give you two guesses who always played the priest! You got it! Sammy! And the more I think of it, the more sense it makes. Sammy was always hanging out with the priests, being an altar boy and all. And it didn't end there. He'd sometimes go over to the rectory on Saturdays and do chores for them. I don't know what exactly, but he'd always come home and tell us some weird story, like he saw Father Camera without his collar on or he looked out the rectory's bathroom window overlooking the courtyard connecting to the nuns' convent and saw the nuns' bloomers on the line! Well, that last one really got me because, first of all, I couldn't imagine any nun wearing bloomers, and if they did, why would they hang them on the line for the whole world to see? I mean, isn't that a sin? They're nuns! No one should see their bloomers, especially priests! I get embarrassed for them just thinking about it. Another thing, wouldn't they have'ta go to confession for that? You know, indecent exposure and all? But then who would they confess to? It would be like "Forgive me, Father, but

I hung my bloomers out on the line." And the priest would say, "I know. I saw them."

So anyway, the way that I figure it is that my mother and father made a deal with the church when Sammy started first grade or maybe even when he was baptized that they'd let him be a priest if the church would just call him Sammy and never let anybody know that his real name was Sambino.

There must'a been a real shortage of priests because the church agreed, and from that day on, Sammy was in secret priest training camp, whether he knew it or not. Now I'm not sure what they did to try and convert him into wanting to be a priest because I never saw it, and I'm not saying anything bad about the priests either, but Sammy started developing an affinity for wearing black and loved those high Nehru collars. He started spending more and more time at the rectory on Saturday afternoons when the rest of us kids were outside playing, and I kinda imagined him in some sort of religious FBI.

Now, Sammy started doing great impressions of all the priests and even the nuns, and one day, he did the unthinkable. It was a Saturday, which was confession day, and Sammy got a crazy idea into his head. There was an Irish priest who had a brogue as thick as pea soup, and Sammy sounded more like him than he did. You couldn't tell them apart. His name was Father Chaney. So whad'dy'ya think Sammy did? That's right! He goes into the confessional box with Father Chaney's name on it and pretended to be him. Because he was such good friends with all the priests, he knew all their schedules and knew that Father Chaney didn't say confessions on Saturday, but Father Voger did. So he sneaks in the box when nobody was looking and like a spider waited for his unsuspecting prey.

Only three people know what happened in that box—Sammy, the poor sinner, and God. I don't even wanna know and never even asked Sammy to tell me for fear that I'd go to hell just for knowing how many Hail Marys and Our Fathers that poor innocent sinner had'da say that day. I wondered what they would'a thought if they knew that their so-called priest was a bigger sinner than they were! Anyway, Father Voger caught Sammy sneaking outta the confession box, and all he did was crinkle his eyebrows while shaking his head at Sammy. Then in his usual deep voice said, "Sammy, you sacrilegious clown!" That's it! He didn't get expelled from school or go to jail or anything! They didn't even kick him outta the altar boys. All the priests and nuns loved Sammy because he did such great impersonations of them. Sammy even said that he caught Father Voger making the slightest hint of a smirk that day. He had'da stop himself from laughing.

Now, I can't believe this because it seems to me that there coulda been no greater sin than impersonating a priest, and it warranted excommunication from the church, if not stoning to death or beheading. I mean, look what they did to Joan of Arc, and she didn't do anything half as bad as Sammy!

The evidence confirming my theory that Sammy was somehow promised to the church, seemed to be piling up faster than the phony penance he handed out that day. Sammy had many talents, but math wasn't one'a them, and he was failing fast.

Now, a few days after the confession fiasco, Sammy gets called down to the principal's office, and he was sure that his luck had run out. He thought he was gonna be expelled, but instead, Sister Mary Margaret just asked him to sit down. She even asked him if he wanted some water, and he had visions of the Last Supper in his head as he silently said the Act of Contrition. He thought he was goin' to his death. Maybe the chair. Maybe a hangin'.

Then something amazing happened. She smiled at him. Sammy was sweating like a pig, wiping his forehead with the white handkerchief that my mother always put in his uniform's pants pocket. He looked like Louis Armstrong, another one'a Sammy's great impersonations. Then she said to him, "I hear that you do takeoffs!" Sammy continued to sweat, not understanding what she meant. Then she said, "Impersonations." Well, Sammy didn't know what to do or say and just sat there looking at her like a deer in headlights. Then she said, "Can you do me?" Sammy's mouth opened like he was catching flies. She just smiled at him and said, "I hear that you're having a very hard time passing math and in great danger of not graduating. I'd hate for you not to be able to graduate with your class. You wouldn't like that, would you?" Sammy just managed a grunt that sounded like "no."

Then she said, "I have a proposition for you." Sammy started to get really scared and wished that he could take the whole confession thing back. She said, "We are having a school talent show for the end-of-the-year celebration, and I would like you to be the star performer." Sammy felt like he was in an episode of *The Twilight Zone* and just wanted to disappear. Then she said, "If you have any hopes of graduating, you'd better learn how to impersonate me before graduation day, or you'll be spending another year in the eighth grade." Sammy couldn't believe that he was being blackmailed by a nun! What was the world coming to? Then she added, "I know that you have no problem taking off on Father Chaney, so let's see if you can do just as well with me! You have one week or consider yourself left back! Do I make myself clear?" Then she gets up from her seat and said, "Fine, now have a good day!"

Well, Sammy was the star of the talent show that night. He started with his usual celebrity impersonations, like John Wayne, Louis Armstrong, and Ed Sullivan. The school auditorium was packed because everybody wanted to see Sammy in action. My family and close friends all knew what Sammy did and they were used'ta his shenanigans, but everybody else just heard rumors about his talent or ended up totally shocked. Either way, everybody was peeing their pants, and there wasn't a dry pair of bloomers in the house. Sister Mary Margaret seemed quite pleased by Sammy's impersonation of her and had'da keep wiping her eyes with tissues to dry up her tears from laughin' so hard. I secretly wondered if she peed her bloomers too then secretly blessed myself asking God's forgiveness for havin' such a sacrilegious thought. A couple'a other kids performed before him like John Schmidt, who played the accordion, and Susan Reed, who did a ballet dance, but everybody was really there for Sammy.

He did Father Voger with his deep voice and John Wayne drawl and even Father Camera who wore a cloak like Dracula. But the highlight of the night was when he had the nerve to do the infamous Father Chaney and his Irish brogue. The audience was roaring and applauding so loud that Sammy knew from the stage that he was graduating because, as they say in showbiz, he had them in the palm of his hand. His diploma and cap and gown were in the bag as sure as you could say "Bless me, Father."

When he got off the stage, everybody was congratulating him and telling him that he should go to Hollywood, even Sister Mary Margaret came up to him, saying, "Well, you pulled it off, so I guess I'd better keep my end of the bargain. Don't be late for graduation practice."

After graduation, Sammy didn't spend so much time with the priests anymore. In September, he went to public high school and, shortly after that, stopped being an altar boy.

Sammy never did become a priest but always kept an affinity for the color black. Me and my family were so proud of him on graduation day, and when they called his name to go up and get his diploma, they called him Sammy, not Sambino. Then I knew that my theory had been right all along about my parents giving Sammy to the church. Everybody kept their end of the bargain, and everybody got what they wanted. Sammy got to learn about the church, to become friends with the priests and the nuns, and to live his childhood years with a name that truly fit him, making him comfortable in his own skin. More than that, Sammy got to learn a lot about himself. He found out that he had a talent for impersonations and developed confidence in himself, thanks to Sister Mary Margaret and Father Voger encouraging him to be himself. Then I realized that Sammy woulda been just as great that night in the talent show even if he had been called Sambino. I don't think anybody woulda made fun'a him for his name because they really liked him. I mean, they might'a teased him a little in the beginning like they did with me and my name, but eventually, he woulda gotten through it, just like I did. I was startin'ta think that havin' a strange name wasn't so bad after all, and in high school, Sammy called himself Sambino. He didn't even try to fight it. I think that he was ready for the name.

The priests and nuns got what they wanted too. Even though they didn't have Sammy as a priest forever, they had a lotta fun with him and forever had the memory of him trying to be a priest. In a way, it was the same thing, and they had the satisfaction of knowing that they helped him to become the good person he turned out to be.

Me and Sammy still go to church on Sunday but not confession. Most of the old priests and nuns have gone, but Sister Mary Margaret is still there. She's ninety years old and walks with a walker. Whenever she sees us, she smiles and then winks at Sammy as tears of joy come to her eyes.

CHAPTER 3

The Great Sambino

I was named after a Sicilian witch, a *strega* in Italian, named Michelina who saved my grandfather from ruin, and my brother Sammy (really Sambino) was named after my father's best friend, Sam Bino (pronounced as Beeno).

I told you that my parents had a great sense of humor. Anyway, Sam, or Sammy as we called him, was my father's best friend, and they worked in the restaurant business together. My father, Gino, was a chef and a singing waiter and worked in some of the best restaurants in Brooklyn and Manhattan. Sammy was a waiter and didn't sing—well, not on the job anyway—but you shoulda heard him when he came over to our house for some kinda party or just a regular Saturday night. My grandpa Mike made the best homemade wine in New York, or so I'm told. He had a secret recipe that transformed people into who they were destined to be in life. It was like magic. Grandpa said that it was the grapes, the best that money could buy. Grandma said it was the barrels that were imported from Sicily. Apparently, the combination of the special wood they were made of, and the Sicilian sun that beat down on them, made any grapes that touched them turn into truth serum. Of course, my explanation was, you guessed it, Michelina. That old witch was at it again. Even from the grave, there was no end to her powers.

Now I consider Grandpa's magic wine a good curse from Michelina and whenever somebody drank it we'd stand around watching them like they were a bomb about to go off, or they were changing from Dr. Jekyll to Mr. Hyde. Usually, people just started laughing alot and doing stuff that they didn't normally do. Like my uncle Joe, who, after two glasses, always started doing math calculations in his head, and every sentence he said had numbers in it. It was almost like he was Einstein in another lifetime. We all knew that he sure wasn't Einstein in this lifetime—nowhere near it. Let's face it. He was a sanitation worker, and nobody could figure out how he passed the test. He was a nice guy but woulda never been in the Mensa society, if you know what I mean. Then there was my aunt Sally, who was double-jointed and did handstands. She was always so much fun to be around normally, but after a few glasses of Grandpa's magic brew, the sky was the limit. Literally. Aunt Sally started doing tumble saucers and flips, twirling around the room faster than the speed of light. Everybody got dizzy just watching her. She was like a one-woman circus act and in another life musta been a very famous gymnast. We were happy that there wasn't a high wire in the room because she was literally climbing the walls. Then there was my uncle Pete who always started talking like Shakespeare, and everything he said was a line from one of his plays. He liked being the witch from Macbeth, so we always made sure to remove all cauldrons, knives, and swords from the room whenever he had a few.

    This brings me back to Sammy. Like I said, he didn't sing in the restaurant, but after one sip of Grandpa's wine, he started singing like a canary. He turned into a regular Enrico Caruso singing all the Italian songs, both modern and classical. One day, when he decided to try out his newfound talent at work and hit an operatic high C note, the other waiters started to duck for cover because they knew that it wouldn't be long before glasses started to shatter. One time, a glass broke right in a customer's hand while she was drinking a glass of red wine. Not a pretty sight on her red-and-white polka-dot sundress. She looked like the American flag. Now you'da thought that she woulda been mad, demanding he pay for her designer dress. But no. She just laughed and gave Sammy a standing ovation, yelling, "Bravo! Encore!" Then all the other people in the restaurant got up and applauded for Sammy too.

So what were a few broken glasses to the owner of the Copa in Manhattan? Peanuts. Sammy was a hot commodity and brought in big crowds whenever he worked as a waiter. Customers started asking for his work schedule, and it wasn't long before the restaurant hired him as a full-time singer. As long as Sammy had a few sips of Grandpa's wine before work, he was singing all the way to the bank and never had to wait on another table. Now it was strange that without Grandpa's wine, Sammy couldn't sing to save his life and sounded like a dying cat. So the secret was kept between my father and Sammy, and they never told another soul.

Unlike Sammy, my father, Gino, had a naturally beautiful singing voice, just like everybody else in his family, and probably everybody else from Naples too. It musta been the beautiful Mediterranean, the sun, and the tomato sauce. Who knows? But it's a fact that the Napolitans are the best singers. It's in their blood, like the tomato sauce every Sunday. My father continued to work as a singing waiter and made good tips, but nothing like Sammy after a sip of Grandpa's wine. My father wasn't jealous of him because they were friends, and Sammy appreciated the fact that if it wasn't for the wine, he'd still be a waiter. He tried giving my father some'a his tips, but my father wouldn't take it, so Sammy just bought him things outta the blue. Like the time my father came home from work and found a beautiful baby-blue Cadillac outside our house that said, "Thanks, Paisan," Love Sammy. He couldn't believe it. He didn't even know how to drive. Sammy just told him that he better get a driver's license. "You're in America now, Paisan. You don't have to walk three miles barefoot and climb Vesuvius and ride the *fenicula* [sky lift] to go to work anymore! Enjoy! Salute!" And so it was with Sammy and my father. Best friends, happy for each other's successes, and never jealous… The both of them just kept praying to the Madonna that granpa's magic wine kept flowing and that the boss never got wise to their scheme. And it had'da be the same exact formula because any deviation might not work and coulda been disastrous.

Now, my father started thinking that maybe he'd better start watching how Grandpa made the wine just in case. You never know. After all, Grandpa was getting up there, and if Sammy was gonna keep raking in the big bucks, Grandpa's secret recipe had'da be preserved. There was one big problem. My father and Grandpa weren't exactly comrades, and getting Grandpa to confide in him was gonna take a miracle. Nobody knew Grandpa's recipe, not Grandma, my mother, or my uncles. The secret was between Grandpa and God. Winemaking was an art, especially for Grandpa, who would spend hours in the cellar with his barrels and crates of grapes like he was creating a masterpiece. It made sense; after all, his name was Michelangelo. My father tried buttering up Grandpa by cooking his favorite baked clams oreganata, but the old man saw right through him. And when he offered to help lift the wine crates, Grandpa just yelled, "Vattina (Get out of here)!" He wasn't having any of it. Making wine was his alone time to commune with nature and God, and my father wasn't gonna get in the way of that.

So Sammy and my father continued singing in the restaurant and making Novenas to the Madonna. They even started giving leftover food to some homeless people who hung out around the restaurant in hopes that God and the Madonna were watching.

Now Sammy, unlike my father, came from Northern Italy, in the Alps, close to the Austrian border. Actually, every time he opened his mouth to sing, it would'a been more natural for him to start yodeling, and he did sort'a resemble the father from *The Sound of Music*. Anyway, the northerners hated the southerners, especially Sicilians, and didn't even consider them to be Italians. So Sammy actually had no business drinking Grandpa's hearty red wine as thick as blood and shoulda been drinking Rhine wine or schnapps, but it was making him a'lotta money, so why look a gift horse in the mouth?

They say that wine is the nectar of the gods and the expression "In Vino Veritas" means that there is truth in wine, which actually means that when you get drunk, you say whatever is really on your mind and in your heart. Well, Sammy took this one step further because when he drank Grandpa's wine, he became a psychic and knew what other people were thinking. In particular, he could tell what a customer's favorite song was.

Now this is the part where I tell you how Sammy saved my father's life, and his lustrous job as a singing waiter in the famed

TWO LEFT FEET

Copa of Manhattan. It was a busy Saturday night, and like usual, the crowd was hurrying in to see this crazy new waiter with a magical voice. Sammy and my father always worked the same shift, to make sure that Sammy always had a sip of Grandpa's wine before work in case Sammy forgot his little flask at home. My father always kept a little bit in an empty pill bottle that he kept in his pants pocket. For the magic to work, Sammy had'da drink the wine no less than twenty minutes and no more than thirty before he started to sing. Otherwise, he sounded like a dying cat, and they were sure the boss would have no problem putting him outta his misery.

So the story goes that my father was waiting on a very well-known baseball star. Rumor has it that it was Mickey Mantle, but I don't know for sure. I woulda loved to be a fly in somebody's soup that night. Anyway, my father was so busy carrying so many platters and tripped on the rug, spilling hot red clam chowder on Mickey Mantle's Yankee uniform. Well, unlike the nice lady who Sammy spilled the red wine on, Mickey flipped. He started cursing my father out like he was an umpire in a game. He didn't get burned, but his uniform had one little stain on it. Big deal! He took such a hissy fit like a little baby and not like you'd think a famous baseball player would act. I didn't know him, but I lost all respect for him that night, and if I was there, I woulda clobbered him over the head with a baseball bat! Take that for cursing at my father, you big bully! Anyway, Mickey called the boss over and tried to have my father fired when Sammy sprang into action just like Clark Kent turning into Superman—without the cape, of course.

Because of Sammy's power to know somebody's favorite song, he started breaking into a chorus of Mr. Snooty Mantle's favorite, and it wasn't "Take Me Out to the Ballgame." It wasn't even "The Star-Spangled Banner," but believe it or not, "The Sunny Side of the Street" by Billie Holiday! Nobody could believe it. He sounded just like her, which was, of course, really funny to see a grown man, in a waiter's jacket singing like Billie Holiday. It turns out that Snooty Mickey's mother sang it to him as a baby, and when Sammy broke out into the chorus, Mickey started crying like a baby. You could almost hear him crying for his mama!

Well, by the time Sammy got finished working his magic on him, Mickey forgot all about the stupid stain on his uniform and was throwing dollar bills around like crackerjacks in a baseball game, not only to Sammy but to my father too. Not only that, but Mickey actually started apologizing to my father giving both him and Sammy front-row seats to the next Yankee game.

Yeah, Sammy sure had a gold mine going on, and everybody was happy. The boss was making money hand over fist, and what he didn't know about how Sammy got his magical voice wasn't hurting anybody—least of all, Sammy and my father. He started to be known as the Great Sam Beno, like a magician in a circus.

Their lucky streak lasted a few more years until I don't know exactly what happened. Maybe the recipe changed, or Grandpa started buying sour grapes, or Sammy started having an allergic reaction but Sammy lost his singing powers, and whenever he opened his mouth to sing, people started covering their ears. He sounded that bad! He lost his psychic powers too, and instead of playing a favorite song, one night made the tragic mistake of singing somebody's worst nightmare. The song that was playing when her husband was killed. It was all downhill after that.

Sammy and Daddy remained friends until the end, but neither of them continued to work in the Copa. They weren't fired, but after all the celebrity, it was just too hard working there as a regular waiter. So my father started working in an Italian restaurant in Brooklyn, where he still sang sometimes, and Sammy went to a Northern Italian restaurant in Queens where he felt more comfortable serving polenta and heavy cream sauces over venison. He never sang again, and the only wine he ever drank was Rhine wine. He didn't have an allergic reaction to it. It didn't make him drunk or psychic or anything. He didn't even yodel.

Sammy still came over to our house on Saturday nights, but not that often. And he wasn't the same. He was sad, and no matter what my father did to try and cheer him up, he just wouldn't laugh. Not even when my father would run around the house screaming, "Hey, Sammy!" lifting his leg high in the air and passing gas, or *fots* as we called them. This use'ta really crack him up into tears. Sammy started losing weight, not eating, and getting very sick. He ended up in the hospital, and my father would go every day trying to cheer him up with stories about the fun times at the Copa. But it would just make him sadder.

Sammy didn't live much longer after that. The doctors said that he starved himself to death because of a broken heart.

Sammy never got married and didn't have any kids of his own. We really were the only family he had in this country, and my father and him were more like brothers than best friends. We always called him Uncle Sammy, and I'll always remember how much fun we had with him in the good old days when Grandpa's wine flowed freely. Everybody who drank it shared a bit of their hearts and dreams but none as powerful as Sammy. His powers were special because they not only made him happy but everybody around him happy too.

Nobody else ever learned Grandpa's secret recipe, and it died with him, but not until it was able to give my family and close friends like Sammy years of happiness. I think that Grandpa didn't want anybody else to know the mystery of the magic wine because he knew just how special it was. Was Grandpa a witch like Michelina? I don't know, but if he was, he used his powers for good in creating that nectar of the gods.

Today, I love wine—the redder, the better. But my brother Sammy, really Sambino after Sammy, can't touch the stuff. He doesn't start singing or reading people's minds. Nothing that exotic. He just starts breaking out in hives the size of Sicily. That's the reason he couldn't become a priest. He couldn't drink the wine! Weird, huh?

CHAPTER 4

Phylo the Drunk

My sister, unlike me and my brother, was the only one of my parents' three children to actually be named after a blood relative. Her name is Phylo. That's right, like the Greek pastry. She was named after my grandma Fannie, whose real name was Philodendron. That's right. Like the plant! Now I know that Philodendron doesn't sound like your average Italian grandma's name, and most of my Italian/Sicilian friends called their grandmas Maria, Carmella, or Josephina. Well, that's because I didn't have an average Italian grandma. There was nothing average about Fannie. That's for sure! And there was nothing average about any of our names. Of course, my family had'da be different.

I already told you how I was named after Michelina, the witch, and how my brother was named after Sam Bino, the singing waiter. So my sister was named Phylo after Fannie (really Philodendrum). Your typical American family, right? Wrong! The dictionary says that a "philodendron" is an American climbing plant, which kinda explains a few things. We all know that Fannie was a Gypsy and always climbing outta her skin fleein' towards her next great adventure. Okay, so she wasn't American.

Fannie came from the part of Sicily with a large Greek influence—Siracusa. This explains the Greek name and also explains why she preferred feta instead of mozzarella on her lasagna and eggplant parmigiana. It also explains why she always wore those housedresses that looked like togas. Now this also explains my great affinity for all things Greek and why I've always envisioned myself on a Greek island or visiting the Parthenon. I love stuffed grape leaves and Spanikopita, and whenever I'm in a Greek diner, I try to converse with the waiters, very proud of the few Greek words that I've learned, namely "Good day," "Please," "Thank you," and "You're welcome." My plan for the immediate future is to increase my knowledge of the Greek language so that when I finally get to Greece, I'll be able to communicate with the natives just as if I was born there myself. At least as if I had a grandmother that was born in the part of Sicily with a large Greek influence.

So I wondered why my sister was named Phylo and not me. I guess that my mother didn't notice when I was born that I'd be the one who loved everything Greek, unlike my sister who couldn't tell a Greek olive from a pimento. The only resemblance she had to anything Greek was like Phylo pastry, she sure was flaky! Other than that, not a single thing. My sister Phylo couldn't even find it on a map! She wasn't exactly *Jeopardy* material. Let's put it that way.

Me and Phylo never really spent too much time together. I'm four years older than her and when you're a kid, that makes a big difference. Unlike me and Sammy who always hung out together and had the same friends on the block, Phylo was just our annoying little sister. The only time we talked to her was to tease her and get her to ask our parents for stuff that they wouldn't give us because she was the baby, and they were more likely to give in to her. In a way, she was our little guinea pig and we used her for experiments, like the time Sammy and me were so bored on a rainy Saturday afternoon. My mother and father were next door in Grandma and Grandpa's house, and we were in charge of watching Phylo. What a joke! What were they thinking?

Obviously, they weren't! In fact, they were probably tastin' Grandpa's latest batch of red wine, and we were pretty sure that they wouldn't be comin' back in for a while. So me and Sammy did a little taste testing of our own. We knew the cabinet in the china closet where our parents kept the liquor. Now being Italian, we grew up on Grandpa's wine, and Grandma always gave us some mixed in a glass of Coca-Cola, especially on holidays. But we never tasted all that other stuff in those big glass bottles with fancy labels that they hid for company. They didn't even know that we knew where it was! Wow! They'd better start keepin' a closer eye on us!

Anyway, Sammy tried to open a bottle that said scotch whiskey, but it was sticky and stuck and wouldn't budge. So he gave it to me to try. Sammy wasn't what you'd call Hercules, but I was. It must'a been the Greek thing, and everybody knew that I was really strong for a girl and probably stronger than most'a the boys on the block too. So I gave it three sharp twists, and it opened. It smelled like the rubbing alcohol that my mother put on us when we had a fever. We opened the china closet where my mother kept those little pink-colored glasses that I saw her pour liquor into for company, and we carefully took one out. Then I poured a little drop into the glass and dipped my pinky into it to taste. I gently touched my pinky finger to my tongue, scared'a what it would taste like. And just like I expected, made a face, and said, "Ugghh!" It tasted like poison. Then Sammy did the same thing. He yelled and tried to spit it out onto the floor. I told him to shut up before they heard us. So we figured let's let Phylo try it. She hated regular food and, in fact, use'ta hide it from my mother by throwing her sandwich behind the china closet.

She had so much food hidden back there that she could'a fed a small Greek island. After about a few weeks, it started to smell so bad that my mother thought there was a dead rat in the house. There was a rat all right, named Phylo. My mother finally figured out where the smell was comin' from and moved the china closet away from the wall. Lucy also possessed a Herculean strength. She couldn't believe all the sandwiches that she found. From that day on, she gave Phylo a diet consisting of only drinks. She made her malteds, ice-cream sodas, and protein shakes. She hated to eat but loved to drink!

So what better experiment to try? Would Phylo also love to drink that awful-tasting liquid that me and Sammy just spit out? And if so, would that mean that she'd grow up to be an alcoholic? (whatever the heck that is) Or would she act like any other normal kid and spit it out? We had'da find out if she was destined to always be flaky little Phylo. So we told her to dip her finger in the glass just like we did. She tried it, then licked her lips, and said, "Mmmm!"

Not a good sign. So we gave her a little sip, and she asked for more. Then she had another sip and another. Phylo was really loving this stuff! Before we knew it, she started dancing around the room and breaking into a chorus of The Supremes's "Baby Love"! At that point, we stopped giving her sips, but it was too late. Phylo was drunk! She started walking all crooked and tripping all over herself like the drunken man we saw on Liberty Avenue.

Me and Sammy stopped laughing at her and started to get scared. We tried to make her lie down on the couch, but she kept waving her arms over her head, saying that she was chasing away the birds circling her head just like in the cartoons. We tried to give her a pillow from the couch, but she kept crying for a bed pillow, all the while singing a rendition of Supremes's songs. Me and Sammy knew that we had'da think fast because any minute now our mother and father would be coming back from drinking wine in Grandma's house. And we knew that if we could bet, we'd win a million dollars that they were nowhere near as drunk as poor little Phylo. I also knew that no matter how drunk our parents might'a been, there was no way that they wouldn't notice how weird Phylo was acting. Even for Phylo! There was no way in heck we'd be able'ta cover it up.

So I did the only thing that an honest Catholic schoolgirl could do under the circumstances. I decided to come clean and spill the beans before they could break my legs. I left Sammy in charge of Phylo, which wasn't saying much for my judgment. I went into Grandma's house and summoned up every bit of acting ability hidden within me. And in my most convincing voice, I started to scream, "Mommy, Daddy, Phylo is acting weird! Something's wrong with her."

My mother turned around and just said, "Phylo always acts weird. She's flaky!"

But I kept yelling that I thought she was sick, and then they finally put their wine glasses down and came running into our house with me. Grandma Fannie was running behind them to see what was going on with her namesake. Grandpa just kept sitting at the table and poured himself another glass of red wine, talking to himself, as he said, "Salute!" He was already immune to all our family drama.

Meanwhile, genius Sammy forgot to put the bottle back in the cabinet like I told him to and was just pacin' back and forth, talkin' to himself and scratchin' his head. You could always count on sweet little Sammy to remain cool and calm in an emergency. There were two things that I knew for sure. Sammy would never become a brain surgeon, and Sammy would never become a criminal. He didn't have steady hands, and he couldn't lie. I guess it was all the years of being an altar boy. Whatever! If there was ever any dirty work to be done, I had'da do it myself if I wanted it done right!

Well, as soon as they saw Phylo twirlin' around the room singin' "Baby Love," they knew that somethin' was up—especially gypsy Fannie, you couldn't hide anything from her. Then they all saw the bottle, and I wanted'a kill Sammy. But I was too late cause my father had him on the floor, kickin' him in the butt. My mother, on the other hand, chose me for her prey. And in her usual fashion, got me on the floor hogtyin' me by the ankles, til I squealed like a pig! Still, Phylo sang "Baby Love!" My mother slapped my thighs, and I had rug burn for a month.

There was no use in deny'in it or tryin'ta explain. They knew what we did, and as Ricky said to Lucy on *I Love Lucy*, "I caught you red-handed!" Unfortunately, our hands weren't the only things that were red—so were our butts and thighs! In those days, there was no such thing as child abuse. If you did somethin' wrong, you got a beatin'. That was it! End of story!

There was no goin' out to play after school for a long time. There was no TV, not even Ed Sullivan on Sunday night. And guess who was on this Sunday night? You got it! The Supremes! Phylo was sure happy cause she was the only one'a us who could watch it. Phylo and Grandma Fannie. And they both sang every word of every song. After that day, they locked the liquor cabinet.

CHAPTER 5

Queen of the Gypsies

When I was ten years old, my grandpa Mike, in an effort to escape another smoldering summer in the city, bought a mansion (or so he said) in the country—Marlboro Country. That was the name of the town. So despite our deep dismay at leaving our city friends behind and led by the iron hand of my grandfather, we threw caution to the wind, packed up our caravan of misfits, and proceeded onto the New York State Thruway. Embracing the butterflies in our guts and our sudden craving to explore the unknown, we were about to discover a strong part of our Sicilian family's heritage. The vagabond syndrome. We came from a long line of gypsies, especially on Fannie's side where Gypsy blood ran as thick as the Sunday sauce we were required to consume under penalty of death.

We started our journey before the crack of dawn at the end of June, the first Saturday after school got out for the summer. Our freedom day had come, or so we thought. Like an overstuffed sardine can, the tribe consisting of my grandparents (who were not small people); my brother, sister, my mother, and me; my three cousins; my aunt and my uncle, the navigator all packed ourselves into his gray Plymouth Belvedere. We were like a circus clown car, and thinking about it now, I realize it must'a been illegal in at least a few states, and the fact that we weren't arrested is as much a mystery as it was a crime.

Sitting on each other's laps, barf bags in hand, we proceeded towards our preconceived notion of cowboys on horseback, swinging saloon doors, and giant billboards of red cigarette boxes. Like most childhood fantasies, our balloon was about to burst because, despite its name, Marlboro wasn't some wild western city that packed up its spurs and saddles, and giddyupped into the sunset relocating in Upstate New York.

The ride up there was uneventful enough, except for the occasional horse and cow sightings, accompanied by the appropriate oohs and aahs, along with a random barf attack, afflicting one of us kids. This was our first experience in the wild blue yonder, and just as our spirits suffered the anxiety of treading on virgin territory, so did our stomachs, and we had the car upholstery to prove it! Something our uncle would never let us live down.

The road was in our blood and part of our Sicilian history, as my grandmother told tales of ancient times in Sicily, where our ancestors fled the many conquerors of the times. They'd be running down a cobblestoned road, knife in one hand, a loaf of bread in the other while screaming, "Come on, pack up. Let's get outta this place!" And so it was with our modern-day gypsy clan whether we knew it yet or not. Although the times and situations were different, the urgency to flee would always remain just as powerful, the vagabond syndrome rearing its head in all of our lives sooner or later.

The most notorious gypsy was my grandmother Fannie, and she didn't come by her title easily or accept the honor lightly. Most of her brothers and sisters were gypsies in their own right, her brother, my uncle Jack, traveling across the country with his sons, selling all kinds of stuff out of the back of a caravan like a traveling show / medicine man. He did this well into his nineties when he was tracked down on the Lower East Side of Manhattan by himself dealing a game of three-card monty. Then there was her sister, Aunt Grace, who always flew in and out like a whirlwind, never taking her coat off for fear she'd cool her heels. She always carried a shopping bag full of fruit, bread, and cheese because she only ate on the run.

Fannie was a unique and interesting character, full of the usual grandmotherly advice, bits of wisdom, and kitchen of comfort, but there was something almost supernatural about her, not in a scary way but mystical. It must'a had something to do with her piercing crystal-blue eyes that just saw right through you, and she was our parents' built-in lie detector test. If our parents detected foul play, they'd just send us to Fannie. We'd walk into her living room, hands covering our eyes, trying to shield ourselves from her power, but it was no use. She saw right through us. After a couple of minutes alone with us, the words just came pouring out like a faucet. There was no badgering involved, no loud threats. Just her translucent look and we were putty in her hands. I think without realizing it we looked forward to those meetings with her in her living room, even needed them, needed her to be our confessor. Our parents started the game that we willingly played and that she mastered. They were sending us to our confidant, comforter, and best friend, and there were no losers in this game. If played correctly, we would all be winners in the family game.

One incident that led me to believe that Fannie was a gypsy happened early one Saturday morning. While painting the kitchen ceiling, she climbed down from the ladder and complained of chest pain. Now she did this all the time on account of her being so dramatic and we couldn't tell if she was playing wolf or not. Well, when the doctor showed up saying that she had to immediately go to the hospital, she laughed in his face while grabbing the phone to make airline reservations, insisting that a change of climate and a visit with her baby brother in California was all she needed. Her bags were packed, and before you could say "California, here I come," the gypsy was gone, and we all stood there, shaking our heads and eating her dust! The doctor put up a fight and was baffled while we just smiled, receiving a postcard two weeks later, saying, "Having a wonderful time. On my way to Vegas. Glad you're not here!"

That was the way it was with Fannie, and we thought it was normal for our grandmother to fly off on a whim, trying to escape a heart attack. Then there were her crazy superstitions and old-world remedies like the day I came home from school to find the kid down the block lying on the kitchen table while Fannie was massaging his belly with olive oil and carving crosses on his skin with her thumbnail. She said he had worms. You couldn't put shoes on the bed (why would you?) or a pocketbook on the table—the Italian bread could never be upside down, and God forbid, your knife and fork were crossed. She'd say, "L evetila stu crucia," which in Sicilianish meant "Get rid of that cross!" Bad luck. *Malocchio*. Then there was the time on the stoop when Josie down the block came by with her newborn baby in the carriage. Lena across the street went over to look at the baby, and Grandma jumped down the steps and almost clawed her eyes out. She blocked the baby and said to Josie, "Where's the red ribbon and the red horns?" She gave Lena the *malocchio* sign, pointer and pinky fingers of her right hand practically jabbing her in the eye, and shooed her away like a cat in the backyard. Then she ran into the house to make sure she got a red ribbon and horn for Josie's baby before anyone else laid eyes on her. If you made a funny face, the angel was gonna pass, leaving you like that forever—on and on it went.

Come to think of it, Fannie had a strange liking for violin music, and when cleaning day came around and she had her red bandana wrapped around her head, you could picture her looking into a crystal ball. Her blue eyes peering out, hypnotizing, reminded us to obey our parents' silly rules, believe in our heritage, and no matter how weird it seemed to follow the gypsy code, whatever that was.

The one exception in which she told us to deny our gypsy ways was when we finally arrived at our newfound mansion in the country. The car stopped on top of a mountain, and although we had a panoramic view of the majestic Hudson River before our eyes like a picture postcard, unfortunately, our hearts stopped, and our mouths dropped. My grandfather bolted outta the car, jumping for joy, as he raised his hands in adoration, waiting for our signs of approval. The palace we imagined was nothing more than two oversized barns with chest-high weeds and bushes, and poison ivy was rampant. My grandmother gave us one of her sly smiles along with her twinkling eyes, and we knew why this was one of the times we had to deny the gypsy impulse to run for the hills or from the mountain to the nearest highway and hitch a ride outta Marlboro. She said a true gypsy knows when to run and, more importantly, when to stay. She taught us that and many other lessons on our visits into her living room. We learned about honor, loyalty, and tradition. That's why we got outta the car, climbed over the mountain of rocks that was supposed to be a driveway, and resisted the overwhelming urge to fly with the wind. Instead, one by one, we all looked our grandfather square in the face, smiled, honoring his heroic efforts, and thanked him.

Then the craziest thing happened. After about a week of getting up with the birds, chopping bushes, and clearing broken tree branches, something started to happen. Without realizing it, we actually started to like this place even though there weren't any cowboys on horseback with red cigarette boxes and swinging saloon doors. Every morning at the crack of dawn, after my grandfather drank his glass of vermouth with two raw eggs, we'd start our chores (or *servisa*). We painted the houses and the chicken coop then cleared the land of rocks and stones to plant a big vegetable garden, and before we knew it my brother, sister, cousins, and me were having fun. We climbed the apple and cherry trees, stared at the old ghost house across the road, and counted the cars going by as we sat and watched the river run. We later realized what made this place special was that we did it together day by day, chore by chore, lesson by lesson. Our grandparents had given us the gift of themselves, and we'd someday realize what an important part this place and the time we spent there together would have on our future characters. We learned the love of hard work, perseverance, and commitment and that a true gypsy never runs from those he loves or the ones who love him.

After all our chores were done and we spent a whole day in the sun, my grandfather would give us money to walk down the steep mountain to the little store in town to get ice cream. It was usually a half gallon of butter brickle, frozen solid, so we'd take turns throwing it on the road to soften it as we walked back up the mountain. I think those nights of sharing dessert with my cousins was the best ice cream I ever had. Sometimes I still think that Fannie must'a gotten her heritage mixed up, and if, in fact, her ancestors came from Sicily, it had'da be the northeastern most part facing Romania, wavin' a flag at it, yellin', "Hey, wait for me!"

CHAPTER 6

"Che Eh"

Sometimes on Sunday afternoons, after church and our big meal of macaroni and meatballs, along with all the other stuff, we'd take the bus to visit my father's mother, Grandma Connie, also known as the old lady by my aunts and uncles, but I just called her Che Eh. We'd get off the bus across the street from her house and ring her bell. After what seemed like forever, we'd hear, "Che eh?" which meant "Who is it?" She knew we were coming over, so I don't know why it was such a big production every time. It wasn't like Avon or the Fuller Brush man was calling, and it sure wasn't the Encyclopedia Britannica trying to con her into a lifetime subscription of books. It was a Sunday and it wouldn't even happen on a weekday cause she couldn't speak English, and I'm not even sure if she could read and write. I never saw her reading *Il Progresso*, the Italian newspaper that Grandpa read, and come to think of it, she always had a magnifying glass when she was trying to inspect something up close like a dollar bill (trying to make sure it wasn't counterfeit).

Before she buzzed us in, she'd go all the way down the line, listing every person in the family, starting with her kids down to her grandchildren, and I'm glad she didn't have any great-grandchildren! Now she acted like she couldn't hear, but I think she was playing games with us like the TV show *What's My Line*. In this game, there were no winners, and by the time she buzzed us in, it was dark out and time to go home. It was like we were entering Fort Knox and had to know the secret password, or we were crooks trying to crack a safe. If it was winter, we came prepared with extra warm gloves, hats, and scarves so we wouldn't freeze to death. Wouldn't it have made more sense if my father just had a key? But that would'a been too simple! When we finally got the final *Jeopardy* question right and she was satisfied with our answers, she buzzed us in, and like Dorothy entering Emerald City, we jumped in before she changed her mind. She stood on top of the second-floor landing, her beady brown eyes watching us climb the stairs, still not 100 percent sure who we were or if we were a threat to her. So now you know that she could hardly hear or see and was maybe a bit distrustful, but that's just the tip of the iceberg.

She wasn't what you'd call huggy-feely, and if Grandma Fannie smothered us in her marshmallow bazooms, Che Eh gave us a little obligatory bird peck on the cheek scared she was gonna catch our cooties. If it was one'a those rare Sundays that we were eatin' there, she had a giant bowl the size'a Sicily in the middle'a the table, and it overflowed with Linguine in red sauce. She guarded it like it was the crown jewels or a famous painting by Leonardo da Vinci, afraid the Nazis were coming to confiscate them. Years later, I'd learn that they were so poor during the war in Italy that they banged empty plates together so that their neighbors thought they had food to eat. Then she kinda made sense, and I felt bad for her.

Before we could eat, she had'da take her pills, which was more of a production than gettin' buzzed in the door. She had a problem swallowing them and ground them down to powder with a meat tenderizer and then wrapped them in communion host that she said were blessed by the pope in Rome. Now I found that hard to believe because I'm sure the pope had more important things to do than to bless hosts and have them shipped all the way to Brooklyn because an old Italian lady couldn't swallow pills! If anything, maybe the priest down the block at St. Rita's blessed them, and who even knew if he had the time!

First, she got the host soaking wet, practically giving it a bath in the kitchen sink. Then she sat at the table like a scientist, trying to get all the crushed-up pills inside the host, folding it back and forth like a Japanese lady doing origami or a Chinese lady making dumplings. By the time she got it to stay closed in a little circle, we were starving, and the linguini was a cold sticky mess. Maybe she should'a wrapped the host with the linguine. Even crazy glue would'a been faster! Then she had'da swallow it, which was like the guy in the circus who swallowed fiery swords. It took about twenty giant gags and heaves before my father or my uncle practically forced it down her throat while cursing in Napolitanish that we were all dyin'a starvation! "Morta de famma!" It sounded funnier the way they said it. They'd tilt her head back and hold her nose like she was being baptized in the Mediterranean Sea. Too bad, John the Baptist wasn't around to help her swallow the host. She had'da drink about a gallon of red wine and Coca-Cola mixture just to get it down, and by the time she stopped choking, it was getting dark and almost time to go home.

Now I couldn't understand why she just didn't swallow the pill. Wouldn't it have been easier? It would'a been easier for the rest of us. That's for sure! I guess she thought because it was holy, God would help her swallow it? Who knows? Then there was the way that she looked. God forgive me, but she wasn't exactly a beauty queen, and I kinda had the feeling that even as a teenager she wasn't on the cover of a magazine. Years later, I heard rumors that my grandfather had a *gumada* (girlfriend, oh yeah! That's the other meaning of the word!), and well, I can't say that I was too surprised.

Her hair was in a big white bun sitting on top'a her head like a giant bagel, and she wore a long black dress, with black stockings, and shoes. She was short and had a hunchback like Quasimodo and except for the white hair could'a been a blackbird. And then there was her tooth! It had a life of its own, long and brown, front and center. It was razor sharp, like a deadly weapon, and looked as if she could use it to saw through wood like a beaver. When we finally got to eat, she'd gnaw on the heel of the Italian bread all day long and wouldn't let it go like a dog with a bone.

She was cute though, and still my grandmother, brown tooth and all. Another way that she was different from Grandma Fannie was that unlike Fannie, I couldn't picture her shielding me with her body, blocking me from my mother when she was on the warpath.

Che Eh would'a probably just shrugged her hunchbacked shoulders and stepped aside, so Lucy could get at me. Different. Apples and oranges, I guess.

One time, when Sammy, Phylo, and me were playin' confession with my cousins, she really scared the heck outta us. We'd sit behind the big armchair, taking turns going into the confessional, and guess who always had'da be the priest? That's right! Father Sammy. She came walking outta her bedroom, and her white bun was hanging down to her hips in a long straggly mess. With the black dress, hunchback, and the tooth, we all started screaming. "Help! It's the witch!" She looked like Cousin Itt from *The Adams Family*, and we all started praying, even Father Sammy, that we'd be good and never do another bad thing for the rest of our lives!

Now it's not nice to talk bad about your grandmother, and she wasn't really mean or anything. She didn't hit us, but thank God that was the first and only time we saw her with her bun down. After we finally got to eat, my mother washed the dishes, and I had'da dry them. Well, I had a few problems'a my own. There were certain kinds'a cotton dish towels that I couldn't touch.

If they had a fuzzy kinda material, I'd get the heebiejeebies, chills all up and down my arms, and not in a good way. I'd end up dropping the towel and whatever dish or glass I was holding. My mother didn't have a full set'a dishes, because most'a them ended up splattered on the kitchen floor. Now we finally learned not to use those dish towels anymore, and my mother threw them all out but always forgot to bring one if we were visiting somewhere, or at least inspect it before I tried touching it.

Anyway, before I thought about it, I had my slippery hands on Che Eh's giant linguine bowl imported from Italy, and before you could say O Sole Mio, it ended up splattered all over her kitchen floor, creating a beautiful mosaic tile. My mother gave me her look, and I gave it right back to her because it was her job to stop me, wasn't it? What was she thinking? Well, that was the last time I dried dishes in her house. Che Eh just threw her hands up over her head like she was under arrest and kinda squealed in an almost witchy way, "Eeehhhh! Ou Shame-ou!" That didn't mean "What a shame!" It was kinda the Napolitano version of Grandma Fannie's *scimunita*, meaning "fool," "clown," or "dumbbell." Take your pick! When Grandpa Mike first saw me drop a dish and towel, he just said, "Ma, no sai fa ou servisa!" which basically meant "You don't know how to do work," another variation of my mother's old standby, "But you can't do nothing right!" Basically, they all had the same message and, obviously, not too much positive reinforcement for a kid. But regardless, I still learned how to walk and talk at the same time, among a few other things.

For dessert, Che Eh had a big bowl of peaches on the table, and when I saw them immediately looked at my mother, both of our eyes popping out. I made sure to steer clear of that and not just because I didn't wanna break another bowl.

If cotton dish towels gave me the chills, peaches gave me the shakes like an epileptic fit. Just looking at the fuzz made my teeth chatter like a typewriter. Forget about ever touching one! If I ever became a spy and they wanted to torture me to spill the beans, peaches were the way to do it. Peaches and cotton towels! Lucky for me, Che Eh also had the really good chocolate candy on the table from Italy, the ones with all the nuts in them. I had no trouble holding or swallowing them, that's for sure. Come to think of it, neither did she. She was tossing them down like M&M's and maybe she shoulda wrapped her host in chocolate.

She wasn't a bad grandma, just different. Grandma Fannie was big like a football player, and Che Eh was fast like a soccer player, or even better, hunched like a boccie player! I realized we were all a little nutty in this family tree. I looked over at my father who couldn't leave the house without kissing every saint statue or making sure that all his dollar bills faced the same way in his wallet. Then there was Sammy who was so obsessed with being a priest he carried his portable, fake priest collar around with him to play confession. Maybe he could bless Che Eh's host? Not to mention Phylo who loved the taste of whiskey, and then Che Eh who'd rather spend two hours trying to swallow a host from the Vatican (I still wanted proof of that one) than just swallow one little darn pill!

Oh, and then there was me who couldn't touch cotton towels or peaches. I loved canned peaches, by the way, smothered in syrup. We weren't so different after all. Everybody had something. We were just a different kinda nut in the same chocolate box. It was really weird that just like Che Eh, I'd one day grow up to have a problem swallowing pills, having to throw my head back so many times I gave myself whiplash. I just never bothered the pope. I figured he had enough'ta worry about!

CHAPTER 7

The Earl

On Saturday afternoons, the whole neighborhood went to the Earl Movie Theater down the block from my house. You got to see a double feature along with tons of preview cartoons, and our parents were happy because, for a couple'a hours, they were free and clear to do whatever they wanted with us outta their hair. Our ritual began by first going into the ice-cream parlor to get a bag of penny candy for the movies because movie candy was too expensive, and anyway, they didn't have all the good stuff the ice-cream parlor had. Now I wonder how they let us all in with candy we bought from the ice-cream parlor cause it would never happen today, and I'm sure they'd inspect all our bags first.

We had the best penny candy back then, and for twenty-five cents, you could chew for two hours and still have stuff left over. The line was always out the door, and if you wanted to see the show on time, you had'da get to the ice-cream parlor early. I always got the black licorice pipes and malted balls. Then for a nickel, I got a Turkish Taffy, usually vanilla, and either a Sugar Daddy or a Bit-O-Honey, and I always made sure to get Mary Janes. Yeah, everything that'd make your teeth fall out, and I'm sure that's the reason our dentist Denny Dunny always had his office packed with kids. Sammy wasted his money on Pez and candy cigarettes because he wanted'a make believe he was smoking, but he never knew how to save a penny anyway. My mother told him he couldn't chew Bazooka bubble gum in the movie anymore because it was annoying every time he blew a bubble and always got stuck in the hair of whoever was dumb enough to sit next to him. It sure wasn't me. On the days Phylo had'da tag along with us, she always got those stupid rainbow button candies on the long white page or the ones that looked like a fake necklace. Then, of course, she wanted the wax red lips that you couldn't even eat, and the wax bottle with liquid in them, probably cause she thought they were little bottles of whiskey. Dumb, flaky Phylo.

The best part of the movies was that in between the two shows, they had races and every kid got a number on a ticket from one to ten. It was a movie where ten old guys dressed like jockeys raced horses, and if your number won, you got a prize. Now I can't believe they were allowed to do this. Was it even legal? They were teachin' us how to become gamblers, and I wondered why Uncle didn't come with his friends from the track! We were all screamin' and jumpin' up and down calling for our number just like Uncle at the track. But even if he won, what was he gonna do with a box'a Colorforms or a game of Twister? That woulda been funny! I always won on number two, who was a fat guy that looked like Hardy from Laurel and Hardy. Sammy always got mad cause he never won, and Phylo didn't know what was going on. I used'ta try and get kids to trade their ticket with me if they had number two til they got wise that I had the lucky winner. This was really stupid, though, cause two was lucky for me and wasn't lucky for everybody else, just like Cassie thought number nine was her lucky number, and he was so old and skinny. He looked like a big wind would send him flyin' off the horse and into the audience. But he worked for her. We all just had'da figure out who our lucky rider was.

The Earl had a matron named Bessie, like the cow. Now I'm not sayin' she looked like a cow, but she was kinda chubby on the hips, and a lotta the kids teased her when she patrolled up and down the aisle with her flashlight. As soon as the movie started and the lights went out, she'd start sayin', "Quiet in there, or I'll kick ya to the curb!" All the boys would start yellin', "Mooo!" then start laughin'. I have'ta admit, whenever I looked at her, I thought'a milk duds! She wore a long white dress, kinda like a nurse, with white stockings and shoes too. Bessie had a sidekick named Mel, and he was the manager. He was short and roly-poly with long straight hair. He wore a tuxedo and waddled like a penguin and looked just like the man on the Monopoly game. The one that sent you straight to jail without passin' Go! Come to think of it, Monopoly was another game I won at the races. Unlike Bessie, Mel didn't yell or even have a flashlight. He just walked up and down, smilin' and noddin', doin' his penguin walk, and brushin' strands of his stringy white hair outta his eyes.

The hardest part about goin' to the Earl was after the show was over. You'd try'ta get up and go but your feet were stuck to the floor and everybody's Mary Janes, Turkish Taffy, and Bit-O-Honey, along with Juicy Fruit and Jujubes. If it was sticky, it was on the floor. Maybe when kids were laughin' so hard at the cartoons or the races they started droolin' all over themselves or they were just pigs and spit it out on the floor cause it was the first and last time they tried a candy they didn't like. Stupid! Either way, you were stuck like quicksand, and I made sure to wear the oldest and junkiest shoes I had. Then I thought, what would we do if there was a fire? We'd all be stuck in our tracks and burn to a crisp, unless we ran out barefoot, our feet stickin' to the ooey-gooey mess! I made sure to wear shoes without laces just in case, easier to get out, and sat on the end of the aisle close to the back. Maybe I was lucky winnin' on number two in the races, but I didn't wanna press my luck!

CHAPTER 8

George

Our ice cream man's name was George, and every day at the same time, he'd drive down our block in his Bungalow Bar truck, ringing his familiar bell that was magic to our ears. We didn't run in the house and say, "Ma, can I get ice cream?" or "Ma, can I get Bungalow Bar?" We just said, "Ma, can I get George?" because, to us, George was ice cream, and ice cream was George. One didn't exist without the other, and none of us kids could ever imagine another ice-cream man sitting behind his wheel, and we just hoped that he'd never get sick or move.

George was special from his white cap and uniform down to his white socks and shoes. Now our milkman was named Willy, and he wore white from head to toe too, and we really liked him but wouldn't cry like it was the end of the world if we found out another milkman took his place. First of all, we hardly saw Willy cause he showed up at the crack'a dawn when most'a us kids were still dreamin' about ice cream.

There was somethin' really weird about George cause he always knew exactly what everybody wanted without havin'ta ask us. It's what they called photographic memory, but I called it magic and would try every chance I got to trick him. He'd say, "Hi, Mikey, how you doin' today?" and just hand me my vanilla-ice-cream sandwich. So I'd say, "I think I wanna try somethin' different today," and he'd say, "I know. Don't tell me. A vanilla cone," and he'd always be right. Then I'd try to trick him by sayin' I was gettin' somethin' for my mother, and before I could say a word, he'd say, "So does your mother want her usual coconut pop today or the toasted almond?" Now he knew that those were her two favorites, but how did he know what I was thinkin'? Then he'd wink at me like a twinkling star and chuckle in a singsong way while I just stood there, scratchin' my head. Then he'd just hand me the toasted almond cause he knew all along that's the one she wanted. So why did he even ask? Was he playin' games or a male witch (they were called warlocks) like Dr. Bombay on *Bewitched*?"

So I asked him, "Ha'ddy'ya do that?"

"Do what?" he said, smilin' a crooked smile like a crescent moon.

"You know!" I said. "You always know what everybody wants before they tell you."

"Well, it's my job to know what my customers like, isn't it? What kinda ice-cream man would I be if I didn't keep them happy? That's what I'm here for!"

For a second, I thought to myself, *Maybe he's Santa Claus?* then snapped myself out of it by saying, "Yeah, I guess so," but the wheels were turning in my head.

I didn't believe him as far as I could throw his white cap, and before I could walk away from the truck, I saw him already grabbing two chocolate dixie cups for the Connor boys standing behind me. They never said a word, so I knew I had'da do a little investigating like the spy that I was.

Cassie always got the chocolate éclair, and it didn't take a magician or a photographic memory to know that's what she was gettin' every day, rain or shine. God forbid, she'd ever try somethin' new, and George knew it too. I asked her if she ever tried to trick George by gettin' somethin' different, and she just looked at me like I had two heads.

"Why mess with somethin' that's perfect?" she said as her tongue had a party with her chocolate eclair.

"Don't you think it's weird that he always knows what we want?" I asked.

TWO LEFT FEET

She just shrugged her shoulders flippin' her blond ponytail outta the way of her ice-cream pop and said, "He sees us every day, Mikey, just like our parents and teachers. Of course, he's gonna know! Stop bein' a detective and eat your ice cream!"

I was so desperate that I asked Crazy Charlie who was havin' a conversation with his chocolate cone. "Do you think George has superpowers?" I asked him as his feet squirmed up and down the curb like a worm on an escalator.

He looked up and said, "What? You been in the sun too long, Mikey! He's just George. Not Superman!"

I said, "We got about a hundred kids on this block. How does he remember everything, and what if we change our minds or get somethin' for our mothers? He knows that too! Come on! Think about it!"

He just started singin' "Be My Baby" by the Ronettes to either his drippy ice-cream cone or his imaginary girlfriend. I'm not sure which one.

Then I thought, *I wonder how many other blocks just like ours he sells ice cream to? Does he memorize all their orders too? Maybe he wasn't just our George after all?*

So Crazy Charlie said, "Well, how about Father Voger in confession? Maybe he has superpowers too!"

"What?" I said, not believin' my ears even though this was Charlie talkin'.

"How come every Saturday in confession he always knows my sins before I even confess and always gives me the same penance? How does he do that, huh?"

I shook the question marks outta my head before answerin' him. "Everybody knows your sin every week. You beat up your brother and start fights with every kid on the block. You don't have'ta have a photographic memory for that!"

Whatever! Either I was Nancy Drew or nuts (maybe both) and the rest'a the clowns on my block were in *The Twilight Zone* cause I knew George had superpowers, and I was gonna find out, or my name wasn't Mikey Drew, private eye! So I followed his truck around the corner to Autumn Avenue when he was done with my pack'a losers and hid on line behind a bunch'a kids so I could listen, and sure enough, he knew all their names and what they wanted without them sayin' a word. I was like a snake in the grass, and my antennae were shootin' up to the sky. I saw Jenny from the other fifth grade and told her my suspicions, and of course, she said, "He knows us all from when we were little like our uncle George!" Blah, blah, blah! She just looked at me like "What are you doin' on our block?" as she slobbered her strawberry shortcake. Who eats that anyway? Old ladies. Maybe it was for her mother or grandmother and she couldn't resist or George finally made a mistake givin' a kid an old lady ice-cream pop.

Then I looked up, and he saw me. He just smiled and winked the way he always did. When he flashed his pearly white teeth, it was like sunshine peekin' through a window, and his wink was like the flash of a Polaroid camera, leavin' my eyes blinkin' in the glare. "What happened, Mikey? Did Grandma change her mind and send you over for a vanilla-ice-cream sandwich? Hope she's feeling okay and not too tired to walk to Woolworth's today for the vanilla, chocolate, strawberry waffle-ice-cream sandwiches that she loves so much or the lemon ices from Joe's Pizzeria?" There was that smile again like he knew that I knew his secret.

All the kids ran up to his truck, callin' out his name, and he called out theirs right back as he continued to read their minds. I'm sure of it. I realized he wasn't just our George but the whole neighborhoods. Maybe even the whole world. Who knew? I knew I wasn't ready to give up tryin'a find out even though the rest'a the numbskull kids on my block didn't have a clue. I wasn't done yet, or my name wasn't Mikey Drew, girl private eye! Somewhere, I heard somebody playin' "A Walking Miracle" by the Essex.

CHAPTER 9

Rock and Roll

One day in May, right after my eleventh birthday, me and Sammy were walkin' home from school just like we did every other day. Sammy's birthday was in April, and I was just eleven months older than him. So for one month outta the year, we got to tell everybody that we were the same age. And then, of course, the logical reply would be, "Oh, you're twins! That's funny. You don't look alike. You must be fraternal." This conversation was always with an adult, usually one of our friends' parents who we were tryin'a impress with our interesting white lie since none of our friends would know words like fraternal. We didn't even know what it meant and just looked at each other, shruggin' our shoulders. Then we'd tell them the truth, and they'd just laugh and say, "Oh, Irish twins!" Then we'd both say while shruggin' our shoulders, "No, we're Italian twins!"

Phylo was only six and just started first grade. Ever since the whole getting Phylo drunk incident, there was no way in heck that my mother was gonna trust us to walk her home from school. So she just walked her home herself unless she was working. Then Grandma Fannie walked her home. Sometimes our friends walked home with us—usually Cassie. But today it was just Sammy and me. On the way home, we stopped in Inkelbrinks' candy store, which was a block away from school. I had a quarter in my pocket that I took outta my piggy bank, which was actually a cow, but I never heard the word cowie bank, so I couldn't call it that. I had money saved from my birthday, unlike Sammy who never saved a penny. My mother said that money burned a hole in his pocket, whatever that means. So I bought a Bit-O-Honey for me, which was ten cents, and a Bazooka bubble gum for Sammy, which was only a nickel. That still left me with ten cents left over. I always shared my money with Sammy even though he never spent a penny of his money on me. In fact, all the money that he got for his birthday in April from Grandma Fannie and our other relatives was gone already. I don't know what he spent it on. I secretly thought that Sammy was a gum-a-holic because he always had a piece of Bazooka bubble gum in his mouth. You'd be talkin' to him and, in the middle of a sentence, turn around and he'd pop you in the face with a big bubble. He'd be laughin' his silly chuckle that sounded more like the evil villain in the cartoons, and I'd be stuck tryin'a peel his sticky, icky gum off'a my face. He'd fall asleep with gum in his mouth and wake up with gum in his mouth. He always got in trouble for chewin' gum in school, and my mother told him that if she had'da go up to school one more time cause of his gum chewin', she'd wire his mouth shut and tube-feed him!

So anyway, me and Sammy were gettin' up to our house when I noticed that comin' up the block, walkin' right toward us, was Rock and Roll. Now that wasn't his real name, of course. Nobody knew what it was. They called him Rock and Roll cause if you yelled out the words rock and roll, he went crazy! Now I didn't know who told me this bit'a wisdom, or what it was that he actually did, but I did know that I was itchin'a find out. So as we were climbin' the first step onto the stoop, I told Sammy, "Look, it's Rock and Roll!" Of course, he just blew a bubble in my face and said, "Who?" So I climbed up to the top step and stood under the red awning, hidin' and holdin' my breath so that I could hardly breathe. As Sammy stood next to me just blowin' and poppin', I silently counted to three and waited until Rock and Roll passed our house and was already two houses down before I did it. I stuck out my head, and as loud as I could, yelled out, "Rock and Roll!" Well, he stopped dead in his tracks and spun his head around so fast that I thought it was gonna fall off. Now, I have'ta explain what he looked like. He was real tall, way over 6 feet, and big, real big. He looked like Mr. Clean with a big bald head, and the only thing missin' was the earring. He made up for that with all the tattoos runnin' up and down his arms. He wore a white undershirt and had giant arms like the statue of the Greek god Apollo. And he carried a portable AM/FM radio on his left shoulder that he held with his left hand so that it looked like he was talkin' on the phone, or touchin' his head like he was playin' Simon Says. The only thing was that I couldn't picture him playin' any kind'a game that didn't involve him seriously hurtin' somebody.

Now I was suddenly sorry that I opened my big mouth and blurted out those seemingly harmless three words, "rock and roll." But it was too late. The damage was done, and the bull was in the ring! It took a split second for me to see the glare in his eyes, and before I could say, Jesus, Mary, and Joseph, he took two giant steps without sayin' "May I" and was almost on my stoop. I turned as fast as I could to grab the doorknob, but my hands were shakin' so hard that I couldn't turn it. Meanwhile, dingbat Sammy, who stood there lookin' like a clown in the Barnum and Bailey Circus, with his blue eyes poppin' out and a giant bubble poppin' outta his mouth, stepped on my foot, pushin' me outta the way. Sammy got the door open and escaped into the hallway faster than I could say three-ring circus. Once again, my superhero brother decided'ta save his own skin and leave me alone to slay the dragon—in this case, crazy Rock and Roll! Well, I didn't have'ta look cause I felt his dragon breath on my heels. I prayed to the Blessed Mother to give me the strength, and I guess that she musta heard me cause the next thing that I knew, I was in the vestibule. But then I panicked cause I realized that I had'da ring the bell for my father to buzz me into the hallway since we didn't have keys. As I awaited my impending doom, I thought to myself, Sammy has sold me out once again, and if by some miracle I survive this, I'll never buy that little brat another piece'a gum as long as I live!

Then, as if hearin' my thoughts, Sammy redeems himself by opening the door so that I can get into the hallway before Rock and Roll grabs my ponytail. The door slammed on his big fat hand, and just when I thought I'd be able to take a breath, I heard a buzzer sound. I immediately knew that some simpleminded person in my building buzzed Rock and Roll into the hallway. I hoped that it wasn't my father cause it was bad enough to be sold out by my bratty brother and couldn't bear to have two people in my immediate family contributing to my early demise. I could understand if it was Grandma Fannie cause she was old or maybe the fruit man on the second floor cause he was fruity. But please, God, not my father! Anyway, before I could take a step, Sammy was already up the stairs, poppin' his gum like it was the Fourth of July. I reminded myself to really let him have it!

I started up the staircase and was screamin' for my father. I suddenly reminded myself of the story about "Jack and the Beanstalk," except Jack called for his mother and was climbin' down. Like Jack, though, I silently screamed for my father to get the ax. The only problem was that I knew he didn't have one. And let's face it, even if he did, he was no lumberjack! He was a waiter and a chef. Maybe he could beat Rock and Roll to death with his wooden spoon! I got up to the second-floor landing and didn't have'ta look back, even if I had the nerve cause I felt the thunder of his massive feet poundin' only a few steps behind me. And cause he was a giant, he was takin' the stairs two at a time!

I saw Sammy up ahead, makin' his way to the third-floor staircase, runnin' so fast that his crew cut stood straight up in the air like he was bein' electrocuted. Of course, he was still chewin' like a cow and blowin' more bubbles than *The Lawrence Welk Show*. Now we were both screamin' for my father, and as I made my way to the third-floor staircase, I turned my head for an instant and was sorry that I did! He was just a few steps behind me, lookin' wild like a spooked stallion. He still carried the radio on his shoulder, but now he was just screamin' at the top'a his lungs, "Rock and roll!"

I was almost paralyzed with fear and managed two steps up when I lost my shoe. I hesitated for a split second to try and slip my foot back in when I felt him grabbin' for my ponytail. Sammy was almost to the top'a the stairs, and we were both screamin' like crazy. Everybody else in the building was pokin' their heads outta their doors to see what the commotion was, but my father still didn't open the door. If I knew him, he had somethin' on the stove and didn't want it to burn. Well, if he didn't open the door soon, I'd be burnin' with Rock and Roll's fiery dragon hands around my throat!

All of a sudden, and not a second too soon, my father opened the door, screamin' and cursin' in Italian. And just as I suspected, he had a wooden spoon in his hand. If only it were one hundred times bigger and made of brick! Sammy scurries under his raised arms like the little rat that he is and safely gets into the house.

Then my father saw me two steps away and suddenly stopped cursin' in Italian cause he saw a big scary monster two steps behind me. Then by some miracle, I made it to the landing, and before my father got some crazy idea in his Napolitano head that he could actually slay the dragon, I did the impossible!

I charged right into my father like a bull on a matador. I don't know where I got the strength. Maybe it was the Blessed Mother. Maybe it was Michelina. But before my father could say "O Sole Mio," I pushed him inside the door, fallin' on top'a him.

I managed to scramble to my feet and double-bolt lock the door. After that, it all happened so fast and was sort of a blur. From the hallway, Rock and Roll screamed and banged on the door as my father yanked on my ponytail. His Italian curse words that day were ones I'd never heard before, and I was sure that he was makin' them up on the spot. He didn't even know what he was sayin'. All the while, Sammy just stood there, smirkin' his silly smirk, just chewin' and blowin' and poppin', like he didn't have a care in the world. Well, not for long, cause my father let go'a me and grabbed Sammy by his crew cut so fast that his glasses fell off. And faster than Sammy could say Bazooka, my father slapped his giant bubble, leavin' Sammy with a big pink circle on his face.

Still, Rock and Roll banged on our door! And we didn't care that our father was lettin' us have it. We didn't feel a thing cause we knew that a couple'a whacks with my fathers' wooden spoon was nothin' compared to what Rock and Roll woulda done to us. In fact, we were happy as pigs in you know what and felt safe. We were even smilin', which got him even madder. Then he started cursin' in Italian again, and we'd start laughing again. On and on went this relentless cycle, and we loved it cause we knew that our Napolitano father was harmless and a wimp at heart til my mother got home and he told her what happened. Then we'd get scared and start sayin' our Hail Marys.

Eventually, Rock and Roll left, and we were just happy that our father didn't open the door, or I wouldn't be here to tell this story! After that day, I couldn't stand the word "rock and roll." I loved the music, but if anybody said the word, I'd cringe. I never did let Sammy have it, and whenever I had money, I still bought him Bazooka bubble gum even though my parents said that he wasn't allowed to chew it anymore. He was still my brother, and the only one that I had, brat or not.

My friend Cassie told me about a crazy guy in the neighborhood that went nuts when you yelled out the words "One, Two, Three." I just ran away from her screamin', "Stop it! I don't wanna hear it!"

CHAPTER 10

Poor Leonard

I was six and a half years old when I started first grade. My birthday was in May, and I started school in September. There was no preschool or kindergarten. There was no formal introduction or lengthy preparation into the world of education, and just like every other unsuspecting kid my age, I was thrown headfirst into that vast sea of learning to sink or swim. The decision was totally up to me. Like an unfit flounder, flailing and flopping around, the choice was clear. Either grow some gills or drown.

No, the kids of my generation weren't pampered and lead by the hand like sweet little lambs into their first day of school. We weren't trained and programmed from the minute of birth to become superhuman brainiac children, competing for the gold medal in the Baby Olympics. Our parents didn't quiz and test us. They didn't fill out lengthy forms and applications when we were two years old in the hopes of us someday being accepted at Harvard or Yale. Our parents didn't lie about our addresses so that we could be given the best opportunity at a better school in a better neighborhood. They didn't stab their neighbor in the back so that we could trump their kid outta the last seat in the best school in the city.

No way! Are you kidding me? We went to the school in our neighborhood that was closest to our house. And in my neighborhood, almost all of us went to Catholic school, and that school was St. Sylvester. Now I gotta say that Sylvester was a saint that I never heard of, and I never even heard of a person named Sylvester, definitely not one'a the kids in the neighborhood. As a matter of fact, the only one I knew with that name was Sylvester the Cat from the cartoons, and I'm sure that he wasn't a saint, no matter how good he was.

Unlike the kids of today, kids in the 1950s and 1960s started first grade virtually unprepared according to today's standards and might as well have been blindfolded with cotton stuffed into our ears for the amount of knowledge that we had accumulated up to that point. But knowledge is relative. There are book smarts and then there are street smarts. Granted, we probably didn't have much of either at that point, except for what we learned at home, and we all know that most of us have spent most of our lives trying to unlearn most of that information.

The point is that it didn't matter because we were all the same. We all started at square one, and no one had the upper hand with an ace hidden in our back pocket. The only card game we knew was Crazy Eights or Old Maid and the Italian card games like Sweep (*Scopa*) and Brisk because our grandmothers taught us on rainy Saturday afternoons, and like the naive children we were, so proud of ourselves for knowing our ABCs song. I was personally proud of the fact that I could count by fives in that sing-song way, even if it was only up to thirty. My grandma Fannie taught me that, along with many other immeasurable things, just as my friends' grandmothers taught them special things no one else knew but them.

We all started first grade as equals, simple kids who weren't simpleminded, just lucky enough to still have our innocence intact. More concerned about winning a game of tag than winning a race to the front of the classroom, we were smart enough to know that there was a time and place for everything. And although this was a school that we were entering, our place in the world was that of children, and it was still our time to do childish things. Our lessons to be learned in the outside world were just as important, even more so than the ones we were to learn in school. We had the smarts in our head, like an uncooked recipe, the ingredients were all in there, just waiting to be simmered and stirred. We didn't need poking and prodding. Our parents didn't have the time or energy, and the nuns had about fifty-eight other kids in the class to deal with. Not exactly an ideal situation for individualized attention. And yet, somehow, we survived. Some of us even excelled. All in due time. There was no sense of urgency to stuff our brains with as much information as possible in as little time as possible. We weren't running for the finish line because our lives were just starting. It wasn't the end of the world—just the first day of school.

We lived in a melting pot, each one of us adding our own special spice to the stew, so we learned from each other. If I ran out of oregano, I borrowed some caraway seeds from my friend Cassie who was German/Irish, so we learned about each other's different cultures.

On our first day of first grade, we were six years old, and we all wore the same navy-blue uniform with navy-blue knee socks and brown Oxford shoes. Our families all came from the same lower middle class, and by today's standards, we were poor. But we were rich because we were happy. There was no need to compete because there was nothing to lose. We didn't push and shove each other outta the way unless it was the last day of school, and we couldn't wait to go out and play. Then we'd push each other down the stairs to see who could get home first to change out of our school clothes and be first in a game of "I Eat!"

I'm not a political person, and other than performing my civic duty to vote in whatever election is happening at the time, I steer away from politics altogether. But I grew up in the 1950s and 1960s, two of the most chaotic and life-altering decades of all time. So it would be impossible to talk about my childhood without mentioning the crazy world around me.

I started first grade in 1958 and was only six years old, so of course, I was shielded from the media like all my friends and totally unaware of what was going on in the world. In those days, kids didn't watch the news or read newspapers. Our world consisted of the happy life of Donna Reed and the zany antics of the Three Stooges. Ignorance was bliss, and we had no idea about the Korean War or Communism. We didn't know about Fidel Castro and Cuba, and the only thing that we knew about the Russians was that Speedy and the other Lithuanians on the block—we're glad to be away from them. We didn't know about Julius and Ethel Rosenberg, the atomic bomb, or the FBI. The only Ethel that we knew was Lucy's best friend and we couldn't wait for the next episode to see what trouble they'd get into next. We didn't know about all the civil rights marches in Washington, DC, and that Black people were still being beaten and tied to trees in Alabama and Mississippi. All we knew was that on *The Little Rascals*, Buckwheat and Stymie were just Alfalfa and Spanky's friends, that Carla played with all of them, and that Mrs. Crabtree treated all the kids in her class the same. We loved to watch *Amos 'n' Andy* and didn't think that there was anything wrong with the picture of Aunt Jemima on the pancake box.

But then again, we were dumb little poor kids. So what did we know? We knew that something was going on because every time a plane flew overhead really low, Cassie Meehan would start screaming, "The Japs! Run for cover!" This statement was really silly because, first of all, the planes always flew overhead very low since we lived less than a mile away from Kennedy Airport, which was called Idlewild at the time. Secondly, the Japs, as Cassie called them, were long gone with World War II. She was probably thinking of the Koreans, who were our latest Asian threat but just remembered her parents yelling about the Japs.

The main reason that we knew something weird was going on was because we always had air raid drills in school. Now this was such a strange phenomenon that it comes under the category of "Did that really happen, or did I just imagine it?" But it did happen during my early grades, probably up until the fifth or sixth grade. There was so much turmoil going on in the world at the time. Between the Bay of Pigs and the Cuban Missile Crisis, and then Russia with Khruschev, President Kennedy had his hands full. It was also the beginning of the Vietnam War. But like I said, we were naive little kids. So when the alarm first sounded, we didn't know what was going on.

All we knew was that we heard a sound so earth-shattering that our eardrums ached, and you could imagine every dog within a ten-mile radius spinning in circles, trying to look for cover and ready to commit dog-a-cide. It was the kinda eerie alarm that you heard in movies about the Holocaust or prison courtyards warning the inmates that fun time was over.

But the craziest part was after the alarm went off, Sister Mary Margaret, or whoever was our teacher at the time, blew her little whistle, the same one she used for choir practice, and screamed for all of us to take cover under our desks. We had the old dark wooden desks at the time with an opening underneath on one side, and the other side was where we kept our books. Now the amount of space under there wasn't too big unless you were a small dog or one of the skinny kids like Donna Palmetto, who was in third grade but still looked like she was six years old. Most of us kids were big—tall and chubby. It musta been all the Hostess CupCakes and Twinkies.

But unfortunately for him, nobody in the class was as big as Leonard Summers. He looked like a grizzly bear, and the sight of him trying to squeeze himself under his desk was hilarious! It was like a Great Dane trying to squeeze into a miniature poodle's doghouse. Even Houdini couldn't get him in there! As we all scurried to get under our desks, we heard a loud thumping sound. Now Leonard's desk was in the row to my left and about two seats behind me, and since his opening was on the same side as mine, I got a perfect view. All you could see was his giant baby elephant butt sticking out of his desk as he desperately tried to squeeze it in. He looked like a small planet—*Uranus*. And like trying to squeeze ten pounds of potatoes into a five-pound bag, it just wouldn't work. Now, he was stuck in there, and like a bull at a rodeo, he started bucking up and down, trying to free himself and send the imaginary cowboy on his back, flying across the room. Then everybody in the class started turning their heads, trying to see where the loud thumping sound was coming from, and some of the kids who could see, like me, started giggling.

That's when Sister Mary Margaret started yelling, "What's going on back there? Stop all that giggling right this instant! Don't you children realize that there is a serious drill going on?" But by that time, the sound was getting louder, and Leonard even started crying, "Help me! I'm stuck!" I felt bad for him, but I couldn't help laughing because it was just so funny to see. His desk just kept jumping up and down like it was on springs. And then there was his butt, so big and bouncing around the room from side to side. Well, Sister finally crawled out from under her desk to see what all the commotion was about. She shoulda traded desks with Leonard. He woulda fit under her desk, and she had a better chance of fitting under his, even with her long black habit on. By now, all the kids were laughin' and getting up to see Leonard's butt sticking out. When Sister saw what he actually looked like from *behind*, she turned beet red and tried to murmur somethin' comforting to him like, "Don't worry, Leonard, we'll get you outta there." But we all saw her turning her head and twisting her mouth to keep from laughin'. She tried her best, but I guess that nuns are human after all because, all of a sudden, she let out a sound like a horse's whinny. We couldn't believe it! Our heads snapped to look at Sister, and sure enough, she was laughin' too! Then she started apologizing, saying, "Please forgive me. I'm so sorry!" and we didn't know if she was talking to Leonard or God. Maybe both.

Then as if things weren't funny enough, the unthinkable happened. Leonard was crying and squirming so much that the desk kept jumping around the room as his butt twisted from side to side. Well, I guess that his navy-blue Catholic school dress pants, which were tight already, couldn't handle all the action, and they just split right down the middle of his butt. Sister gasped out loud, then started calling for Jesus, as she frantically blessed herself. Houdini couldn't get him into the desk, and now even Jesus couldn't get him out.

All the while, the alarm kept sounding for what seemed like forever, and even John Dobson, who usually just sat in his seat eating crayons all day long or trying to set his desk on fire, started laughin' so loud he sounded like a hyena.

When the astronauts landed on the moon, they placed an American flag there, to stake America's claim. Now, as I hid under my desk, hysterical at the crazy shenanigans going on and peeing my underpants with the days of the week on them, I imagined the Cubans or Russians shooting a giant arrow with a flag of their country right into poor Leonard's butt. If they were gonna attack, he woulda been the first target they'd see. From way up in the sky, they woulda had a clear view directly into my classroom, landing firmly into Leonard's butt, staking their claim on our country as if he were our designated mascot.

TWO LEFT FEET

After the alarm finally stopped, and we all laughed as hard as we possibly could, and every last drop of pee had trickled its way onto the floor, Sister Mary Margaret managed to regain some sort'a composure in the classroom. Sister tried as hard as she could to try and pry Leonard out from under the desk, but all he ended up doin' was kickin' her like a mule. She probably wanted to kick herself for not bein' able to better control the situation or her own impulses to laugh. She'd be in confession before the day was over, that's for sure.

Sister called Victor, the janitor to our class, to see if he could get Leonard outta the desk, but he thought that he was just comin' up for his usual daily mopping because Karen Panza peed her pants every day. It was like clockwork. Every day at the same time, she'd stand up and in the middle of the aisle just start to pee like a water faucet. Well, today, she was like Niagara Falls. But before he could get to his chore of mopping up the flood in the room, Sister led him over to Leonard. Well, I guess that janitors are human too cause Victor starting roaring out loud like a lion.

Meanwhile, poor Leonard musta had some crick in his neck from being stuck in there so long, and we were all starting to wonder if he'd ever get outta there alive. Victor pulled and tugged as hard as he could on Leonard's exposed butt but laughed every time he saw his white Fruit of the Looms. One thing Leonard could be grateful for was that he wore clean underwear that day and that God forbid, it would'a been one'a those days when you ran outta underwear. What a nightmare that woulda been! Not just for him but us and Sister! We woulda all passed out for sure, just lyin' there waitin' for the enemy to capture us!

As Victor pulled, he got a couple'a the big boys to help by holding the desk down so that it stopped floppin' around the room. Now we were all just standing around, watching and hopin' that Leonard wouldn't die under there, of embarrassment or anything else. Sister was praying on her rosary and pacing back and forth. It was kinda like a woman in labor. It seemed to go on forever, and poor Leonard just wasn't budging. He was stuck, like the big fat baby that he was. Victor tried for a long time then started talking about greasing him up like a turkey so that he might slide out. Then he said somethin' about maybe havin' to call the fire department and needing the jaws of life to get him out.

When Leonard heard this, he started screamin' hysterically, and we thought that he was a dead man for sure. Then I started wishin' that Superman was a real guy and not just a fake TV show cause poor fat Leonard could'a really used him then. We would'a taken Mighty Mouse at that point. Then all of a sudden, it looked like he was startin'ta budge a little. I guess between all his tears, sweat, and snots, and who knows, maybe even some pee too, Leonard was lubricating himself up enough to get slippery and slide himself right outta there, like a home run sliding into third base just in time.

Victor and the two boys pushed and pulled one last time as hard as they could. Then all of a sudden, we heard a loud pop like a champagne cork, and out popped Leonard, like a giant baby bird emerging from his shell. Everybody tried to help him up cause he was wobbly like a spinning top. Sister came over to see if he was all right. They helped him to a chair, Sister's chair, not his desk. He was still whimpering like a puppy and embarrassed about his pants being ripped open. Sister told him not to worry and that she'd call his mother to bring him another pair'a pants. They brought him some water, and we all just looked at him like we were seein' him for the first time.

Leonard's mother came up to school with new pants and took him home. Sister let us have an early dismissal. We left quietly and orderly. Nobody was laughin'. After we all left, Victor was there for hours, cleaning up the mess. He had'da use a whole bottle'a Lysol on the floor to get out the smell'a pee. Leonard stayed home from school for a couple'a days, and when he came back, none of us teased him about what happened. It was weird, but we all asked him if he was okay, even John Dobson stopped chewing on his Crayola crayons long enough to grunt at him and mumble, "Hey, you all right?"

I guess that Catholic school was startin'ta have a positive effect on us and that we were all developing a conscience and somethin' else too—compassion. Who knew? We all went home that day grateful for two things: one was that Leonard was still alive, and second, that we weren't attacked and bombed by the Russians or Cubans or Koreans or whatever other bad guy was out to get us that day.

CHAPTER 11

The Jew and the Shiksa

Like most kids on my block, I went to Catholic school along with my brother and sister. In those days, Catholic school was practically free, and it didn't matter how many kids were in your family cause you got a discount for every extra kid in your household. This worked out just great for the Irish families cause we all know how many kids they had. On average, it was seven. Instead'a tuition like today, where the cost of nursery school is equivalent to the cost of an Ivy League college back then, all our families had'da do was given a donation to the church every week.

Sure, they asked for a certain amount, but my mother just went up there to talk to whoever was in charge at the time and gave her a sad story about not havin' enough money, and they just said, "Okay, my dear, the Lord will provide." And I guess He did cause I know that the mothers of every other kid on my block went up there with a similar story and was told the same thing. We just had'da give an envelope to the church on Sunday. And everybody did too. So I guess that the Lord did provide for my whole neighborhood cause none of us paid tuition and we didn't go hungry either. Between selling chances, raffle tickets, and Friday night bingo, along with cake sales, spring carnivals, and bazaars, the church made enough money to stay open.

There musta been a few public school kids on the block, but for the life'a me, I can't remember a single one, except for the one Jewish kid who lived in the apartment house and was named after a show about a horse. He had a long neck like a horse, so we called him Mr. Ed. His real name was Eddie Horowitz. He was a few years older than me and already in high school. He never played outside with the rest of us, and while we were outside screamin' and fightin' in a game'a red light, green light, or ring-a-levio, like the hoodlums that we were, he'd just pass by with his big black glasses on his face and his yarmulke on his head. (We called it a beanie.) Then he'd smile a crooked little smile at me, give a half-hand wave, like he was reluctantly raising his hand in class, then shake his head, and walk away.

Now I know that he was a little older, but so were some'a the other boys, so I could never figure out why he didn't play with us. He didn't even go to the Earl Movie Theater on Saturday afternoons for the races and prizes. He clearly was different but interesting. He was tall and thin with jet-black hair and kinda cute in a nerdy kinda way but never said two words to me or anybody else for that matter. He'd just smile then walk on by with his armload of books.

A while later, my mother told me that his mother stopped her on the sidewalk one day to talk. She said that Eddie really liked me and had a crazy idea of marrying me someday. Then his mother got mad, yelling at my mother, practically spitting in her face with her breath that smelled like fried onions. She told my mother that there was no way in hell that her only son was gonna marry a ginny Gentile and that I'd better keep my *shiksa* hands off'a him. Now my mother never heard of that word but took it to be the Yiddish version of the Italian *putana*. His mother was short and skinny with wiry gray hair, and except for the black glasses, she didn't look at all like Eddie. She wore black sweatshorts with nylon stockings rolled around her ankles and held up by rubber bands. Not a pretty sight! His mother went on to say that Eddie was very smart, studying at Yeshiva (a Jewish school) and that he was preparing for an Ivy League college, and that there was no way a little greaseball was gonna get in the way of his education. So I should get any ideas of marrying a rich Jewish boy outta my head because over her dead body would it happen.

My mother was keeping calm up to this point, but that last line about her dead body started filling her head with wild thoughts. It was one thing for this skinny little witch to call her daughter a ginny and a greaseball, but my mother knew that I was no *putana*, and whatever kinda Jewish curse she was spittin' out at her was no match for what my mother kept in her back pocket.

Now my mother was not a violent woman, except for when she yelled at us kids, and she didn't wanna cause a scene, right out there in front'a all the neighbors. But it didn't take long before smoke started comin' outta her ears, and she started thinkin' of Fannie and Michelina and all the famous Sicilian curses or *malocchios* that were cast in our family's history. Her palms started sweating, and she started mumbling in Sicilian under her breath. She thought to herself what would my grandmother do, and before you could say *malocchio*, my mother was givin' her the horns and pullin' that wiry gray hair outta her head. Like a whirling tornado, Eddie's mother never saw her comin' and, just like Dorothy, had nowhere to hide.

Thank God, my father happened to be comin' up the block and got there just in time before my mother pulled every hair outta her head. He pulled my mother off'a her and dragged her into the house. He didn't even wanna hear her side'a the story about what happened, and that's strange cause my father was very protective of me. Mrs. Horowitz just stood there, eatin' my mother's ginny dust and rubbin' her head…

They never talked to us again, and Eddie even stopped waving at me. As far as I know, my mother's curse never took on his mother. I mean, we never saw her walkin' down the block limpin' or anything. She didn't lose an eye, and her hair was still gray instead'a blue and purple.

About a year later, we found out from another lady who lived in the apartment house that Eddie was goin' to a very snazzy college in Indiana, that he got all kinda scholarships, and was studyin' to be a brain surgeon. I never saw him again. So that's the story of how I almost married a Jewish boy without ever really wantin' to.

Sometimes when my mother gets really mad at me, she'll yell out, "You shoulda married that Jew boy!" And then I'll think to myself, "But, Ma, you put a curse on his mother. I somehow don't think that it woulda worked out!"

CHAPTER 12

I Eat Fish Eyes

I told you about Eddie Horowitz, the only Jewish kid on my block. Other than him, the rest of us were Irish and Italians. There were a couple'a families like my friend Cassie, who were mostly Irish with a little German sprinkled in—sort'a like the Irish part bein' the banana split and the German part bein' the rainbow sprinkles, so we just called them Irish. And then there were the Lithuanians. It was kinda weird cause there were only about three or four families in all, and they were strategically placed in every other building, almost like they were tryin'a hide from the Russians.

Now I don't know alot about politics, but I do know that they tried to escape Communism, and what better place to hide than Looney Lane? The Russians would never find them here, among the rest of us average, run of the mill, lower-middle-class citizens, like lookin' for a needle in a haystack. If our block was a melting pot, then the Lithuanians were the hot spice sprinkled in. They were the paprika on our egg noodles. I wondered what made certain people of certain nationalities pick a specific area to move to and if they all knew each other. I decided that they must'a all known each other, and the first one'ta move there told the next one and so on.

In the building next door to me must'a been the first Lithuanian to arrive on my block, and his name was Speedy. Now that wasn't his real name, of course. Nobody knew his real name, except for maybe the other Lithuanians. The reason we called him Speedy was really funny or seemed funny when you were a stupid kid. The fact was that it literally took him about a half hour to walk down the block. Now that might'a seemed pretty mean'a us kids to tease him that way, but he wasn't your typical fragile old man. Yes, he did have a cane, which was more like a giant club, or a tree branch that he carried over with him from the old country. I can just picture him tryin'a check it as baggage on the airplane or putting it in the overhead compartment as a carry-on. But I guess that he must'a come over by boat, and that would'a made it a little easier for him to smuggle it over. But he most probably just got it here, maybe from the tree around the corner. Whatever. The point is that he carried a weapon and wasn't afraid to use it on poor innocent children. Okay, maybe we weren't so innocent, but we were poor.

I don't think that Speedy actually hit anybody with his tree stump, but not cause he didn't try. He was just never able'ta get close enough. He was just too slow. I can't remember what we did that could'a been so bad for him to wanna kill us. All I know is that whenever we saw him come outta his house or saw him walking up the never-ending mile which was our block, we'd all scream, "Aaahh! here comes Speedy! Run for your life!" as if he could ever catch us!

He did get pretty close to me one time when we were all hidin' inside his gate, which was like an oversized pigpen. We saw him comin' up the block and knew that it would probably be dark before he reached us, so we had plenty'a time to just wait before screamin' "Aaahh!" But we must'a gotten distracted plannin' our next big scheme, or Speedy was on roller skates cause, all of a sudden, we looked up, and there he was, standin' outside the gate. He was cursin' at us in Lithuanian and wavin' his tree stump over our heads like he was king of the mountain.

Everybody scurried like dirty rats tryin'a climb outta the gate. We pushed and shoved each other outta the way, trampling on heads to get to safety. Forget the Three Musketeers' motto of "All for one, and one for all." We were unscrupulous pirates, and our motto was "Every man for himself!" So who'da'ya think was left standing there alone? That's right. Just like that silly song about the cheese standing alone, you can call me mozzarella! Better make that Roquefort, it's stinkier.

So there I was, trapped inside the gate, with Speedy wavin' his big tree stump over my head as my so-called friends stood outside, watchin' and gigglin'. I was in the ring, the main attraction, and they were the spectators. The sad thing was, I think that they were itchin' to see my blood all over Speedy's stick. Some friends! I'd have'ta take care'a them later. First things first. How to escape? The only thing on my side was that my opponent wasn't in the ring with me. That was my ace in the hole. Speedy was mean, and maybe even crazy, but there was no way that he was gonna climb into the gate with me. That was for sure.

So was my strategy to wait it out til he gave up cause he was too tired, or had'da go to the bathroom, or did I do the brave thing and try'ta make a run for it? That would'a shown my so-called friends a thing or two, wouldn't it? After all, success is the best revenge, and I really wanted revenge against those losers so bad that I could taste it. If I wasn't so busy tryin'a escape, I woulda tried to conger up a curse from Michelina. My dead *strega* (witch) of a namesake, where was she when I needed her most? Maybe helpin' some other poor girl who got herself in a pickle. I sure hope that she wasn't laughin' at me and how gullible I could be.

Anyway, I decided'a go with plan B and make a run for it by distracting Speedy. I just yelled out at the top'a my lungs, "Speedy, look out! The Russians are comin'!" Well, the poor old guy cowered to the ground, coverin' his head, and started mumblin' somethin' that sounded like prayers, and I climbed over the fence onto the stoop and ran down to the sidewalk on the other side'a Speedy. He never even noticed me making a run for it. I felt kinda guilty about the way I scared him and all. After all, he scared us all the time, right? Why should I feel sorry for him? But I did.

Who I didn't feel sorry for was that pack'a losers I used'ta call friends, especially that idiot Charlie Desanto, the usual ringleader in any crazy shenanigans. He was the first one'ta jump inside the gate and the first one out. What a coward! Meanwhile, he was always tellin' me how he wanted me'ta be his girlfriend and marry him someday. Yeah, right! Like I'd ever! Especially not now! He could just marry Suzie O'Flannagan for all I care! He tells her he wants'ta marry her too. On the days that he can't find me. Why doesn't he make up his stupid mind already? I don't think that she can stand him either. Good for him! That's what he gets for pickin' daisies from old man Mancuso's garden for Suzie and me. Not only a coward but a thief! No thank you. If and when I was ready for a boyfriend, it was gonna be somebody better than him.

I wanted'a clobber Charlie and the rest'a those kids over the head with Speedy's tree stump that day, but I didn't. Somethin' stopped me. Maybe my conscience, maybe Michelina, or maybe my fear'a goin'a juvenile hall. I didn't do well in closed spaces.

I never did tease Speedy anymore. After that day, it just didn't seem funny. The other kids still did. But I couldn't control what they did. I was still tryin'a control my own silly impulses to do stupid, childish things. I was changin' somehow, hopefully for the better. Maybe this was what growin' up was all about. All I knew was that I didn't like the way it felt to see Speedy so upset and scared that day. I knew that it was wrong, and I promised myself that I wouldn't deliberately hurt anybody's feelings that way again—at least I was gonna try not'ta.

We all thought of Speedy as a monster who we needed to fulfill our childish games, but I realized that he was just a frightened, lonely old man in a strange country who maybe needed a friend. I also realized that our ideas of monsters and friends can change on any given day. I needed my friends to help me that day, and they acted like monsters. And then there was Speedy, who we all thought of as a monster, but maybe he only acted that way cause we treated him that way. I didn't know and was confused. I went over'ta Speedy that day, tryin'a pat him on the shoulder and help him to his feet when I saw him cryin'. We were so mean, and I felt so guilty.

Now maybe Speedy was just a mean old man after all. I don't know for sure, but I like to believe he was just lonely.

If Speedy was the first Lithuanian to arrive on Looney Lane, then Mr. Apamadis was the second. He lived in the same building as Speedy and most probably was shipped over by Speedy as back up on the war against us kids. But unlike Speedy, Mr. Apamadis was not mean and scary and didn't take all day'ta walk down the block. In fact, he was his total opposite. Just like Dr. Jekyll and Mr. Hyde.

Mr. Apamadis was fast like lightning, tall and thin, and he scurried around like an Eastern European elf. He was the super of the building, and you'd always see him smilin' and wavin' at us kids as he carried giant bags of trash or heavy planks of wood. If Speedy's big idea was to have Mr. Apamadis as his comrade in scaring the life outta us kids, he was dead wrong cause Mr. Apamadis was kind and gentle. On more than one occasion, he had'ta calm Speedy down, preventing him from clobberin' one'a us over the head with his tree stump. In a way, Mr. Apamadis was kinda like the Lithuanian Superman. He helped to keep peace and order on our block and was our hero.

There were two other Lithuanian families on the block. One was a brother and sister named Leja and Lukas. Leja was eleven just like me, and Lukas was twelve. She was in my class, so I guess they were Catholic too. Leja had long light-brown braids that hung in front of her and went all the way down to her waist. They were strong and thick like heavy ropes, and I could imagine them comin' in handy if you were trapped down a well. She'd lower them down and pull you up to safety, kind'a like a Lithuanian Rapunzel. She also reminded me of the girl on the label of the Vermont Maid maple syrup. Leja and Lukas played outside with us sometimes but were not regulars in our gang'a misfits. Lukas had a short crew cut, and the hair on top'a his head stood straight up like a porcupine. Leja had a high-pitched squeal like a bunch'a seals and would start soundin' her alarm for Lukas to help her whenever somebody said somethin' to her that she didn't like. All of a sudden, you'd hear "Luukkeee!" and he'd come runnin' like her own personal superhero. It didn't have'ta be anything bad either. Maybe she was mad cause she couldn't go first in hopscotch or we didn't curtsy at her feet when she came outside, but she thought that she was a princess. She mighta been one in her country, but her crybaby routine wasn't gonna work with us. She had'da wait her turn just like the rest of us. Like it or lump it, as we said.

Now Leja was annoying and a real sissy, but we usually tolerated her with no problem cause she didn't play with us all the time anyway. I think that she and Lukas went to a special Lithuanian school on Saturdays to keep their culture alive. Anyway, unlike Leja, Lukas was quiet and easygoing. He was the Mr. Apamadis to her Speedy.

But one day, while pickin' teams for a game of I Eat, which was like red light, green light, except you had'da call out different foods that you would or wouldn't eat, Leja took the biggest hissy fit of all time. Somebody called out I Eat fish eyes, and Leja started runnin'. When she was called "Out!" she started squealin' like a pig for Lukas to come to her rescue, like she was bein' murdered or somethin'. She started jumpin' up and down, her braids flappin' through the air like elephant ears, insisting that in Lithuania they ate fish eyes along with the eyes of other creatures. All of us unanimously yelled, "*Uuugghh!*" reminding her that the rules in this country were different cause we didn't eat fish eyes no matter how poor we were. If things got that bad, we'd just stick to mayonnaise sandwiches and, in the case'a the Connor family, sugar sandwiches.

But before Lukas could come to her rescue, Suzie O'Flannagan, who was a tough girl on the block, ran up to her and started yankin' on her braids like she was churnin' butter or ringin' a church bell. Leja's braids stretched all the way down to the sidewalk, and she was cryin' so hard that nothin' came outta her mouth. She just stood there with her eyes and mouth wide open like she was at the doctor's office, and he said, "Say aaahhh." Nothin' came out. No high-pitched squeal. Nothin'.

By the time Lukas reached her side, her braids were all outta their rubber bands, and there was hair all over the sidewalk. He came over just shruggin' his shoulders and shakin' his head as he looked at us, as if to say, "Sorry, kids, try livin' with her!" He led her by the elbow like the big protective brother that he was, all the way upstairs to their apartment on the third floor. It took almost fifteen minutes for us to hear the loud screams comin' from her window. At least we knew that she was still alive.

After that day, whenever Leja came out, she had her braids wrapped up on top'a her head like two flyin' saucers. She never came out alone and always had Superhero Lukas by her side. She hardly played with us anymore either. Whenever I saw her in class, she'd quickly look over at me then turn her head back real fast as if I didn't notice. I felt bad for Lukas cause he didn't come out to play either. Her loyal subject 'til the end. Oh well, as they say, their loss!

CHAPTER 13

Winston

The other Lithuanian family on the block were two brothers who lived on the top floor of Cassie's building. Their names were Jonas and Tomas, but we called them Johnny and Tommy. Like Leja and Lukas, they went to Catholic school with us and Lithuanian school on Saturday. But unlike them, they played outside with us without creating a scene. There weren't any tantrums, just two nice brothers who liked to have fun and knew how to play by the rules. You'd think that Jonas and Tomas would'a been best friends with Leja and Lukas, bein' that they came from the same country and had a lotta things in common. But they weren't. In fact, I hardly ever saw them together, and they never stood around talkin' in their native language. I think that Jonas and Tomas couldn't stand Leja's superior attitude any more than we could, and just like us, she made them want'a barf. That's for sure. They were full-blooded Americans as far as we were concerned. They played baseball, ate hot dogs, and definitely didn't eat the eyes of fish or anything else on the planet! Uggghhh! Too bad Lucas didn't come out without annoying Leja. We missed him.

Jonas and Tomas were good sports and funny too, especially when it came to Winston. Winston was the craziest character on the block. If we took a survey among all the kids, he'd win, hands down. He lived in the building next to Cassie. He was a grown-up with kids of his own but acted like a kid himself. He wore an old hat that was folded in the middle so it looked like he had it on sideways, like a brown banana on his head. He'd come out onto the stoop and fold his fingers together in a weird way so that he could start whistling from them.

The sound that he made sounded more like a bugle call. If we were in the army, he was the wacky general, and we were his obedient soldiers. Not only did he come out and blow his crazy horn with his hands, but every day, he'd come out with a different snack for us. Like the Pied Piper, he knew how'ta make a block full'a hungry mice come scurrying.

One day, he'd come out with a bag'a chocolate chip cookies and a half gallon of ice cream. He'd take two cookies outta the bag and spoon some ice cream in the middle. We didn't know it then, but he was the original Chipwich inventor and should'a become rich for creating it. He didn't have any plates or napkins and just leaned on his knees to make the sandwiches. It was very unsanitary, and it's a wonder we didn't all get sick and die. What was even more amazing was that our mothers just let us run to his stoop every day and devour whatever crazy concoction he invented that day. Either we were poorer than we thought and our parents were happy that it was one less meal they had'da worry about feedin' us, or they didn't care what we ate or who was feedin' us as long as we were outta their hair. Either way, do the words child abuse sound familiar? And if they were abusive, every mother and father on our block would'a been in jail. Then where would we all go? Foster care? Better to take our chances with Winston.

He was definitely weird but harmless—at least that's what we thought and our parents hoped. Whenever he came out and started tooting his hand horn, we'd all scream, "Winston! Let's go!" It was exciting cause we never knew what sort'a goodies he'd have every day. We looked forward to it. So what if we were covered in melted ice cream that dripped not only from our mouths but from his filthy hands? What was a little food poisoning compared to a lotta fun? We were tough kids and survived eatin' worse, especially Charlie Desanto who practically lived on dirt and worms.

Another day, he came out with a big barrel'a grape jelly. He started pouring water into it from an empty milk gallon and mixing it with a big wooden spoon. He was makin' his very own special kinda Kool-Aid. After mixing, he'd spoon some into little paper cups and hand one out to each of us. Thinkin' about it now, it reminds me of a little massacre in a place called Jonestown, where another guy who seemed harmless made his special Kool-Aid concoction too. Only that story didn't turn out so well! It's a wonder we're all still alive!

Besides his magic whistle and interesting variety of snacks, Winston also made weird sounds. He'd come up to you in the street, carrying an armful of different colored balloons tied to long ribbons and start purring like a cat or barking like a dog. Mostly, it was just the cat thing. He'd say, "Hey, pussycat! Meeooww!" then wink and make clicking sounds with his tongue.

Come'ta think of it, maybe he wasn't so harmless after all. Maybe we were just stupid, naive kids, starving for a little excitement and a lotta candy. In defense of our parents, none of us kids ever told them about the pussycat and meeooww thing cause we knew that they'd make us stop runnin' every time he came out to call. And that would mean no more messy ice-cream sandwiches, jelly Kool-Aid, or whatever else he had up his messy sleeve. Anyway, some of the parents went for free snacks too, especially Mr. Connor. He ran up there with us all the time and sometimes even pushed to get in front'a the line. I guess even he was gettin' sick and tired of his wife's famous snack of Wonder Bread with sugar on top. Anything Winston dished out had'da be better than that.

If nothin' else, Winston sure provided us with a lotta entertainment, like the time the police had'da come cause they thought that he was hangin' in his front window. What happened was, he moved outta the six family building and across the street into the row of three private houses. His was the house in the middle, sandwiched between Sandy Matone's house and Millie DeFalco's. Maybe he did make money on the Chipwich after all cause he bought his own house.

The houses were small, with the top roof, and another sort'a ledge that extended outta the upstairs bedrooms. One day in the summer, we were all outside playin' like usual when somebody looked up at Winston's window and started to scream, "Look! It's Winston. He's hangin' in the window!" Well, of course, everybody started to run over to see what she was screamin' about and to make sure that it wasn't just some hysterical girl. But it was Suzie O'Flannagan, and she was tough and wouldn't start screamin' for no good reason. When we looked up, there was a brown shade in the window and a silhouette of what looked like Winston hangin' there.

Well, before we knew it, the block was swarmin' with cop cars. They even sent out the SWAT team, whatever they do. All of a sudden, everybody and their mother was out, even the grandmothers. For sure, my grandma Fannie was there, inching up to get a front-row view. The older she got, the more of a news reporter she became, and I knew that she'd be taking mental notes. Police officers started climbing up the house onto the ledge to get to the window. They started yellin' for everybody to get back and to remove small children cause it might not be a pretty sight. They musta been kiddin' and didn't know who they were dealin' with cause there was no way that anybody who lived on Looney Lane was gonna run away from excitement like this! This was what we lived for, and even though none of us wanted'a see Winston hangin' and dead, we were sure enjoyin' the show. I'm surprised that somebody didn't start selling popcorn! If Winston wasn't the one in the window, he woulda been down in the street handin' out the snacks. I sure hoped that he wasn't dead. Not just cause we'd miss the goodies either. He was fun too.

All of a sudden, a police officer screamed, "Everybody, back up!" He started breakin' the glass with an ax, and glass started splattering all over the sidewalk. We all started to scream, half in fear of what they'd find and half in anticipation. He gave it a couple'a good whacks, and the glass came flyin' out. Then we all saw it and let out a big "Aaaahhhh!"

It wasn't Winston hangin' from a rope after all. Instead, it was Winston's shirt hangin' on a hanger! Everybody was pushing to the front to see what it was. We heard people chuckling and sayin', "Oh man!" "What a gyp!" like they wanted'a see him hangin' there!

The cops starting yellin', "Okay, folks, it's all over. Go home. There's nothin' to see!"

Even Fannie said, "Aaahhh!" and waved her hand in front'a her face like she was shooing mosquitos away.

It was weird. We were happy that he wasn't dead, but it was a letdown at the same time. Pretty pathetic, wasn't it? How boring were our lives that we were actually excited about the prospect of a man hangin' in his bedroom window?

I don't know about anybody else, but all I can say is that I'm glad that the cops didn't carry out a dead body that day. Everybody stood around murmuring and gigglin' about how stupid the cops musta felt goin' through that whole big scene just to find a shirt on a hanger. It took a long time for the crowd to slowly disperse. Like Romans in an ancient arena, they were contented to throw Winston to the lions.

CHAPTER 14

Vicky and Lilly

The block that I grew up on was a melting pot of wacky characters, and my friend Cassie Meehan's building just sizzled and boiled with loons. If there was a contest in which building on the block had the most wackos, Cassie's would win. I was a little jealous of her good fortune in this contest, but I knew that my building was a close second, so I didn't feel so bad.

On the top floor of her building lived two sisters, Vicky and Lilly. Vicky was more our age, but Lilly was maybe two years older, thirteen or going on fourteen. And there was a world of difference between us, if you know what I mean.

Me and Cassie were still two stupid little fat kids (although we were both startin'a slim down a bit), and they were what you'd call streetwise. They knew things we never even heard of and were sure as heck ready to school us.

It musta been a Saturday afternoon and me and Cassie were outside playin' stoopball when Vicky and Lilly were comin' into the building and asked us if we wanted'a go up to their house for a while. Like I said, we were what you called two naive, innocent Catholic schoolgirls who said a Hail Mary every time we even had a bad thought. Neither one of us had gotten our so-called "friend" yet, and our idea of a good time was dunkin'a pack'a Oreos into a glass'a ice-cold milk.

So we were really surprised that they invited us up since we never really hung out with them before, but we said okay. When we got up there, we noticed that their mother wasn't home and that they were alone. Lilly went into the kitchen and came back a couple'a minutes later with a loaf'a Italian bread sliced lengthwise into two halves that she slobbered with tons of butter. She also had a giant mug'a hot tea with the tea bag hangin' off the side. She set all this out on a snack table then sat down and started dunkin' each long piece of buttered bread into the hot tea. Well, I thought this was the craziest snack I ever saw! Give me a Hostess CupCake anytime. She told us to sit on the couch but didn't offer us any of her snack, which looked more like a meal for a lumberjack. Vicky was sittin' on the couch, just gigglin'.

I started gettin' a weird feeling in my belly, not hunger but somethin' else that I couldn't name. All this shoulda been some indication of what we were in for, but like I said, two dumb, fat kids. They were both what you called developed with big boobs, and Cassie and me knew that they both went out with boys while we still wore trainin' bras, and the only thing we did with boys was fight.

All of a sudden, Lilly tears herself away from her feast, stands up, and asks us if we wanna see somethin'. So we figured that she had the new Beatles poster or the *Hard Day's Night* album. I saw the movie seven times and screamed so loud I almost fainted. Meanwhile, Vicky gets up and goes over to a small table and turns a little lamp on. It has a long flexible neck that she bends, and I notice that the bulb is red, which I find very weird. Vicky plays a weird record on the record player that I never heard before then closes all the venetian blinds so that it's really dark except for the stupid red light. Me and Cassie look at each other and shrug our shoulders, not knowin' what's going on. Then Lilly starts walkin' slowly across the room, wiggling like she just got off a horse and doing a bad John Wayne imitation. Then she turns around and makes a strange kinda face, not a smile, really, but scary like the face of the fat lady in the fun house. Then Lilly starts shakin' her shoulders up and down, and with the scary face, I think that maybe she's havin' a seizure. I knew about seizures on account'a Johnny Muller in my third-grade class took one once, and he was flopping all over the floor like a goldfish out of a bowl. But no. Instead, Lilly starts slidin' the shoulders down on her blouse, one at a time, and I think that maybe she feels hot and we should open a window so she can get some air. She was gettin' hot all right, but stupid me had no idea that it had nothin'a do with the temperature in the room. Me and Cassie got all excited when we thought we were gonna see a new Beatles poster but had no idea that Lilly was also excited!

So now Vicky is following Lilly around the room with the red light as she starts opening the buttons on her blouse. She was wearin' a black bra, somethin' we didn't even know existed, cause we thought they were all white like we wore and like the ones that our mothers wore. I looked at Cassie, and I think that we were both in shock cause all we wanted was to see a new Beatles poster and maybe get a couple'a Mary Janes, but we were sure gettin' a whole lot more than we bargained for. Then Lilly starts grabbin' her boobs with her hands like she's rollin' out pizza dough, pushin' them together, and we see this long line down the middle of her chest that they call cleavage.

Then I think, okay, maybe this is a dance that she had'da learn for school, like a class project about dances from around the world, but what country would do a dance like this? I reminded myself that I'd never visit there when I grew up. All of a sudden, she pulls her left boob outta her blouse and starts jigglin' it back and forth like it's on a seesaw or somethin'. I thought that I was gonna barf and knew that it had nothin'a do with school—not the kind that I went to anyway. I thought of Sister Margaret Angela and said as many silent Hail Marys as I could. I looked over at Cassie who was as white as a ghost, and I thought she was gonna pass out. Now she was normally white, being Irish and all, but she looked like a sheet out on the clothesline. Our feet were like cement, and we couldn't move if we wanted'ta, and we wanted'a fly like the wind. We just sat there with our mouths open like we were in a trance. Lilly was in a trance too, swayin' across the room, poppin' one boob out and then the other, givin' them equal time in the show, then puttin'em back in again like a magic act or a baby bein' put in his crib for a nap.

She did this over and over again. In and out they went. Now you see'em. Now you don't. Up and down they went, playin' peekaboo, or like a juggler with oranges. Make hers cantaloupes or even watermelons! I never saw anything like it in my life. Lilly was what they called well developed or voluptuous. Me and Cassie just called her a pig, and we knew that we'd have a lot to talk about in confession this Saturday! Meanwhile, Vicky, her assistant in this crazy show, kept shining the red light on her, following her around the room with it, and I realized that I was at the craziest circus in town! Lilly was still playin' with her balloons, like it was her very special birthday party when I started sweatin' and gettin' dizzy. The room was spinnin' around me, and I knew that we had'da make a run for it if we were ever gonna escape her boobs that were startin'a look like the eggplants Grandma Fannie cooked or, worse, like the long loaf'a Italian bread on her tray.

Then all of a sudden, we hear footsteps in the hall and voices that sound like Vicky's mother with somebody else. They hear it too, so me and Cassie start silently thanking God for rescuing us. And like magic, Vicky turns off the lamp and puts it back on the table as Lilly pops her little (I mean big) puppies back into their cage, and goes back to her snack table and her disgusting Italian bread with butter like nothing ever happened.

We heard the key in the door, and Vicky's mother came in with shopping bags of groceries, but we just scrambled past her, barely grunting hello. We scrammed outta there as fast as our fat little Catholic schoolgirl feet would carry us. We wished that we had wings and could fly down the two flights'a stairs to Cassie's house and were almost tempted to slide down the banister but knew that Mr. Catapano, the super was home, so we ran as fast as we could, trippin' over each other and takin' two steps at a time.

When we got to Cassie's door, we stood there for a long time just tryin'a catch our breath and prayin'ta erase that horrible memory from our eyes like an imaginary eraser on a blackboard. When we got in, Cassie's mom asked us if we wanted a snack, and I secretly prayed that it wouldn't be Italian bread with butter. I didn't eat Italian bread for a month! When she pulled out the Oreos and milk, my eyes lit up, and my mouth watered. I have'ta say that those Oreos and milk that day were the best I ever tasted in my life. We savored every morsel just dunkin' and eatin' and drinkin'. We laughed at each other's milk mustaches as we sat at Cassie's miniature plastic table and chair set and were so happy like pigs in you know what!

We were happy that we were safe, that we were still kids, and that our virginal virtue was still intact, at least for a few more years. We never hung out with Vicky and Lilly again, and we both musta said at least one hundred Hail Marys that night. We never told our mothers what happened, but both told it in confession even though the only fault we had was being two naive little chubsters.

Whenever we bumped into Vicky and Lilly in the hallway or out on the stoop after that day, we just quickly turned our heads away, ignoring them. A couple'a times, they tried to say stuff to us like "Do you wanna know what girls do with boys?" and we just gave them the cold shoulder, turning our heads, and in unison like the team we were, yelled out as loud as we could, "No!" because we knew what girls did with boys—they had fights!

CHAPTER 15

Queen of the Block

One of the interesting families living on our block in Brooklyn was the O'Flannagans. They were about as Irish as you could get, even their house was painted Kelly green, with ivy running up and down the sides. There were seven kids. Come'ta think of it, most of the Irish families had seven kids. It musta been a lucky number with some significance to the old country. It woulda made more sense for their lucky number to be four, as in four-leaf clover and all, and probably a whole lot cheaper too since it doesn't take a genius to figure out that feedin' four kids was cheaper than feedin' seven! But whatever! Go figure the Irish!

Anyway, the Flans, as we called them, had a mother named Bunny and a father named Tim. I use'ta hear Tim call Bunny (Bunny Hop) and thought it was kinda corny, but I guess it was kinda cute and a term of endearment. So they had six girls and one boy, and you woulda thought that the only boy, Timmy, woulda been the Irish king with a crown made'a shamrocks, right? But wrong! The oldest daughter was named Peggy, and she was the queen'a the house. She even thought she was the queen'a the block—maybe even the whole world!

Peggy Flan would walk down the block. I should say glide down the block like she was walkin' in a dream. Sleepwalkin'. That's what she looked like. And she commanded attention like she was the queen of England! Or I should say Ireland (if they even have queens).

Each foot was strategically placed one in front'a the other, like tryin' to avoid a land mine or balancing on a tightrope.

She was so stiff that it looked like a long stick was shooting up her butt, and instead'a lookin' uncomfortable like a normal person, she just smiled a plastic mannequin smile like a doll in a store window. She turned her head from side to side in a queenly manner but looked more like a fan that blows back and forth across a room. The only thing missing was the tiara and the queenly wave. She did try to pull off the wave but looked more like a school crossing guard.

Peggy was so tall and skinny like Olive Oyl from *Popeye* and not pretty at all like Cassie and me, the neighborhood chubsters. But there was something about her walk that made everybody on the block stop what they were doing to look at her—and not to laugh either. It was like she thought she was the queen and was convincing us of it too like she had some kinda magical power over us. It was weird. Years later, I realized that she was just projecting her dreams and aspirations onto us, and like simpleminded sponges, we absorbed them.

Peggy wanted to be a supermodel, and we were her cheering squad. She was the little engine that could—skinny body, homely face, and all. And we, her loyal subjects, waved our imaginary pompoms in the air, chanting rah-rahs of encouragement in a chorus of "You can do it!"

Secretly, we were cheering for our own personal victory and that little glimmer of hope in all of us that there was something bigger and greater than ourselves out there. Peggy was our mascot, so to speak, because everybody loves a winner, and sometimes everybody needs a hero. So when all the other Flan kids got so excited to see her come walking up the block, returning from her long hard day at work in whatever mysterious job she had in New York City, we were all excited too because there is strength in numbers and we were all fighting for the same cause even if we had no idea of what it was. Maybe to the Flan family, she was just another meal ticket and the difference between mayonnaise sandwiches and a little ham between their two slices of Wonder Bread. Let's face it, Mr. Flan was the only breadwinner in that household, and with seven kids, even in those days when the cost'a livin' was cheaper, Peggy helped put food on the table, even if it was only mayonnaise sandwiches. No wonder they thought she could walk on water and saw her as the female Jesus. They did everything for her but kiss her feet. Well, maybe they did that in the house. I don't know cause nobody was ever allowed in there. It was off-limits to the rest'a us kids, and we always wondered what it was like in there. The closest I ever got was in the vestibule one time, waitin' for Clare or Suzie to come out. I tried to peek through the Irish linen laced curtain to see what mysteries lurked in there but couldn't see a thing. There were rumors of green elves and leprechauns runnin' around, but I can't say for sure. We thought of it like The Munsters's house on TV, spooky and exciting at the same time.

Mr. Flan worked for Cadbury's Chocolates, which sounded like a great job. I wondered if he got to bring home free samples of chocolates for the kids, and if so, it would kinda explain Clare's acne problem. But I guess he couldn't bring home that much, and how much chocolate could you eat anyway? I hope that they at least got free Valentine heart candy, but I can't remember ever seeing him carry them home. Yeah, the Flans were a strange clan. They even had an Irish dog, an Irish setter named Pat, who was really very pretty, with long red floppy ears. They made up weird stories too. Well, they do say that the Irish have the gift'a gab. Their daughter Barbara, who was the only one to really have a significant amount'a fat on her, came up with a doozie one time. Well, actually, she had a big fat jelly belly and said that it was cause all the kids in her family were born with extra ribs. I had'da shake my head a little when I heard that one cause I'm no Einstein, but even I know that there's no such thing. Let's face it, she was the first one to the dinner table every night and probably the last one up too. Whether it was mayonnaise sandwiches or filet mignon, we all knew who was gettin' the lion's share. But I felt sorry for her though cause, one night, she came out five minutes after she went in for dinner. When I asked her "How did you eat so fast?" she just said that they had a really big salad for dinner. In those days, before the world was health-conscious, nobody ate just salad for dinner unless you were Bugs Bunny. And besides, I know that

Cassie and me were considered the two chubsters on the block, but at least we had it evenly distributed and didn't look like a lady who was gonna have a baby.

I saw pictures on TV of starvin' kids in Africa who had their bellies all swollen from malnutrition and hoped that Barbara didn't have that. Wow! Just how poor were they? Now I really hoped that the extra rib story was true cause I'd feel guilty for laughin' at her if she was really starvin'. I secretly started concocting a plan to smuggle in a care package'a macaroni and beans. That would'a filled'em up, if not given'em a bad case'a gas. I could sneak outa the house at night after everybody else was asleep and leave it on their stoop. Nobody had'da know it was me. Sister Margaret Angela in school said that we should all try to help the poor and that God would bless us if we did. Well, I wouldn't do it just for the blessing, but let's face it, it couldn't hurt. I mean, my life wasn't all peaches and cream either. We weren't starvin', but I wouldn't mind puttin' in a request for a more interesting menu at our house.

You know, I realized that we were all in the same boat really, and luckily, it wasn't the *Titanic*. The whole block, all of us kids, came from poor families. We just didn't know it cause we had hardworking families that cared for each other, and most of all, we had fun—lots'a fun!

I never did tell anybody my theory about Barbara Flan's jelly belly and never did bring over the care package either. I figured I'd save it for a really poor family, not one of us cause nobody that lived on Looney Lane could ever be poor. Peggy continued to be our source of inspiration, at least for a couple'a more years, until we were old enough to develop dreams of our own. But until then, she proved that no matter how much we loved this exciting block with all its flavorful characters, there was another great big world out there, full'a opportunities, even for a semipoor kid growin' up on an overcrowded city street, and like the Frank Sinatra song about wishin' on a star said, no one was better off than we were!

CHAPTER 16

Crazy Charlie

It was the end of July and 102 degrees in the shade. People were droppin' like flies, and you could fry an egg on the sidewalk. Not that I ever tried it, but so I've heard. It was the summer right after my eleventh birthday, and although we spent most of the summer Upstate in Marlboro Country, we alternated back and forth with the city so that our parents could take care of chores and we could see our city friends. The worst part about bein' in the country was missin' our friends cause we didn't have any up there. It was just my brother and sister and my cousins. That's it. We had no choice but to play with each other unless you wanted'a sit under a tree and count how many cars went by. And you could do that for just so long before 'ya started talkin' to the trees! Believe me, I know. This was probably our family's ulterior motive, anyway. They'd isolate us in the middle'a nowhere, surrounded only by country bumpkins and beautiful scenery, in the hope'a us bondin' and becomin' best friends forever. Well, I have'ta admit that I did have fun with my cousins and sometimes even with Sammy and Phylo, but if I had'da spend one more hot country night swattin' flies and playin' war with Sammy and Phylo, I was gonna scream!

So thank God, here I am stuck on Looney Lane on one'a the hottest days in the summer. Unlike the country, where we have a three-foot pool, here in the city, all we have is the johnny pump and Rockaway Beach if my mother takes us. Since we don't have a car, gettin' to the beach is a big deal cause we have to carry tons'a stuff on the bus or train. Thinkin' back on it now, I don't know how my mother did it. My father usually didn't come with us, and he didn't drive anyway, so my mother had'da lug three kids, blankets, a cooler, snacks, and sandwiches, along with who knows what else up all the train station stairs, or wait at the bus stop forever since the bus to the beach came only once an hour. She never complained and took us all over the place.

Anyway, today we were in the johnny pump with all the kids. Cassie was there along with the O'Flannagan kids. And of course, annoying Charlie Desanto had'da sit on the hydrant, stoppin' the water from shootin' out, and just when you went up to his face to yell at him, he'd jump up so the water shot you right in your eye. He was always doin' stuff like that, just like the time he stuck a stick in my eye. Of course, he said that it was an accident as he squirmed around in that wiry, jumpy way'a his, like a worm walkin' on hot coals. You could never believe anything that Charlie ever said cause he was what they called a compulsive liar. He couldn't help it. He just loved tellin' stories. One day, he'd tell you that his uncle was the prince of Arabia and that he was flyin' over on his magic carpet any minute now, and if you promised'ta marry him, he'd let you be the first one'a his friends to ride on it. Then before you knew it, you had a stick in your eye! He use'ta walk along the curb with a big stick in his hand, holdin' it sideways like a steerin' wheel, and makin' believe that he was drivin' a car. Of course, it was a Cadillac, a light-blue one. He walked up and down the street, balancing himself on the curb, one foot in front'a the other like on a tightrope, yellin' out, "Brrrmm! Beep! Beep! Get outta the way!" And in my case, I didn't move fast enough, so his stupid steerin' wheel, which was really a stick, ended up in my eye. He started sayin' he was sorry, but I just ran past him into the house. My mother put a cool rag on it, but my father was really mad and wanted'a let him have it. Come'ta think of it, everybody's father wanted'a let him have it at one time or another. I even heard his own mother call him a juvenile delinquent once. It was the time that he climbed up onto the train tracks of the El Train on the corner. Everybody heard that he was up there, and the whole block ran to the corner to see what Crazy Charlie was doin' now. The rumor was that he wanted to see if he could fly like Superman. He was up there, all right. We all saw his skinny little body wavin' down at us like he was a movie star on stage, and the wind was blowin' his curly black hair straight up in the air like corkscrews. He wasn't wearin' a Superman cape, though. Just his usual shorts and T-shirt. The crowd was gettin' bigger and bigger, and we watched like it was a circus act, the one where the fat man wearin' a skinny bathing suit jumps down from way up high into the little two-foot pool'a water without killin' himself.

But this was no circus act. This was Charlie. And he wasn't a big fat man but a skinny little kid. So if he jumped, he'd probably get blown away like the house in *The Wizard of Oz*. Then I started'a wish that his uncle would fly by on that magic carpet. Charlie really could'a used the ride. He was really annoying, but I didn't wanna see him splattered all over the sidewalk. Gross! He just kept standin' up there, smilin' and wavin' at us like he was Elvis Presley til the police went up there to carry him down.

Charlie didn't come out for a while. He was punished, and his father really let him have it. We heard his mother tell my mother that he couldn't sit down for a week. She said that if he didn't stop his crazy pranks, she was gonna put him in reform school. Now I wasn't sure what reform school was, but I pictured the kids from *Our Gang Comedy*. Mugzy with the hat and Sach who made those weird faces with his cheeks. I hoped that Charlie didn't have'ta go there cause we'd miss his crazy shenanigans. He wasn't in my class, but I knew that he was always in trouble in school. His mother and father were always up there, and the rumor was that Sister Thomas Joseph almost threw him outta the window one day for causing such a ruckus in class. Everybody knew that he was a troublemaker. But he was our troublemaker, and what would we do without him? Who would we fight with? Sure, there were other kids to fight with, but it wouldn't be the same as fightin' with Charlie. Like it or not, he was special and an important piece in the jigsaw puzzle of our block.

About two weeks later, we saw Charlie outside again. It was another hot Saturday afternoon, and like usual, he was runnin' along the curb with his stick, which, of course, was a steering wheel to him. Although I was so happy to see that he was alive and not in reform school, I made sure'ta steer clear of his light-blue Cadillac. Everybody did.

CHAPTER 17

The Good Pirate

About a month before the whole Charlie and the train tracks fiasco, at the end of June just before school got out, there was another incident that almost blinded me for life. This time, it involved my mother and a schoolbag. Let me explain.

There was less than two weeks left of fifth grade, and I had just turned eleven in May. As usual, the classroom was as hot as Hades, and we were all roasting in our uniforms. Those navy-blue jumpers were murder, and I wondered how Sister didn't pass out under that long black habit. I'd heard that dark colors attract the sun, so I wondered why the nuns didn't wear white habits in the summer months. This made a lotta sense to me, but who was I? I guess that the laws of St. Sylvester stated that the nuns had'da suffer along with us kids, and I also wondered if it was penance for some mysterious sin they had committed. But what could a nun do that was so bad? I couldn't imagine.

This was long before the age of air-conditioning, at least in our poor neighborhood, and there weren't even any ceiling fans in our classroom. The principal's office had an old brown one over her desk that was so rickety it sounded like it was gonna fall right on her head. I never saw it cause I didn't get into trouble in school, but my brother Sammy saw it firsthand on many occasions. So on this one day, Sister was sittin' up there, fannin' herself with the church bulletin and gettin' no relief at all. Her face was so beet red, and she was trapped inside that black habit that went from head to toe. Only her face was exposed, and even that was all scrunched up like a prune that had been boiled in oil. Her headpiece was so tight around her head and face that she looked like the inside of a patāda squeezin' out of its skin or a Vienna sausage that plumped right out of its casing. I think that the worst part for her was how tight the collar was around her neck cause she kept pullin' and tuggin' at it like she was choking on a chicken bone. She started scratchin' and clawin' at her neck like a dog diggin' for a bone. All the while, her face got redder, and sweat was pourin' down her cheeks. She started clearin' her throat and coughin', and I wanted'a run out and get her a drink'a water, but we were in the middle of a science test, so I wasn't even supposed to be lookin' at her. At that point, I didn't even care if I failed the test cause I couldn't take my eyes off'a her. She was the biggest science experiment in the world, right before my eyes.

Then I started staring at her like she was a fire-breathing dragon, waitin' for the smoke and flames to come pourin' outta her nose and mouth cause they couldn't come outta her ears since they were taped shut. Her ears never had any problem hearin', though. That's for sure, especially when one'a us mumbled a joke under our breath. Instead'a taking my science test, I just sat there, elbows on my desk, chin cupped in my two hands, watchin' and waitin' for her to explode.

Then as I was sittin' there with a dumb grin on my face, she caught me. All of a sudden, I heard her yell out, "Decrescenzo, is there something you want to share with the class? Have you finished your test already? It seems like you're smarter than the rest of us! Do you want to come up here?" She snapped me back into reality, and my head snapped back toward my test paper like a turtle returning into his shell.

I just mumbled somethin' like, "No, Sister."

I failed the test but didn't care. It was worth it.

Before I got sidetracked on Sister lookin' like a boiled sausage cause of the heat, I was talkin' about how I almost lost my eye in fifth grade. This time, Charlie wasn't the culprit but my mother. What happened was my schoolbag handle broke. In those days, kids didn't have fancy backpacks slung over their shoulders designed with TV characters and superheroes but regular schoolbags that you carried with a handle. They sort a looked like a briefcase but not so fancy. Mine was dark brown, and as I was gettin' ready for school one morning, I told my mother that my handle broke the day before. Of course, she answered by saying, "Whaddy'ya telling me now for at the last minute? You should'a told me last night!"

But my mother, being the jack-of-all-trades that she was, came up with a temporary makeshift solution to my problem. She got some rope and tied it from one end to the other in place of the brown plastic handle. Imagine a kid today using a schoolbag that looked like that? It woulda never happened. They'd call it child abuse. Anyway, the rope was too long, and she had'da cut it. She couldn't find a scissor handy, and since it was gettin' late, she grabbed a knife. She held the knife in her right hand and the rope in her left, cuttin' the rope with the knife underneath it, the sharp side pointing up toward the ceiling. She was using a lotta force to cut it and, me bein' the nosy kid that I was, stood right over her. Well, she probably didn't know her own strength cause the knife cut the rope but continued traveling upward, right into my eyeball.

It happened so fast that I didn't even feel anything and was more scared'a the way my mother was screamin' than anything else. She screamed so loud that she woke up my father who was workin' nights at the time. He came runnin' in and in his Napolitano accent that we always made fun'a said, "Ma, wha happa?" which meant "What happened?" My mother was still standin' there, screamin' like a loon as I just shrugged my shoulders at him. My eyeball didn't fall onto the floor or anything, and as far as I could tell, it was still in its socket, so I didn't know why she was so hysterical. I didn't have any pain but felt a little wetness on my lower eyelid. When I put my finger up to touch it, she started screamin' again, and I noticed a drop'a blood on my fingertip. I just said, "Uugghh!"

My father saw the knife and rope along with the broken handle, and before he could say, "O Sole Mio," he was cursin' at my mother in Napolitano. He might'a been an immigrant but was no dumbbell. Knowing all too well about my mother's crazy need to create new inventions outta nothing, it took him two seconds to realize that she had her seamstress hands in this somehow. The next thing I knew, they were both grabbin' me, throwin' a white dish towel over my head, and pushin' me outta the door before my father had a chance to kiss his saint statues goodbye. My father was neurotic before we even knew what the word meant, and he had'da kiss all his saint statues before he left for work every day. He had about twenty'a them ranging from St. Joseph to St. Linguini and was always late for work cause of his obsession. He also got fired from a lotta jobs cause of it. For him to leave the house without kissin' his statues was like him leavin' the house without his underwear on. So now he really wanted'a let my mother have it, not only cause she probably blinded me for life, but also cause he was gonna have bad luck for the rest'a the day since he didn't get to kiss his statues. I wanted'a tell him, "Hey, Dad, I was just stabbed in the eye with a knife, how much worse can your luck get today?" But then that was my bad luck, not his, right?

Anyway, before I knew it, I was runnin' down the block with my mother and father on either side'a me. I still had the white dish towel over my head, and I felt like Casper the Friendly Ghost floating down the block. All the kids who were late for school rushed past us, turnin' their heads as they ran to see why I had a towel over my head. Then down the steps came Cassie, her ponytail flopping back and forth as she made a mad dash to get inside the school doors before the final bell rang. If I didn't have this dumb towel over my head, I'd be runnin' with her cause the two of us were late every day. It was our routine, just like my father and his saint statues. Cassie looked over at us, and of course, I couldn't see her, but she raised her hands up over her head lookin' like a priest on the altar givin' his final blessing. Guess she figured I sure coulda used one. All she asked was "What?" as my mother brushed her off with a hand wave. All the while, my father kept rantin' and ravin' in Napolitano.

Lookin' like a boxer in a ring or somebody bein' smuggled across the border, my parents continued dragging me through the streets with the towel over my head until we reached the train station. It was the longest six blocks'a my life. They pushed me under the turnstile, tellin' the token booth clerk that I was only six even though I just turned eleven cause they wanted'a save the twenty-five cents. We sat on the bench down in the station and waited fifteen minutes for the next A train. My mother kept peekin' under the towel to make sure that my eye wasn't bleedin' and that it was still there while my father alternated cursin' and sayin' the rosary in Italian. I guess that he wasn't sure which one was gonna work best and wanted'a cover all bases. Of course, it was my luck that the train was makin' all local stops, and between its stallin' every few minutes like an old lady runnin' outta breath and the fight that broke out between two rival street gangs on Broadway Junction, East New York, it took forty-five minutes to reach Brooklyn Eye and Ear Hospital in Downtown Brooklyn.

Now the A train was notorious for havin' the wackiest of characters as passengers, and on that day, I fit right in sittin' there with a towel over my head like a scary monster from an Alfred Hitchcock movie or somebody who just escaped from a mental hospital. Usually, whenever I rode the train with my parents into Manhattan to Radio City or the Central Park Zoo, we were scared'a some'a the weirdos that we saw, but that day I thought to myself, "Wow, they're all scared'a me! Cool!" The ride was so bumpy that I kept expecting ta'see my eyeball roll onto the floor and imagined it rollin' up and down the car like a runaway marble. But that never happened.

We finally made it to the hospital and waited in the lobby for the eye doctor to come out. He took us into an examination room with bright lights and a machine that looked like a robot. My father started blessin' himself again as my mother started cryin'. Of the three of us, I was the sanest, and I'm sure that the doctor noticed cause he addressed his questions ta'me and not my parents like I thought he was gonna. He had on a white coat and black glasses and kinda looked like Ben Casey, who I loved better than Dr. Kildare. He told me to rest my chin on the robot machine and look into the little hole. Then he put drops into my eye. It didn't hurt, and yet my parents continued to fall apart.

He gave them a strange look, and so did I cause they were startin'a act guilty, and I wondered if they were really scared'a me goin' blind or of them goin'ta jail for child abuse.

In those days, parents didn't go to jail for child abuse like they do today unless it was for somethin' really bad. If I went blind, that woulda been really bad, but I knew that it was an accident. The doctor didn't, though, and kept lookin' at my mother and father like they were on the witness stand. Then all of a sudden, he said to them more than me, "Don't worry, it's not so bad and could have been a lot worse! Luckily, the knife went into the iris, the colored part of the eye, and not the pupil, the black part, or she might be blind right now."

Well, my mother started cryin' again, and my father started prayin' in Italian and wishin' that he had all his saint statues handy to kiss. I just smiled at the doctor, imagining myself on an episode'a Ben Casey, and he just saved my life. He put some ointment in my eye and then a white patch over it so that I looked like a good pirate instead of an evil one. He said that I had'da wear the patch for a month and then come back for a checkup. I could take it off to sleep but had'da wear it all day long.

This is where the good part comes in. He said that I could watch all the TV that I wanted but couldn't read cause it was too much strain on my eye. I couldn't believe it and wanted'a kiss him and thought for sure that my mother would fight him about all the TV. I wanted business, but she just nodded and said, "Yes, Doctor." My father kissed his hand, and I was so embarrassed. The doctor wrote me a note for school that said I should sit in front'a the class so that I could see better.

And then I asked him, "Doctor, can I do homework?" I can't believe that I had the nerve.

He said, "Do you get a lot of homework?"

And before my mother could say anything, immediately answered, "Yes, tons!"

So he said, "Well, in that case, maybe we should excuse you for a while just to make sure. You seem like you're a pretty smart girl in school and should have no trouble catching up. Whad'dy'ya think?"

Well, for sure, I wanted'a kiss him then and imagined myself married to him someday if only he'd wait for me. So he wrote me a note that said I was to be excused from homework until school got out for the summer! I couldn't believe it and imagined that this was what it must feel like to win the lottery! My mother was so relieved that I wasn't gonna be blind, that she woulda gone along with anything I wanted at that point, and I started to realize that gettin' stabbed in the eye might turn out to be not so bad after all.

When we were leavin', the doctor said, "You're a very lucky, young lady."

And I said, "I know, feelin' almost as lucky for not havin' to do homework and for all the attention I was gonna be gettin' lookin' like a pirate than I was for not going blind. Crazy, huh?"

It was a Thursday, so he told me to go back to school on Monday. When I did, I felt like a celebrity cause all the kids wanted'a know what happened, and I told the story so many times that I felt like I was reciting lines in a play. I gave my teacher the note, and Sister kept lookin' at it to see if it was real to make sure that I wasn't tryin'a trick her. When she read the part about no homework, she started'a twitch, and I thought she'd start to scream, but it was also signed by my parents, so she had'da obey it. Wow, I was really startin'a like all this power. I sat in front'a the class and took notes and took tests, but if I started'a get tired or bored, I just stopped and said that my eye hurt. She had'da believe me cause I was wearin' the eye patch to prove it. When the other kids wrote down their homework assignments, I just sat there grinnin', and I knew that she secretly wanted'a let me have it with the ruler but couldn't.

Now I wasn't a liar but knew that I was tryin'a manipulate the situation and considered confessing in confession on Saturday but then convinced myself that I wasn't doin' anything wrong. After all, the doctor did say no homework. Right? Why couldn't I enjoy it? I deserved it after gettin' stabbed in the eye.

When we got home that day, my mother made my favorite for dinner, homemade pizza, the way that Grandma Fannie made it. And the next day, she took me'ta Woolworths with Grandma for her favorite snack. They made these great ice-cream sandwiches outta toasted waffles with Neapolitan ice cream in the middle. They called it Neapolitan cause it had vanilla, chocolate, and strawberry stripes and not cause it came from Naples. The combination of the hot waffles and cold ice cream was great, and I knew why it was Grandma's favorite snack. We sat on red-and-silver stools that swung around at a counter and were served by a lady wearin' a white dress and a pointed white hat on her head. She let us pop a balloon to see how much we had'da pay for our ice cream waffles. It wasn't a penny but a quarter. Still a good deal. It was so much fun'ta be there with my mother and grandmother and not in school like my friends. When we finished our ice cream, my mother bought me my favorite Colorforms, the ones with the Mickey Mouse Club, and then Grandma Fannie bought me the Lennon Sisters cutout dolls. I was so happy and wondered if it had'da take me almost losin' an eye for my mother and grandmother to be nice to me but knew it wasn't true. Still they were bein' extra nice.

    I told my friends outside the truth about what happened, but when it came to Charlie Desanto, I decided'a tell a little fib. After all, he deserved it for all the tricks he played on me. I told him that I got a part in a movie as a pirate and had'da practice with the eye patch on to make it seem more natural. Of course, he wanted'a know what movie and could I get him into it too cause he loved pirates and was one last Halloween. I told him no cause they only needed girl pirates, and of course, he said that he'd wear a dress. Then I couldn't take him anymore and told him the truth. Then he started chasin' me with his stick that was his steerin' wheel, and I said, "Hey, get away from me. My mother almost blinded me once, and now you're tryin'a do it again? Isn't that enough for one lifetime?" I guess not 'cause a month later he'd finally stab me in the eye with his steerin' wheel that was really a stick.

    All the kids started laughin' and playin' a game'a Johnny on the Pony. I just watched. I wanted'a play, but was no dumbbell. I already had two close calls and didn't wanna go blind. I needed my eyesight to keep watchin' all the crazy shenanigans that went on. This was the best block on earth! I heard Lesley Gore singin' She's A Fool.

CHAPTER 18

The Ugly Duckling

Every Wednesday afternoon, we had an early dismissal from school so that the public school kids could have religious instructions. After all, why should we be the only ones to benefit from a Catholic education? I saw some'a those kids hangin' out on the corner by the ice-cream parlor and in the school park late at night when I was passin' with my mother or father ta'buy ice cream. All I can say is that I'm not sure what they were doin', but it didn't look like they were sayin' the rosary. They reminded me'a the movie *West Side Story* that I just saw with my mother and aunt Teensie, and I wondered if they were Jets or Sharks. Now there weren't any Puerto Rican kids in my neighborhood that I knew'a, so I figured if they were in a gang, it would'a been the Jets. Anyway, I loved that movie, and I'm kinda surprised that my mother let me see it, but she said that it had great music, which it did, and a lotta fightin' too.

Anyway, gettin' back'ta religious instructions, I sure thought that those kids could'a used a little alone time with Sister Mary Margaret. A couple'a minutes alone with her would'a certainly straightened 'em out, and if they were in a boxin' ring with her, they'd be down and out before the ref called one. She sure was a tough cookie and even the big boys in eighth grade were scared'a her ever since she hung Salonzo out on the flagpole. Everybody was still talkin' about that one. I was curious to see just how tough these public school kids really were, and wished that I could'a snuck into their class.

Bein' that it was the end'a June, this was our last novena of the school year, and we couldn't wait for summer vacation. On Friday morning, we went into school as usual, then collected our report cards and test scores. Then Sister would probably give us a little speech about havin' a safe summer, blah, blah, blah, Father would give us a little blessing, and then, if we were good, we'd get a little going-away party to say goodbye to our school friends for the summer. We all brought in different snacks to share, and I was bringin' my favorite, Mary Janes.

Anyway, all of us were so excited. So on the last day'a school, we had a snack in school at twelve noon instead a'goin' home for lunch. This was our routine every Wednesday, and at one o'clock, we lined up in a single file and followed Sister down the stairs, outta the building, and across the street to the church.

We silently filed into the pews with our heads reverently bowed, like the obedient children that we were or we were forced to be! Now if we thought that the classroom was hot, the church was an oven. The windows and doors were all closed, and there wasn't a breath of air. I glanced over to look at Sister, just to see if she was turnin' into the dragon again. Her face was red, but no more than usual, so I looked over at Suzie DeBano, who sat to my left cause she came right before me alphabetically and always sat in front'a me in class. She was fannin' herself with the choir book and opening the top button on her white cotton short-sleeve blouse. So was Jane Denker, who sat on my right cause she sat behind me in class. She was normally very white, and her face had big red welts on it. She said that everybody in her family had a reaction to the heat. I turned my head around, and everybody was fannin' and squirmin'. Meanwhile, Father Voger said, "Everyone, please stand," and between the heat and the smell of the incense, I started'a feel nauseous and was glad that I didn't drink any milk with my Oreo cookies for snack.

I thought I was gonna barf for sure and didn't wanna do it all over Suzie cause I liked her and we went to Girl Scouts together. I didn't wanna do it to Jane either but woulda been more embarrassed if it was Suzie. Her father gave us a ride to Girl Scouts on Thursday afternoons, and I was scared that if he found out about it, he wouldn't let me in his car anymore.

As if things weren't bad enough, all of a sudden, the most horrible thing happened. We were all standin' up and sayin' the rosary out loud. Just as we got to the Glory Be to the Father part and up to the word Son, somebody let out a yell that sounded like "Augghhh!" It was so loud that we all turned around. It was comin' from about four rows behind me, so I couldn't see or hear exactly what was goin' on, but it didn't matter cause we all started'ta smell what was goin' on. Karen Panza was at it again. This time, it wasn't just the usual number one but number two, and it smelled so bad that it should'a been called number one billion. That's right, Karen Panza decided'ta end the school year with a bang and a boom. She had the Fourth'a July right in her pants and was givin' us a royal send-off, a little present to remember her by as if we could ever forget her.

Now I silently said a prayer of thanks that her last name began with the letter P, which was very appropriate, since that was all she ever did, except for today. Today, she did her *duty* as a Catholic schoolgirl to make us as sick as we could possibly get and still be alive. Now everybody in her pew started standin' up and jumpin' around to get away from her as the horrible smell made its way up to our aisle. Maryanne Peterson, who sat on her left, looked like she passed out while Judy Powers, who was on her right, scrambled to get outta the pew and make a mad dash for the door. So that's why they call it a PEW!

Meanwhile, Father Voger was still up there, sayin' the billionth Hail Mary, and if I thought it would'a helped ta'get the smell out, I woulda said a million more. Then I was prayin' that he'd cover me with incense and wouldn't even mind takin' a bath in it, if I ever got outta there alive. All the kids started coughin' and chokin' as Karen Panza just sat, holdin' her rosary beads in her hand as if she wasn't responsible for one'a the worst disasters of all time. The atomic bomb had nothin' on her, and God forgive me, but I wanted'a choke either her or myself with her rosary beads just ta'end the misery.

Finally, as Father, who still seemed totally unaware of what was going on (maybe it was the incense), got up to the last Our Father,

Sister Margaret Ann, with her hand coverin' her nose and mouth, ran up to Karen's row and dragged her out. She climbed over the last two kids in her pew who were either too obedient or stupid to abandon ship before now, and while still firmly clasping her rosary beads, Karen waddled out into the aisle like a duck. By now, most'a the kids were outta their seats and huggin' the wall alongside the Stations of the Cross, and I looked up at Jesus and wondered how he woulda handled this. Then the whole church was lookin' over ta'see what was goin' on. Lucky for them that they couldn't smell it. I felt a little jealous. Sister continued ta'cover her face as everybody on our side'a the church gasped for air, and still, Father prayed.

Like the ugly duckling that she was, Karen Panza waddled down the aisle, starin' straight ahead with that dumb blank look'a hers as she left a trail'a little brown duckling eggs all over the church. Sister scurried her outta the side door as fast as she could and motioned to Sister Thomas James, who was sittin' with her class, to come over. Sister told Karen to stand in front'a the door and not to move, and she didn't. She didn't cry or feel embarrassed or anything. She just stood there, prayin' the rosary out loud all by herself as she continued to drop the last of her vile pellets. Meanwhile, Sister Thomas James, who I'm sure was sorry she found out about our little fiasco, tried'ta evacuate us as fast and orderly as possible without a stampede. Row by row, we hurried out as fast as we could as if on a sinking ship. We covered our noses as we jumped over her brown trinkets as if on a land mine or playin' a game'a hopscotch.

When we were finally all outside, Sister walked Karen over to the grotto by the statue of Mary. Mary was so pure and beautiful, and I prayed that she couldn't smell it. At least we were outside now and had some air. Then Sister Thomas James walked us all over to the grotto, too, but not too close to Karen. Thank God. Novena was almost over, but everybody else was still in the church. Sister Thomas James stayed with us while Sister Margaret Ann went over to the rectory to use the phone and call Karen's mother. She told her to bring her some clean clothes, and her mother didn't seem surprised, except for the fact that Karen usually had her accident earlier in the day—twelve o'clock on the dot. She musta gotten confused today with early dismissal and all, or maybe she had a really good snack, or maybe she was just so excited cause she loved novena so much. Either way, her insides decided'ta save her present for church instead'a the classroom, and instead'a her usual water fountain that Victor the Porter cleaned up every day, today was her special surprise. Like Hansel and Gretel, she left her very special trail ta'follow. But who in their right mind would wanna? Not me or anybody that I knew. That's for sure, and we were just glad that we'd survived.

Karen's mother showed up with two'a Karen's younger sisters, and they all waddled off together, like a little family'a ugly ducklings, not side by side but all in a row, one in front'a the other. They all looked the same, except Karen was the only one droppin' brown eggs. She never even bothered to change her clothes. I guess that her mother was used'ta it by now, and no matter what, she still loved her.

The rest'a us kids were dismissed as usual but not til we could see Karen and her family waddlin' down the block. We all went home happy to start our summer vacations and knew that we had'da interesting story ta'tell our friends. When I went back to school in September, Karen wasn't in my class anymore cause she got left back and had'da repeat fifth grade. I kinda felt sorry for her but, in a way, more sorry for the kids in her new class.

CHAPTER 19

Castro Convertible

Saturday was the first day'a summer vacation, and all the kids swarmed outside like hundreds'a bees breaking free'a their hive. School was our hive, and the street was our honey. The noisier and dirtier it was, the sweeter it tasted. After the long cold winter and boring rainy spring, we were like wild animals let out of a cage. Summer was finally here and not a minute too soon.

I couldn't wait ta'tell everybody about the Karen Panza fiasco in novena on Wednesday even though I still got nauseous just thinkin' about it. This was too good a story, and it had'da be told. It was hot out, but not hot enough for the johnny pump. They didn't turn it on until the Fourth'a July, anyway. So after breakfast of just toast with grape jelly, I asked my mother if I could ring Cassie's bell ta'see if she could come out. My mother said that she had'da take me shoppin' for sneakers at John's Bargain Store, which she called Cheap John's. They had Keds on sale for $2.99 a pair, and if I didn't wanna be barefoot all summer, we'd better get down there before all the size 6s were gone. I guess size 6 was a popular number and sold out fast. Cassie never had a problem in this department cause she wore size 9s, and the shoe salesman always teased her and asked if she wanted oars with her shoes cause they were as big as canoes.

Anyway, I begged my mother if we could please go a little later, just til I at least got ta'tell the Karen Panza story. She said okay cause she was busy doin' chores in the house anyway but reminded me not'ta blame her if there weren't any sneakers left when we got there.

I said thanks then ran outta the door. I was wearin' my penny loafers, the maroon ones that had one shiny penny on top'a each foot. I usually wore these with my pedal pushers for goin' out to parties and visiting relatives. They definitely weren't for goin' out to play, so I knew that I'd better get home in time for my mother to take me shoppin' for sneakers. Wearin' penny loafers for one day wasn't so bad, but I'd be really embarrassed if I had'da wear 'em all summer.

So I got outside and saw Leja playin' jump rope with Suzie and Clare O'Flannagan. They were singin' the one that goes "All In Together Girls," which you really were supposed to play with more than three girls since the more girls you had, the better chance you had to sing all the months of the year. This way, they could only sing January, February, and March before they had'da repeat themselves, and that wasn't the right way. They all had polynoses hangin' off the tips'a their noses and looked like'a bunch'a doofus's. So I was glad that I wasn't playin' with them. Barbara O'Flannagan was out riding her pink princess bike that still had trainin' wheels on it, and I thought that it was kinda embarrassing for a ten-year-old to still use trainin' wheels, but that's just me. Actually, it was her sister Clare's bike and then passed down to all her sisters. Good thing that she was the last girl before it fell apart. Her brother Timmy, bein' the only boy, had his own bike. It was an old black one without trainin' wheels and musta been passed down from his father and, from the looks of it, maybe even his grandfather if they had bikes back in those days.

Now I shouldn't talk cause I didn't even have a bike and had'da bug my brother Sammy for rides on his, which of course, he didn't wanna part with. I was kinda mad that last Christmas, Sammy got a bike and I got a stupid doll carriage, which I hated.

Unlike most'a the girls my age, who had tons'a Barbie dolls and suitcases full'a Barbie clothes that mixed and matched in shiny, shimmery colors, I'd rather ride a bike anytime. So why didn't my mother know this? After all, she lived with me. Wasn't she payin' any attention to me at all? She sure had no problem noticin' when I did somethin' wrong, that's for sure. Anyway, I wheeled my stupid doll carriage around with an even stupider (if that's a word) doll that I didn't even know or care the name of cause it was my Christmas present and I had'da play with it. But I didn't like it and would try'ta bribe Sammy for rides with his favorite Bazooka bubble gum every chance I got.

    Anyway, I kept lookin' to see if Cassie was out but saw Sandy Matone instead in front'a her house doing her Hula-Hoop. She was twirling her hips around so fast that I got dizzy just lookin' at her, and she looked like the tornado that swooped its way into Kansas in *The Wizard of Oz*. Her ponytail was flyin' through the air, and she looked like the teacup ride in Coney Island, the one that made me throw up. She was countin' out loud with every twirl that she did and was already up to 186. She gave me a look like, "Look what I can do!" as if she was in the Hula-Hoop Olympics. I just rolled my eyes and made a face at her as if to say that I wasn't impressed cause I wasn't. What I couldn't understand was how she managed to keep the Hula-Hoop goin' for so long cause she was as skinny as a string bean. I thought it was gonna fall straight down to the ground but didn't. I pictured somebody with big fat hips doin' it and figured that it would'a been easy to keep it up without even trying cause it couldn't pass over your hips. Then I thought that maybe the reason she was so skinny was cause she did the Hula-Hoop all day long and was already up to number 530. I could still hear her countin', even two doors away. What a show-off! I decided that even if doin' the Hula-Hoop was good exercise and made you skinny, I'd just get mine another way. I'd rather roller skate or bike ride. I just had'da hope I got a bike next Christmas. Either that or start givin' Sammy a lot more Bazooka bubble gum, and I had a strange feelin' that I'd have a lot more luck workin' on Sammy than I would tryin'a convince my parents that I needed a bike.

    So I went into the vestibule of Cassie's building and rang her bell. Her father buzzed me in, and I went in to knock on her door. Cassie answered the door, and she was chewin' somethin', but I couldn't tell what it was. I asked Cassie if she wanted'a go out and play stoopball cause I just got a new pink Spaldeen and it was really bouncy and great for hittin' fly balls. In stoopball, it was five points if you hit the ball on the flat part of the step and caught it on a bounce and ten points if you caught it on a fly. If you hit the ball on the point of the step and caught it on a fly, that was twenty points, and if you were ever lucky enough to hit the ball on the very top step next to the door and catch that on a fly, that was a whopping one hundred points. But nobody ever hit that one. Not that I ever saw, anyway. These were the game rules. I don't know who made 'em up, or when, but this was just the way it was.

Cassie said that she had'da finish her lunch first. She was sittin' at her little miniature table and chair set and eatin' a ham-and-cheese sandwich the way that her mother always made it for her. First of all, it was Wonder bread with the crusts cut off, and it was cut into quarters but cut diagonally so that she had four equal triangles. Then her mother put French's mustard and butter on both slices of bread so that the mustard and butter mixed together. Now when I first saw this, I thought that it was weird, but when I tasted it, changed my mind. It was good. Cassie drank her usual egg cream that her mother made with Bosco and milk and squirted seltzer from the big silver bottle with the nozzle that was delivered to her door every week. In those days, we had milk delivered to our door every week, and our milkman's name was Willy. He'd pull up in his white truck and come out in his white uniform and cap and carry a crate up to our doorstep. Cassie had soda and seltzer delivered too, but we didn't, probably cause my mother just bought the cans'a soda and mixed them with a couple'a drops'a wine cause Grandma said that Grandpa's wine was better than medicine. Come to think of it, we didn't go to Dr. Altruda's office unless we were really sick, which wasn't too often. He was the doctor for the whole neighborhood and not only the kids. All the grown-ups went to him too for every kinda ailment known to man. There was no such thing as a specialist. He did it all. He brought us into the world and sometimes was there to watch us go out too. He knew everything about everybody. There were no secrets.

Anyway, I watched Cassie finish her lunch and sat in the other miniature chair next to her. I didn't wanna tell Cassie this right now while she was eatin', but we were both too big for this table and chair set. There was nothin' mini about either one of us, and it would take only a few more of her ham-and-cheese sandwiches with mustard and butter before this set fell apart, just like Goldilocks. I noticed that Cassie had mustard on her lip and was just about to tell her when she picked up an extra slice'a Wonder Bread that was sittin' on a plate and wiped her mouth with it just like it was a napkin. I never saw her or anybody else do that before, and it would be somethin' that I teased her about for many years to come. I told Cassie to hurry and finish eatin' so that we could go out and play stoopball and that I had a really funny story to tell her. I didn't wanna forget to tell her about the Karen Panza story, and I was startin'a get a little nervous because I knew that I had'da get home for my own lunch and then go shoppin' for sneakers with my mother. But Cassie had'da finish the end of her egg cream, which was all sudsy on top.

Meanwhile, Cassie's mother was in the kitchen washin' clothes. She had a weird washin' machine that I never saw before since we just washed clothes by hand and hung 'em out on the line, or if there was a lotta heavy stuff and it was rainin' or snowin', we went to the Laundromat. Her mother was takin' the wet clothes outta the bottom part and then slidin' them through a big roller that squeezed the water out. It was like a giant typewriter, and instead'a puttin' the paper through, she put the wet clothes into one end and then pulled it through the other. Her mother was always washin' clothes since they had seven kids and all. Her father was sittin' in the livin' room reading the newspaper, and he looked a little like Captain Kangaroo with straight white hair and a white mustache to match. In her livin' room was a Castro Convertible couch that was still opened since it was Saturday, and whichever one'a her brothers slept on it musta just gotten up. She had four brothers, and they were all cute, but especially her brother Jimmy, who sang doo-wop on the corner and looked a little like Ricky Nelson from the Ozzie and Harriet show. He had one'a those big pompadour hairdos too, the kind that took the guys hours in front'a the bathroom mirror to get it just right, and also the kind that made all the teenage girls swoon as they passed by wearin' their poodle skirts.

Anyway, Cassie finally finished eatin'. Her mother was still doing laundry in the kitchen and cleaning the kitchen table. Cassie's father worked for Ehler's spices, and the kitchen table was always full'a different kinds'a spices. They had everything from paprika and oregano to curry and caraway seeds. Being that Cassie's mother was German, she used a lotta caraway seeds and put it in her sauerkraut that she made from scratch. So Cassie gets up and asks her father, who was still readin' the paper, if we could jump on the bed. He just nodded and smiled as he motioned with his hand toward the direction of the sofa bed as if we couldn't see it. He was a very nice man who didn't talk much and usually just sat on the stoop smokin' cigarettes.

So I took off my penny loafers and again reminded myself that I had'da get sneakers with my mother. Cassie was already barefoot, so the two of us climbed up and started laughin' like hyenas as we jumped up and down on the Castro Convertible like we were on a trampoline. With each jump, we propelled ourselves higher and higher, and I felt like I was one'a those slinky toys or on a pogo stick. We just kept jumpin' and screamin' as her mother did the laundry and her father read the paper. No matter how much noise we made, they didn't even turn their heads, and I thought to myself, *Wow! This house is fun. They let her do whatever she wants*!' If it was my house, my mother would'a been screamin', and my father would'a been cursin' in Napolitano. But then again, it woulda never happened in my house cause first of all, we didn't have a Castro Convertible, and second of all, they would'a never let me do it. I imagined hearin' my mother yell, "Get off'a there right now before I break your legs!" Then I woulda silently thought'ta myself, "Not if I break'em first, Ma, when I fall off this thing." All the while, my father woulda been pacin' back and forth as he alternated cursin' in Napolitano and prayin' to the Madonna that I didn't kill myself. Then I thought, this is just another difference between the Irish and the Italians. They have caraway seeds, and we have oregano. They drink beer, and we drink wine. They can sit quietly while their kids play, and we scream at the top'a our lungs while threatening bodily mutilation. I guess that variety is the spice'a life, after all—literally.

Anyway, me and Cassie started'a get a little wild, like two monkeys tryin'a break outta a cage at the Bronx Zoo when I started'a feel springs under my feet. Like I said before, neither one'a us were lightweights, and we broke the Castro Convertible. I pictured the girl from the TV commercial, the one with the long curly black hair, who sat on the bed like a gentle little lady and imagined her cryin'. She wanted'a know how two girls could be such tomboys and so disrespectful of her beautiful Castro Convertible, the one that put her in commercials and probably gave her a nice bank account for college someday.

Well, I felt the spring cut my foot then screamed so loud that Mrs. Minghe upstairs started bangin' on the pipes. I fell into Cassie, who was in the middle of a jump, on her way up towards the ceiling. She banged her head on the ceiling and on the way down banged into my head. Now I let out another yell, and so did Cassie. We crashed into each other so hard like two wrestlers in a wrestling ring, then both bounced into the wall. We hit the floor on top'a each other, both trapped between the wall and the once-beautiful Castro Convertible. Cassie had a bump on her head the size'a humpty-dumpty, and my foot was bleedin'. Still, Mrs. Minghe banged on the pipes. Cassie's mother finally came in from the kitchen. She wasn't screamin' but just standin' there lookin' at us with her hands on her hips and shakin' her head as if to say, "You crazy kids." I guess when you have seven kids, by the time you get down to the last one, you've pretty much seen it all, and nothin' makes you crazy. Well, I knew that even if my mother and father had a hundred kids, there's no way they wouldn't'a been screamin' like an episode of *The Lone Ranger* when the Indians attack the lone ranger and Tonto. Cassie's father got up and put his paper down. He came over to help us up and asked if we were all right. Cassie's mother got ice for her head and a Band-Aid for my foot, which was really just a small cut after all. I felt bad that I got blood on the sheet and that we broke the springs. They didn't yell at either one'a us and told me not to worry about it and that the sofa bed was old anyway. I still felt bad, though, and could still see the girl from the Castro Convertible commercial cryin' her eyes out.

I left Cassie's house and walked home feelin' a little embarrassed about what happened and knew that although Cassie's parents didn't seem mad, mine would'a been steamin' mad. Then I wondered if they only acted calm in front'a me and really weren't that different from my parents after all. Maybe as soon as they got Cassie alone, they'd really let her have it. I didn't think so. Her parents were Irish and calm, and mine were Italian and crazy. End of story. We never did get to play stoopball that day, and I never got'ta tell her about the Karen Panza story either. All of a sudden, it didn't seem that funny anymore. Nothin' did, and I didn't know exactly why. I walked towards my house, tryin' not'ta step on the part'a my foot cut by the sofa spring, like I was dodgin' a land mine. Then I started doin' that crazy thing we kids always did when we said, "Step on a crack. Break your mother's back!" All of a sudden I realized why I was feelin' so sad. I was about'ta face the music, and the name'a the song was "My Mother Lucy." It wasn't the theme song from *I Love Lucy* but a different scarier version.

When I rang the bell and was buzzed in, I could tell by how long my mother kept her finger on the buzzer that she was really mad. I didn't know what time it was but knew that I was really late. As soon as I walked in the door, my mother asked me, "Where were you? Do you know what time it is?" and "We had lunch a half hour ago." Then before I could say a word, she asked, "And why are you limping?" Again, I tried to answer when she said, "You can really forget about findin' any sneakers now. I guess you'll just have'ta wear your penny loafers all summer long." So I told my mother the whole story from the beginning. I told her about waitin' for Cassie to finish her lunch but left out the part about her wipin' her mouth with the Wonder Bread. I could tell that she was in no mood for funny stories. Then I told her about how Cassie's father let us jump on the Castro Convertible and how we broke the spring and how it cut my foot. She didn't scream right away and just stood there with her mouth and eyes wide open like in the old-fashioned Silent Movies, but before I could say Castro Convertible, her mouth was flyin' a hundred miles an hour, just like Superman tryin'a rescue somebody. I could sure use him now. Her arms were flappin' too, like a big bird tryin'a get off the ground for the first time. She started chasin' me around the dinin' room table, yellin', "How could you embarrass me like this by breakin' somebody's Castro Convertible? Don't'ya know how expensive those things are!" We were still runnin' around the table when I answered her back saying, "But, Ma, they said that it was old anyway." Well, this got her even madder, so she went into the kitchen to get the wooden spoon, which she usually just threatened us with and didn't use cause she liked throwin' her shoe instead, but why take any chances, so I tried'ta make a run for it, still tryin' not'ta step on my bad foot. Meanwhile, my father who was in the livin' room watchin' his favorite show, *The Abbott and Costello Show*, came runnin' in screamin' somethin' in Napolitano that translated into "You should have to eat a dog!" He was mad that all the noise interrupted his favorite episode, the one with "Who's on First, I Don't Know Is on Second." Grandma Fannie came in cause she heard all the yellin' from her house and, as usual, tried'ta protect me from my mother by shieldin' me with her body. In her usual dramatic way, she'd hide me behind her apron as she raised her hands in the air like she was stoppin' traffic. Then in her Sicilian accent, she'd tell my mother, "Lever lona!" which meant "Leave her alone!" Maybe I didn't have Superman, but I sure had Fannie. Granny always had my back. My father was glad that she came in cause he was sittin' and laughin' in front'a the T.V. again.

My mother called Cassie's house and spoke'ta her mother, sayin' that she was so sorry for what I did and could she help pay to fix it. Cassie's mother told her not'ta worry about it, that it was very old anyway, and that we were just kids havin' fun. I was glad cause my mother finally calmed down, and the smoke stopped shootin' outta her ears. She made me a peanut butter sandwich with grape jelly from the Flintstone's jar and a glass'a milk. She didn't cut the crusts off or cut it into quarters, just two equal halves the way that she always did. Then she said, "Let me see what happened to your foot." I took my shoe off and the Band-Aid that Cassie's mother put on it.

Then my mother asked me if her mother put Mercurochrome on it. I said no, so she went into the bathroom to get the bottle'a orange liquid and another Band-Aid. She fixed me up and then said, "We'd better hurry up if you wanna get a pair'a sneakers."

I was so happy that she wasn't mad at me anymore. I gave her a big hug. My mother could be tough sometimes, but she was mine, and I knew that she loved me. Sammy and Phylo stayed home with my father. They were all in the livin' room, laughin' their heads off, as they watched another episode'a *The Abbott and Costello Show*. Grandma Fannie went into the yard to water her purple hydrangeas that she called Snowballs, where Grandpa Mike sat in his green Adirondack chair, reading the Italian newspaper.

So my mother grabbed her pocketbook and put a little lipstick on in her favorite summer shade, coral, which perfectly matched with her auburn hair that came right outta'a box. Then off we went on a Saturday afternoon mother/daughter shoppin' spree—just the two of us girls, just like in the movies. How exciting!

CHAPTER 20

Two Left Feet

Me and my mother made our way down Liberty Avenue towards John's Bargain Store, or as she called it Cheap John's. It was a Saturday afternoon and the beginning'a summer, so everybody and their mother was out, literally, and their grandmothers too. Families were pushin' their shoppin' carts as they made their way towards Key Food or Bohacks to do their weekly food shoppin'. My mother and grandmother did the weekly food shoppin' at the A&P and would be draggin' me along as soon as me and my mother got back from buyin' my sneakers. We passed Sackson's Shoe Store on the corner, which always had a display'a shoes outside on a rack. I never saw anybody go in there'ta buy shoes, but this was the place where me and Cassie committed our one and only crime. We were repeat offenders cause every chance we got, we'd run down there when nobody was lookin' and knock every shoe off the rack. We'd get so excited, then run away as fast as our chubby little feet could carry us, laughin' like crazy, like we just got away with robbin' a bank. Whenever we got bored, which was a'lotta the time, we'd say, "Let's go knock the shoes off'a Sackson's rack." We snuck down the block and tiptoed past the Old Time Barber Shop with the red-and-white-striped pole outside that looked like a big round candy cane. We wanted'a make sure that neither one'a our fathers were in there getting a haircut or a shave, where the barber puts loads'a whipped cream on their face with a small brown brush. We acted like we were spies or robbers pullin' a big heist. We were two dumb little fat kids, bored outta our minds, and just lookin' for a little excitement with good, clean old-fashioned fun. That's exactly what we said every time we went into the apartment house to ring bells and run. Who were we hurtin'? Nobody. Except for maybe the little old lady who tripped over the rug and broke her hip while scrambling to answer the bell.

Come'ta think of it, were me and Cassie really that different from the neighborhood bad boys who robbed cars and candy stores? They didn't think they were hurtin' anybody either in the name'a good, clean fun. Just like Frankie Sneakers, who was called Frankie Sneakers cause if you didn't do what he told'ya to, he'd take your sneakers away from you and throw'em down the sewer or over the telephone lines. This wouldn't'a been such a big deal, except for the time he did it to Billy Mancuso in the blizzard'a 1962. Not a pretty sight. I think that Billy lost two toes that day! Now of course I didn't know Frankie Sneakers or anybody like him. I was an innocent Catholic schoolgirl, along with my accomplice, I mean sidekick, Cassie. This was just a story told'ta me by my older cousin Mickey, who was two years older than me. The story goes that Frankie Sneakers stole so many sneakers out from under people's feet that he got a case'a cold feet himself durin' his last attempt and was nabbed by the police. We heard that he was magically relocated to an unbeknownst location in Upstate New York for an indefinite amount'a time. I can't believe that me and Cassie never went'ta confession for all our crimes against Sackson's Shoe Store and all the innocent old people who lived in the apartment house. I hope that it's not too late now ta'say I'm sorry and that God can still hear me.

Anyway, talkin' about sneakers and feet reminds me'a what I was talkin' about in the first place. Me and my mother were on our way to get my sneakers. The two Connor boys, Ryan and Dylan, were goin' into Joe's Pizza place for a slice and a Coke. For twenty-five cents, you could get both, and Joe cut the slice in half so that they could share half each. They also shared the drink. I saw kids goin' into the ice-cream parlor to buy their penny candy for the Saturday movie matinee. They were showin' *The Three Stooges*, which I hated, so I didn't wanna go anyway. Then we passed Bernard's children's clothes store. It had the scariest-looking mannequins in the window a'kids dressed up in fancy clothes with glassy blue-and-green eyeballs that looked real. I hated going past there cause I kept feelin' like those scary kids were followin' me with their eyes that weren't really eyes at all. At least I hope they weren't! The only good thing about Bernard's was the mechanical horse out front that you climbed on top'a and put a nickel in so that you could go on the ride'a your life. This ride made you feel like a real cowboy or cowgirl, and it was nothin' like those stupid baby horse rides in front'a other stores cause, on this one, you had'da climb up on a high platform and put your foot into the stirrup like a real horse. It had a long rein to hold onto, and the horse even looked real with a long mane and eyes that looked real, just like the mannequins. It was kind'a spooky now that I think about it. Both the horse and the mannequins of all the neatly dressed kids had eyes that seemed'ta follow you around, and it felt like an Alfred Hitchcock episode or maybe *The Twilight Zone*. At least, you could pass the horse real quick without lookin' into his eyes, but when you were up there, it was really hard'ta keep lookin' straight ahead and not turn even an inch to the left or right, or you'd be greeted by those scary kids. I know I wasn't the only kid on the block who got nightmares from them either. Still, we wanted'a ride that horse every time we passed it. Weird.

We finally made our way down'ta the end'a the block and were just about to cross the street in front'a Cheap John's when my mother saw Rosalie Catapano in front'a Rosalie's shop. Now the store wasn't named after her. She just happened'ta have the same name as the owner. Rosalie was real Italian, what they called Off the Boat, whatever that meant, and she was a *gumada* of Grandma Fannie. She had pitch-black hair that she wore in braids piled high on top'a her head, and they circled around and around like Italian sausages. She always wore a fancy dress, like she was goin' to a party, and black high heels with buckles at the ankles. She also wore a lotta real shiny gold necklaces and bracelets and even had a gold tooth right in front. But the strangest and funniest thing about Rosalie was that she wore bloodred lipstick that went all the way up to the bottom'a her nose like she just finished eatin' a messy cherry ice pop. She probably didn't have any lips, or very little ones, and drew one with a pencil or magic marker then colored it in with lipstick. She looked so funny, and she thought that she was beautiful too. But the worst thing about Rosalie, and why I always tried'a hide whenever I saw her, was that she pinched my cheeks. She did this to me ever since I was little cause I was cursed with chubby cheeks, among other chubby body parts. Thank God that she didn't try'ta pinch anything else, or I woulda kicked her in the shins! Anyway, lots'a old people would pinch kids' cheeks but not like her. She'd grab onto my face with her thumb and pointer finger like I was a life preserver and she was drownin'. Then she'd jiggle my cheek back and forth like she was tryin'a wake it up from a nap or like a dog with a yummy bone who wouldn't let go til my face turned beet red and I stepped on her foot.

So when I saw Rosalie comin' towards us, I stepped behind my mother for safety. Rosalie kissed my mother on both cheeks, the way the Italians did, and when she took a step towards me and I saw her hand start'ta go up towards my face, I panicked. All of a sudden, my hand went up'ta block her, and our arms were crisscrossed like fighters in a boxing ring. She looked surprised, and her big red lips formed the shape of a giant Cheerio. My mother couldn't believe it and slapped my hand, sayin', "What's wrong with you? That's not nice. Say you're sorry to Rosalie!" So I mumbled, "I'm sorry" under my breath but didn't really mean it. Then Rosalie, in her thick Italian accent, a hundred times thicker than my father, said, "Na water bowda, da keedsa na lieka. Dasa rieta!" which in English meant "Don't worry about it. The kids don't like it. That's all right." But it wasn't all right with my mother, who gave me one'a her *malocchio* looks and made me kiss Rosalie the Italian way on both cheeks. I didn't care and woulda kissed her on three cheeks as long as she didn't pinch my cheeks anymore.

We said goodbye to Rosalie, and as we crossed the street, my mother pinched my arm, as if to say, "Maybe you got away with it from Rosalie, but you're not gettin' away with it from me!" At least one good thing happened. Rosalie never pinched my cheeks again.

So we finally got in front'a John's Bargain Store, or Cheap John's as my mother called it, and the sidewalk was swarmin' with people. It looked like they were givin' stuff away. The only thing I could see was the sign in the window that said, "Big sale!" "Keds for $2.99." "Hurry, goin' fast!" Then I saw my mother's eyes again, comin' at me like two poisoned darts, and then I felt the pinch. We tried'a make our way through the crowd up to the big wooden bin in front'a the store. Like a giant treasure chest, it held tons'a Keds, white, red, and black ones. Keds were sneakers without laces. They were made'a canvas with thick rubber soles, and your feet just slipped into them like loafers. All of a sudden, we saw Keds flyin' through the air and landin' on the sidewalk as people desperately searched for their size. I heard people yellin', "Do you have a size 7?" "Only in black." "No, I want white." They were gettin' frantic, like the sneakers were food, and they were starvin'. My mother gave me another look as she grabbed my arm, and like a bulldozer, she said, "Come on, I'm goin' in." We were goin' into battle. My mother jabbed some lady with her left elbow and made about two inches headway. Then all of a sudden, my crazy mother yelled out, "Look out! It's a rat!" People started screamin' and tramplin' all over each other, tryin'a scram outta there—big sale or not! Well, it worked cause we were suddenly up to the big wooden treasure chest'a Keds. Now my mother started screamin' at me, "Hurry up, look for any size 6s!" and I said, "But, Ma, I want white." I saw the look again and started scramblin' through the bin.

Now some'a the shoes were paired together, either stapled, glued, or had a little plastic loop, but some, actually most, were just thrown all over the place. My mother found one size 6 in white but not its partner. I found a pair'a whites tied together, but they were a size 7.5. Most'a the shoes that were left were size 8 and 9, and I was suddenly jealous'a Cassie. The lady next'a my mother picked up a pair'a whites tied together, and my mother almost grabbed 'em outta her hand, screamin', "What size are those? Are they 6s? I'll give ya four dollars for them."

The lady just said, "These are mine. I saw them first!"

Then I saw my mother's face get red, and she said, "Don't start in with me lady. I'm in no mood for you today!"

It turned out that she had size 7s anyway. So we kept lookin'. Now most'a the people who realized that there really wasn't a rat were back, but my mother wasn't losing her ground. She found a size 6 in red and said, "Why don't you take one white and one red?"

I looked at her and said, "Like a candy cane?"

She made a face, and we kept lookin'. Then she saw a white pair tied together that had one size 7 and one size 6. We already had one size 6 white and wasn't letting go'a that one. My mother held on to it for dear life. Now we only had'da get that size 6 away from the size 7. My mother tried breaking the plastic loop with her fingers then tried biting it off. When I saw her open her pocketbook, I jumped back cause I knew that she was lookin' for a pair'a scissors or a knife, and ever since she stabbed me in the eye with the knife tryin'a fix my schoolbag, I wasn't gonna be anywhere near her and a weapon. She was always sewing and had a scissor in her bag just in case but realized that she left it in her other bag. Lucky for me. So she puts the pair'a shoes on the ground and tells me to try them on. Well, of course, the size 7 was swimmin' on me but the size 6 fit. So she puts her foot into the size 7, which was her size, then told me, "On the count'a three, pull to the right, and I'll pull to the left." I just looked at her, and she said, "Just do it!" So we did, and it broke.

So my mother pulled the size 7 off'a her foot and sent it flyin' through the air, back into the giant box'a loose, rejected sneakers, silently hopin', like love lost Valentines, for their partner to come and join them. Still, the crowd pushed and shoved, desperate to find their perfect fit. "Good luck!" I wanted'a tell'em. Just like Cinderella's ugly stepsisters, they had no chance.

Then my mother whipped the other size 6 white sneaker out from under her armpit, where she carefully protected it, like a mother hen sittin' on her treasured eggs. She shoved it in my face and said, "Here, hurry up and put this on. Let's get outta here before they kill us!" I put the other sneaker on my right foot, and before I could say anything, she said, "Perfect, let's go!" Then I looked down at my feet, and somethin' didn't look right. They didn't feel right either. I was about'ta open my mouth when she said, "Whad'dy'ya doin'? You're standin' there lookin' at your feet like Dorothy gettin' ready'da click her heels! If you wanted'a go'ta Kansas, you should'a got the red sneakers! Now come on. I'm losin' my patience with you."

Then she looked down at my feet, and I saw her face. Both her mouth and eyes were opened so wide. It looked like she saw a ghost, and I could almost see the smoke comin' outta her ears. They fit fine, but the toes'a the right foot pointed in the same direction as the left one, like it wanted'a follow it someplace. Now we both knew that I had two left feet. I was a great dancer but literally had two left feet! Actually, it was two left sneakers, but why argue with semantics cause when I tried'a walk in 'em, I fell flat on my face. I quickly got up from the ground, and my mother gave me one'a her looks.

"Whad'dy'ya want me'ta do?" she asked. "You wanted white Keds in size 6, and that's what'ya got. Is it my fault that they only had lefts? I'm not a fortune-teller. I don't have a crystal ball!"

I thought to myself, *Michelina did. I should'a gone sneaker shopping with her*!

My mother saw me roll my eyes and said, "What? That's what happens when you wait til the last minute to go shoppin'. You get stuck with whatever is left!"

I got what was left all right! Two'a them!

My mother finally said, "Whad'dya wanna do? Either take these or wear your penny loafers all summer. It's up'ta you."

"I can't walk in'em," I told her. Then I tried givin' her the sad-eyed, puppy-dog face, turnin' down my lower lip for added effect, but she wasn't buyin' any of it. I'd seen this look on TV. It's the one Lucy gave to Ricky on *I Love Lucy* in all those episodes when she was tryin'a get him to forget her latest crazy shenanigans. They called it the damsel-in-distress routine. Well, it might'a worked for Lucy on TV, but it sure wasn't workin' for me. Maybe I just wasn't doin' it right, or maybe I just wasn't a damsel, whatever the heck that was! Anyway, my mother wasn't Ricky. She didn't have a Spanish accent, and I couldn't wrap her around my little finger, whatever the heck that meant. I'd heard'a this expression on TV also. It was usually on a western like *Bonanza* or *Gunsmoke*, and the girl wore a long flowered dress with a big bonnet on her head. She always had long golden blond, curly hair, and batted her eyelashes at Little Joe, Adam, or Hoss like the sun or a big bug was in her eyes. Then she'd giggle like a hyena, and they'd all take their cowboy hats off'ta her, bowin' their heads, and sayin', "Yes, ma'am!" Well, I opened my eyes from my little imaginary escape to find that I wasn't livin' out west on the prairie, like Laura on *Little House on the Prairie* (whose Pa, by the way, was played by Little Joe from *Bonanza*). What a coincidence! No! I was thrust back into reality by the sharp, shrilling voices of what seemed like a million desperate women searchin' for their perfect size 6s in a bottomless pit'a confusion.

Then I heard her, "Whad'dy'ya doing? Snap out of it!"

And just like that, I was back in Brooklyn in front'a Cheap John's with my mother lookin' at me like I just came back from outer space, the gleam in her eyes wantin'a send me right back there. I might'a been only eleven years old, but I knew right there on that day that I sure as heck wasn't and was never gonna be a damsel (whatever the heck that is!) cause the only thing I was ever gonna wrap around my fingers was my own hair!

Never skippin' a beat, my mother continued where she left off. "You didn't even try'ta walk in them. You always give up so easy, Mikey. Just like roller skatin'. Remember how you kept fallin' the first time you tried? I musta used a whole bottle'a Mercurochrome on your knees that day. As soon as you hit the ground, you were ready'ta pack it in, takin' off your skates, and runnin' into the house like a little baby so that Grandma Fannie could make you a potato-and-egg sandwich. Remember? Good thing that I was holdin' the skate key and you couldn't escape. I made'ya keep tryin', and by the end'a the day, you were skatin' circles around that know-it-all, Sandy, the butcher's daughter. What a show-off! You showed her a thing or two! Remember?"

I looked up at my mother and wanted'a say, "Yeah, Ma, but I wasn't wearin' two left feet that day!"

I knew that she wasn't budging, and unless I wanted'a wear my penny loafers all summer long or my black-patent leathers while playin' hopscotch or freeze tag, I'd better figure out how'ta walk in these things and fast. Ladies were tryin'a pull'em off'a my feet, screamin', "Hey, if you don't want'em, I do!"

I looked at my mother and said, "Okay."

She said, "Good girl!" and gave me a hug. Then she told me'ta spread my knees apart a little and try takin' a few steps with my right foot turned out to the right. I looked at her. "Just try it," she said. I felt like a duck but tried my best. "Maybe I can do somethin' with'em," she said. "You know, cut the toes out or somethin'. I'll figure it out. It'll be like our little arts and crafts project. It'll be fun!"

"Yeah, fun for you!" I said out loud.

My mother didn't even notice that I was answerin' her back cause, by now, I could see the wheels turnin' in her head. She was like Scarlett O'Hara in *Gone with the Wind* and loved turning scraps'a material into dresses and could fix anything—well, except for the fiasco when she stabbed me in the eye tryin'a fix my schoolbag. I admit, not one'a her better moments. Other than that, put a needle and thread in her hands, and she was a genius.

So my mother leads me away from the crazy scene and outta the line'a fire. Like her little puppy dog on a leash, she guides me onto the sidewalk in front'a the store. Then she said, "Okay, put one foot in front'a the other like you're balancing on a tightrope and try not'ta trip over yourself this time!" Easy for her'ta say. I was on the risky side'a this nutty circus act while she was just the trainer. So I took a few steps with my left foot in its normal position, like nothin' weird was goin'on, and my right knee bent so that my right foot pointed all the way east like it was hitchin' a ride'ta China. Some people were lookin' at me, sadly shakin' their heads cause they thought that I was crippled and other people shook their heads, thinkin' I just did somethin' really nasty in my pants! How embarrassing!

I wanted'a scream out, "No, you got it all wrong! I don't do that. Only Karen Panza does!"

I suddenly felt sorry for all the times I made fun'a her and silently promised myself that if I could somehow escape this horrible situation, I'd never make fun'a her again—at least I'd try!

And so we kept on walkin' with me stoppin' every couple'a steps to reposition my knees and feet. I felt like a little old lady. Actually, I was the circus lion, jumpin' through the fiery hoop, and she was my trainer, crackin' her whip every step'a the way. We got halfway down the block before my mother realized that she never paid for the sneakers!

"Oh my God!" she said. "I totally forgot. I never paid for the sneakers. Well, whad'da they gonna do, put us in jail for a pair'a $2.99 sneakers? They're not even a real pair!" she said.

Then she started laughin' really hard. I tried not'ta laugh but thought about them handcuffing us as I hobbled off to jail and started gigglin'. Then I told my mother that they'd have'ta arrest us cause I sure as heck couldn't run in these sneakers and that they should pay me the $2.99 for all the pain and suffering I was enduring havin'a wear two left feet!

My mother put her hand on my shoulder and said, "You know, Mikey, you're really smart and should be a lawyer."

I just said, "I'll take it under advisement, Ma!"

Then we both started laughin' really hard as we continued on our lopsided journey home. Every now and then, we looked back to make sure that nobody was chasin' us, then we started laughin' again.

It took us a really long time to walk the two blocks home, but we didn't care cause we were havin' fun. I guess you'd call it mother-and-daughter bonding time. I even started gettin' use'ta wearin' the two left feet, forgettin' about how weird it felt. It felt exciting, almost like me and my mother were partners in crime, and I wondered if this was somethin' to say in confession on Saturday. Like she was readin' my mind, my mother suddenly said, "You know, Mikey, stealin' is wrong and a sin, and I better not ever catch'ya doin' it, or else! You know that this was not stealin', right, but just a weird mistake on account'a the two left feet and all, right? It was just an honest mistake, okay? "Still, just'ta be on the safe side, we probably shouldn't go shoppin' there for a while. You know, I think I'll just bring the $2.99 over there tomorrow anyway to be on the safe side. Oh, and, Mikey, please don't say anythin' about this to your father. You know the way he is. He'll be sayin' a thousand novenas to the Madonna so that the two of us won't go'ta hell for all of eternity! Let's face it, Mikey, I think you're old enough to hear this now. I don't know if you've noticed, but he is a bit neurotic. Do'ya know what that word means?"

I actually didn't but kinda had the feeling that it had somethin' ta'do with the reason why he had'da kiss every saint statue before he left for work every day and why the dollar bills in his wallet all had'da be facing the same way.

"Let's just keep this between us girls, okay, Mikey?" she said. "Your father's gonna give me enough hell, I mean, heck, about makin'ya wear two left feet. I don't need'a fight with him about anythin' else, okay?"

I said okay as we kept on walkin' the never endin' mile of our block, past all the nosy neighbors on Looney Lane, gettin' ready'ta face the music with my father.

CHAPTER 21

Potato Croquettes, Anyone?

As soon as we walked through the door, the fireworks started. It was like the Fourth'a July, except we weren't listenin' to "The Star-Spangled Banner." The music blastin' from my father's old Victrola record player was a tragic Italian opera. I didn't know the name of it but knew my father well enough to know that he only played his opera records when he was sad or mad. From the way he was cursin' in Napolitano, I figured that today was a mad day. My mother looked over at me and gave me one'a her *I Love Lucy* faces. You know, the one when Lucy realizes that she's about'ta get in big trouble with Ricky and says, "Eeeeyyylll!" Well, today, my mother, Lucy, was TV Lucy, and my father, GiGi, was TV Ricky. The only difference was that Ricky cursed in Spanish, and my father cursed in Napolitano. My mother didn't usually have an Ethel to help her out, except for Grandma Fannie sometimes, but today, I was definitely Ethel.

Not only was my father screamin', but Grandma Fannie and Grandpa Mike were also singin' in this concert. In harmony, they all sang at the top'a their lungs, "But where were you?" "Don't'ya know what time it is?" All three'a them had Italian accents, so they added an A after every word. It sounded more like, "But-a here-a wer-a you-a?" It was really funny, and I started'a laugh til my mother flashed me one'a her "Whaddy'ya crazy?" looks, and I realized that this was no laughin' matter. So like lambs to the slaughter, we marched into the house, ready'ta face our sentence.

It was Saturday night, after 5:00 p.m. already, and the natives were mad and hungry. Saturday was usually steak and patāda's night, and that was my mother's meal ta'cook. My father was a gourmet chef but only cooked on Monday or Thursday nights when he was off from work. That's when he made his special sauces with linguine or lobster. Sometimes he just made pasta fagioli (macaroni and beans) or egg noodles with butter, but whatever he cooked was delicious, and we always loved it. He also cooked on holidays or special occasions but never on a Saturday. That was steak night and my mother's job! When we walked into the kitchen, I could smell broccoli, the way that Grandma made it, sautéed with lots'a garlic and olive oil, and I could see the big pot'a water boilin', the giant bubbles waitin' for her to throw the spaghetti in. Grandpa was makin' his famous patāda croquettes, the ones that he mixed with chopped meat and onion. He was forming them into perfect little oval shapes with his bare hands, gettin' ready to put them into the preheated black cast-iron fryin' pan that was in Grandma's family for generations. It was so heavy, more like a weapon than a cookin' utensil, and I pitied anybody who got hit over the head with it.

The tragic opera music kept on playin' 'ta the smell'a sizzlin' garlic when all of a sudden the three'a them stopped dead in their tracks like deer in headlights! Then all heck broke loose. Fiery darts started shootin' outta their eyes, aimin' at me and my mother. Maybe they saw the two left feet or maybe they just realized they were cookin' Saturday night dinner cause me and my mother were out gallivantin' til 5pm, but they started drownin' out the opera music. So were the neighbors bangin' on the pipes. This made Grandpa even madder, and as the cast-iron fryin' pan started'a smoke, so did he. You could see the steam comin' outta his ears, and with his hands all full'a patāda croquette mixture, he started doin' that crazy dance'a his, where he jumped up and down, shiftin' his weight from one foot to the other like he was smashin' grapes. Then he started'a pull out whatever hair he had left on his head, coverin' himself in croquette mixture. Still, the fryin' pan smoked, and the macaroni pot boiled. The opera music played, and the neighbors banged. It didn't look like any'a us were havin' dinner that night.

TWO LEFT FEET

Sammy and Phylo were sittin' on the couch in the livin' room watchin' the Three Stooges. They were laughin' their heads off, not cause the Three Stooges were so funny but cause they knew the show goin' on in the kitchen was funnier than anything the Three Stooges could come up with.

My mother desperately tried'ta make her case, tryin'a get a word in edge-wise between the screamin', bangin', gigglin', and tragic Italian opera music. She tried'a explain about the mob scene outside Cheap John's and how all the good size 6s were gone by the time we got there cause somebody (she gave me a dirty look) was late. But the jury was in, and we were guilty as charged. Then my mother tried playin' the sympathy card (since puttin' the blame on me wasn't doin' her any good). She said, "Look, the poor kid had'da get two left feet. That's all they had left! I thought we were gonna get trampled on like a bunch'a grapes!"

Well, if we thought that they were mad at us before, nothin' prepared us for the wrath of Grandma Fannie. You see, everybody knew that I was her favorite, and in her crystal-clear blue eyes, nothin' was good enough for her Miche-l'e, as she called me (pronounced as Mi-ke-lee with the "I" short like Mickey Mouse.) When she heard my mother say two left feet, her head snapped like a turtle comin' outta its shell. Her neck stretched clear across Grandpa and my father like a giraffe reachin' for food. Her eyes stopped at my new white Keds. Then she lowered her head, crinkling her eyebrows and squintin' really hard to get a better view. She wanted'a make sure that she was seein' straight before she erupted.

There they were. My two left feet, sparklin' clean, shiny, and brand new—perfect, except for the fact that they both pointed in the same direction, towards the door that I desperately wanted'a run outta. Even if I could run with the wind, with my luck, I'd probably trip over my two left feet and break my neck. Then my big plans for a great summer vacation would go down the drain cause I didn't think that you could put your neck in a cast like a foot, but maybe I was wrong.

All of a sudden, her mouth opened wide like Moby Dick, but nothin' came out. Then her hands flew up to her head as she held it like a coconut, shakin' it back and forth. Then she started screamin', half Sicilian, half English. "Ma, che si patsa?" (Are you crazy?) "You make-a the kid-a walk-a with-a two feet-a the same-a? Two left-a! Shame-a on-a you!" My mother wanted'a crawl under the rug like a bug. Then grandma grabbed her heart like she was havin'a heart attack and wobbled back and forth like a spinnin' top gettin' ready ta'stop. If we didn't know her any better, we would'a thought she was gonna hit the floor, and I suddenly thought'a that carnival game where the guy said, "Where she stops, nobody knows!" But we knew her routine and saw her perform it many times before. It was all part'a her show, and just like the boy who cried wolf, she was very good at it. We only hoped that if she ever had a real heart attack, we'd be able'ta tell the difference.

My grandmother grabbed my arm and ushered me over to the couch where she took the sneakers off'a me and examined my feet to make sure that there wasn't any permanent damage. Then she shot my mother an evil look, like fiery darts were shootin' outta her crystal-blue eyes. She started rubbin' my feet, and then while strokin' my long hair, she said, "No worry 'bout-a. Tomorrow, I take-a you to my shoe store. I buy-a you real-a good-a shoes, no this-a cheap-a junk-a!"

Nobody said a word about it for the rest'a the night. Eventually, Mt. Michelangelo stopped spewing lava and everybody calmed down. The pan stopped smokin', and the neighbors stopped bangin'. Grandpa wiped the patāda croquette mixture outta his hair and continued to make his world-famous patāda croquettes in the black cast-iron fryin' pan that nobody got hit over the head with that night (meaning me—pheeww!). Grandma finally boiled her spaghetti, and we ate it with broccoli, garlic, and oil. The steak waited for tomorrow, which was Sunday, macaroni and meat sauce with Lucy's world-famous meatballs day. But sometimes you gotta stray away from the routine a little, and desperate times call for desperate measures. So Grandma Fannie cut the steak up and cooked it in the Sunday meat sauce like steak pizzaiola, which normally was never eaten on a Sunday. They put neck bones in the sauce and sometimes even pig's feet (which made me gag) but never steak pizzaiola.

That was definitely for another day—maybe on a Thursday night with linguine and marina sauce or Saturday night steak night with mashed patādas. We still had the fried meatballs, though. Maybe we could be a little flexible if we had'da when it came to what we ate on what night, but we weren't that crazy! Lucy's fried meatballs were a religious tradition, like goin'ta church. She inherited her meatball gift from the original Michelina, and we weren't gonna take a chance with her wrath. Fannie and Michelangelo were enough for one family to bear!

CHAPTER 22

Fannie to the Rescue
(PF Flyers)

The next day was Sunday, so of course, the shoe store was closed. But on Monday afternoon, right after her favorite soap opera ended (*The Edge of Disaster*), Grandma got ready'ta take me to her special shoe store. I walked into Grandma's livin' room and saw her sittin' on the gold couch with the plastic covers that I hated cause you got stuck to them, especially in the summer. I heard her cryin' and blowin' her nose in her special way that sounded like a foghorn. She always had a little dainty-flowered handkerchief in the pocket'a her housedress just for these occasions. I went up to her, bent over to kiss her hello, like I always did, and asked her why she was cryin'.

She said, "The lady, she gotta run over by the car-a and she die-a!"

I said, "Who?" thinkin' that she was talkin' about one'a our neighbors.

She just snapped back at me, "Stupid-a, Scimunita, the one on-a the show-a with-a the blond-a hair-a. The no good-a bum-a drive away, and leave-a the poor-a lady alone-a in-a the street-a like-a dog-a! She gotta three kids-a, oh my God-a!"

I said, "Grandma, calm down. It's not real. It's just a show. She didn't really die."

She gave me a look that said, "You'd better say one hundred Hail Marys in confession on Saturday, you heartless brat. How'd you like it if somebody did that to your mother?"

I figured that I'd better not argue with her, first of all, cause nobody ever won an argument with her, especially my grandfather. He called her his lawyer, and whenever anybody asked him a question, he'd say, "Speak to my lawyer." Besides, I didn't want her to change her mind about buyin' me new sneakers. I was her favorite and wanted'a keep it that way.

I just hugged her and said, "I'm sorry, Grandma," and she started'a calm down. Then she shut the TV off and went into her bedroom to get dressed. The bedroom was connected to the livin' room on the other side'a the wall where the player piano was. My grandparents had what I thought was a magic piano that played music by itself. The keys would jump up and down as a roll with musical notes on it turned around and around. It was kinda scary like Casper the Friendly Ghost was sittin' there playin' or maybe the invisible man. I tried'a trick my friends one time on April Fool's Day by bringin' Cassie and Charlie up there. I told'em that a ghost lived in my grandmother's house and that it sometimes played the piano, but they didn't believe me. They musta seen a player piano once on an episode'a Liberace.

Anyway, we didn't have any doors separating our rooms. It's what they called railroad rooms like we were hobos living on a traveling train car. Sometimes I wondered how Grandma and Grandpa could sleep at night. I mean, what if the player piano started goin' off in the middle'a the night? Did they get scared and push each other off the bed? Maybe they thought they were at a Liberace concert or just dreamin'.

So I waited for Grandma to get ready and watched her get dressed. She wasn't embarrassed, and neither was I. It was like watching a show. First, Grandma put on her corset, which she pronounced "cor-say." It was peach colored with a thousand hooks and strings in front and back goin' all the way down from her brassiere to her hips. It took forever to put on, and each time she did another hook, she held her breath. It looked like somethin' the Japs mighta used durin' the war for torture, and by the time she was done, I thought she was gonna pass out.

If she did, I was just hopin' that she landed on the bed and not the floor cause, I'm ashamed'ta say, she wasn't a small woman, and there was no way I could'a gotten her off the floor. Grandpa wasn't even home cause he took a walk to the newsstand to get the Italian newspaper.

Anyway, after that was on, she sat on the bed to put on her nylon stockings. Sometimes I helped her roll them up above her knees where she held them in place with giant white elastic bands. When she took'em off at night, she had big red dents in her legs above her knees, and now I wonder how she never cut off her circulation. Grandma never wore those garter belts with hooks on the side that grabbed up the stockin's. My mother wore them and so did my aunt Teensie. When I turned twelve, she made me wear'em too cause she said I was too big for knee socks. I did everything I could to get outta wearin' a dress or skirt cause those things were torture! I hated them! Grandma was lucky that she didn't have'ta wear that garter thing cause I felt trapped in it. But Grandma did have her corset (cor-say) thing ta'wear, and I guess that was enough torture for one person to bear. Grandma also wore a thing they called a girdle! Whoever invented that one had'da be a mean boy like Charlie Desanto. I don't even think the Japs coulda been that mean!

My mother tried'a make me wear the girdle too, along with the garter thing, cause she said, "You need it to hold you in to make your belly flat." What was she talkin' about? I didn't have a belly. I was still a kid who just wanted'a play stoopball and roller skate. I was still tryin'a get my own bike. So what if I was turnin' twelve? Big deal! I imagined myself ridin' on my brother Sammy's bike with the girdle and garter things on. I woulda been so stiff like a statue, my face beet red cause I couldn't breathe. My stomach would'a been killin' me like I just ate a whole bag'a Oreo cookies with a gallon'a milk, and my legs would'a been like wood. Just like Pinocchio, I'd try to pump the peddles up and down, sayin'ta myself, "I am real! I am real!" But I couldn't move cause I was trapped in the prison'a the girdle and the garter! Why did my mother tell me that I had'da wear the girdle and garter things because I was growin' up and not a kid anymore, but when I asked her if I could go outside at night after dinner, she said, "No, you're too young!' There were a lotta things I didn't understand. Like what if there was a fire? By the time everybody put on all the girdles, garters corsets (cor-says), and brassieres, we woulda all burned to a crisp, just like a Girl Scout campfire where you toasted marshmallows. (Only problem is that we'd be the marshmallows!)

Anyway, back to Grandma. It sure took her a long time to get dressed, and I was scared that by the time I got my new sneakers, summer would be over! After the brassiere, girdle, nylons, and famous corset (cor-say), she put on her white slip. Sometimes she wore a half-slip that went from the waist down to her knees, but sometimes she wore a full slip. That was more trouble and took even longer cause she had'da slide it over her head then down and over her shoulders and back. This wasn't easy cause it didn't have an opening in the back like a button or a zipper, and like I said, she wasn't a small woman. That's when Grandma asked me to put talcum powder on her back (she already had it all over her neck and chest and looked like the Pillsbury Doughboy) so that she could slide into it like a baseball player into third base. She was already sweatin' like a pig (her words, not mine), and summer just started. Forget about July and August, she was like a water faucet. Now these were the old days before the magic of air-conditioning. We were lucky to have window fans, and they didn't really help much. By the time she squeezed into the slip, I felt like we went through a war, the Big One, as Archie Bunker from *All in the Family* use'ta say. I didn't say anythin' to Grandma, but it woulda been a whole lot easier if she just had a bigger-size slip (instead'a squeezing ten pounds'a patādas into a five-pound bag). Maybe the next time she went to Rosalie Shop, I could think of a nice way to say it. I could say, "Look, Grandma, that slip is so pretty. You should get one like that." I'd have'ta make sure that she got a bigger size, though. That was the tricky part. I couldn't ask my mother to do it. She'd just sound mean to Grandma sayin' somethin' like, "Ma, you better stop eatin' so much macaroni. You're gettin' as big as a china closet!" My mother would definitely say somethin' like that for sure, and that woulda hurt Grandma's feelings so bad, and I'd never let her do that. She wasn't mean on purpose and didn't realize that sometimes she hurt people's feelings. Anyway, I'd have'ta figure that out another day. I needed new sneakers.

Grandma finally put her dress on which was quarter sleeve since it was the beginning'a summer. Her dresses were always bought at Rosalie Shop, the store where ladies bought nice clothes. She usually wore navy blue or dark tan with polka dots or small flowers. They always had buttons all the way down the front, so she just put her arms in and buttoned all the way down—my favorite part! I was almost home-free! I looked at the clock—almost three.

I was tryin'a help Grandma as much as I could so that we could get there before the shoe store closed. Grandma made sure that her dresses always had pockets in front too, just like her housedresses, so she always had a place for her handkerchief (in case she was still cryin' about the lady on the soap opera). They fit snug at the waist, just like her corset, and she was shaped like the letter V. Then it ballooned out, down around her knees, so she looked like a giant letter O. Ethel, from *I Love Lucy*, wore those kinds'a dresses.

Then it was time for her hair, which was jet black right outta a box. It was soft and fine, and she always pushed it back with pretty mahogany-colored combs. Then she put on her shoes, which she bought, of course, at Red Cross Shoes. She had three pairs, black, navy, and tan. The black and navy were all closed up and high to the ankle like baby shoes, and they laced all the way up, almost like boots. Her tan ones were for spring and summer. They looked nicer than the other ones (if you were an old lady) and had an open toe like peekaboo and a strap that went around to the back so that her heel showed. Her shoes were what I heard people call claw-hoppers (whatever that means). I sure hope she didn't plan on buyin' me any'a these shoes! I'd die of embarrassment. Imagine me playin' red light, green light wearin' those. I'd lose every time. The kids wouldn't even play with me! They'd make fun'a me more than Karen Panza! All of a sudden I felt sorry for her and made a silent prayer to never make fun'a her or anybody else ever again. I didn't even have my fingers crossed.

We finally went into the bathroom, so she could put on her makeup. She put white powder all over her face that came in a little round blue box with a removable lid. She put the powder on her face with a round thing called a powder puff. It flew all over the air and made me sneeze. She didn't sneeze cause I guess she was use'ta it. She looked like Casper the Friendly Ghost, so she took a tissue to dust off a lot of it. Then she put on what she called rouge. It was a small round box with bright red-orange stuff in it that she also put on with a little puff. She dabbed two small circles into the middle'a her cheeks, and she looked like Bozo the Clown. (Grandma sure did look like a lotta TV characters.) Then she rubbed them in so the color went all over her cheeks. Finally, she was done. I looked over at the little alarm clock on her gold-colored bedroom vanity, and it was almost three thirty!

I said, "Come on, Grandma, you look great!" tryin'a push her outta the door.

But she said, "Wait a minute-a. Hold-a you hors-a! I need-a my pock-a-book-a! You think-a the shoes-a free-a? I look-a okay, ma no that-a good-a! I'm a no movie star!" She grabbed her tan pocketbook that matched her shoes. It was square with two handles, and she held it over her left arm on top'a her elbow. We were ready to go out when she said, "Wait-a, it's-a chilly out-a side-a. I betta take-a my spring-a coat-a!"

I said, "Grandma, it's summer. You don't need a coat!"

Then she said, "You always-a gotta carry-a som-a-thing-a. The weather she change-a fast-a. Then-a you gett-a sick-a! I'm-a old-a lady, ma I'm-a no stupida! Listen-a Grandma, Michele!" (Pronounced as Mi-kelee.)

I said, "Fine, Grandma. Why don't you take your beige sweater? It's not as heavy as the coat."

She said, "Good-a girl! Ma where's-a you sweater?" I told her I didn't need one, that I never felt cold, and she said, "Wait-a you old-a lady lik-a me-a, everything-a hurt-a, then-a you say, aahhh, my grandma tell-a me the true. I should-a listen-a when-a was-a kid-a!"

I said, "Okay, Grandma," and ran as fast as I could next door to my house to grab my navy-blue school sweater cause it was the first thing I could find. When I ran out into the hall, she was just lockin' her door. Her house was like Fort Knox. I didn't know what she had in there.

I was runnin' ahead'a her, through the hallway and out into the vestibule to open the door when I looked back to see her lookin' at herself in the big gold mirror that hung over the long table next'ta the stairs. She was fixin' the combs in her hair and puttin' on her red lipstick cause she just realized she forgot to put it on. She didn't make those big fake red lips like Rosalie, the Italian lady, but just a little dab. I couldn't believe it! We were never gonna make it in time, and good thing that it was Monday and my father's night to cook. After the last scene when my mother and me were late, Grandpa would erupt like Mt. Vesuvius if it was Grandma's night to cook. And where'd Grandma think she was goin' anyway? To the ball? We were just goin' to the shoe store. (I hoped!)

I said, "Grandma, come on, you look great! We're gonna be late!"

I think that Grandma was what they called vain and just wanted'a look nice in front'a the neighbors like she was a movie star. And anyway, who has a giant mirror in their hallway on top of a giant table with a white lace tablecloth on it? She had a big vase on the table with plastic flowers in it too. Very spooky!

We were finally outta the door on the stoop! Hallelujah! It was hot out, and we definitely didn't need sweaters. I just wanted'a hurry up and hoped she didn't get sidetracked walkin' down the block. I hoped there weren't too many people out, but was outta luck. Everybody was out, and she stepped off the stoop like a queen gettin' ready to greet her loyal kingdom. Grandma loved puttin' on a show and impressing people. Phylo was playing stick ball outside the gate with Darlene Heany. As soon as I went past her, she stuck her tongue out at me. She always did that. So annoying. Grandma said what she always said when somebody made a funny face.

"Stop-a stupid-a! The angel-a gonna pass-a, e you stay-a like-a that-a!"

The angel never turned me into a pig whenever I made that crazy pig face that Cassie taught me, the one where you pull both eyes down with the two middle fingers of your left hand while liftin' your nose like a pig snout with the pointer finger of your right hand and stickin' your tongue out at the same time. Maybe the angel was too busy passin' over some really mean kids and not kids like me, who made funny faces just'ta make people laugh, not'ta make fun'a them. I guess she was really busy cause I knew that there sure were a lotta really mean kids out there. Maybe the angel did fly over me and just waved her hand over me, flyin' away, laughin' her halo off cause I was so funny. Either way, I'd never met or heard of any kid who turned into a pig or anythin' else for makin' a funny face. I think that was just somethin' Grandma made up to get us to stop doin' it.

We started walkin' down the block and only got two doors away in front'a Mrs. Maynor's house when we had'da stop so that Grandma could say hello to her. She was one'a the other Grandma's on the block, and she wasn't really a lady friend'a Grandma or a *gumada*, but they always talked about the arthritis in their knees or *The Edge of Disaster* cause she watched that soap opera too. I hoped that she wasn't gonna start cryin' again over today's episode. Instead, she started talkin' about Mrs. Maynor's grandson Tommy, who accidentally hit Grandma in the head with a softball about a week before. She was walkin' down the block with my mother goin' to the A&P for Saturday shoppin', and of course, there were a billion kids out like today. Tommy threw a fastball to his crazy cousin Jay, and he missed it cause he was too busy lookin' at some girls passin' by. I hated (I mean disliked cause hatin' is a sin) Jay cause he had small beady brown eyes and always looked at you in a weird way.

Anyway, the ball hit Grandma in the head, and she let out a loud scream that they heard all the way down the block. Then she started cursin' in Sicilian. It's a good thing there wasn't anybody around who understood her, except for Mr. Marino, the old man across the street who was in competition with Grandpa for the best homemade wine. He was on his stoop and started chuckling out loud when he heard the familiar Sicilian curses. Grandma never hit the ground, but Tommy and yucky Jay helped her over to the stoop where she sat down on the second step while Mrs. Maynor went in for an ice pack. Grandma was okay, never went to the doctor, just had a giant egg on her head. She went home to lie on the couch and probably watch another soap opera while my mother went food shoppin' by herself.

Anyway, Mrs. Maynor was still apologizing for it and asked her how she was feeling and all. I kept grabbing Grandma's arm so she'd get the hint to go. Then I looked down at my feet and saw my penny loafers and wondered if I'd be wearin'em all summer after all. At least I wasn't wearin' the two left feet. There's no way Grandma was gonna let that happen. If she'd only get me to the shoe store already. We said goodbye and started walkin'. Janie Connor was sittin' on the pony ride outside her house. There use'ta be a man who had a pony, and for fifty cents, you could sit on it and take a picture. I had one where I was wearin' the cowgirl hat and had a dress on. It was in front'a our gate, and I musta been about seven or eight. Whoever heard of a cowgirl on a pony with a dress on? It musta been a Saturday, and I was going to somebody's birthday party, or maybe it was my birthday, and the pony ride was my present. You didn't really ride it. He just walked it in front'a your house, around in a circle from gate to gate and it sure as heck wasn't worth the fifty cents. Even the horse looked bored outta his mind!

We passed Janie and saw Cassie and Sandy, the butcher's daughter playing ball in front'a Cassie's house. They were doin' "A My Name is Anna," where you bounce the ball and swing your leg over the ball with each bounce. They asked me if I wanted'a play, but I told'em I was goin' to the store with my grandmother. I didn't say I was going to Red Cross Shoes for sneakers just in case somethin' happened and I didn't get'em. Sammy passed by on his two-wheeler and just gave us his usual stupid grin. He was bein' chased by, who else, but Charlie Desanto, who had his usual stick in his hand. Of course, in his wacky mind, it was his light-blue Cadillac convertible, and he was tryin'a run Sammy over. He was always up to no good, even in imagination play.

We were almost down the block when my father turned the corner. He was comin' back from the fish store cause he was makin' baked clams and linguine with shrimp that night. Friday was always fish night, but sometimes he made it on his day off too. He wanted'a know where we were goin' and said to make sure not to be late for dinner. We were eatin' at five thirty. I kissed him goodbye, and we turned the corner. The shoe store was around the block, next door'ta Buster Brown Shoes. The only time I ever saw people buy shoes in there was for Baby's First Shoes, the high-laced white ones that looked like Grandma's. I guess mothers wanted'a make sure that kids got a good pair'a shoes when they learned to walk, and then after that, Cheap John's was good enough unless you were rich, and we weren't. We weren't poor either, and I knew a'lotta other kids were poorer than us but didn't know any kids who got shoes there.

We finally made it to the shoe store, and when we went inside, the salesmen all knew Grandma cause she bought her shoes there for years and years. She said they cost a lotta money, but they lasted a long time. A short man with a gray suit and glasses came up to us and asked us to sit down. He shook Grandma's hand and asked her what she was lookin' for today.

She said, "Oh no, I'm-a here-a for my granddaughter today. She need-a sneaka."

He looked at me, and I looked all around the room at all the shoes on racks lining the walls and didn't see any sneakers—only old lady shoes. I started'a sweat when the man asked me what kinda sneakers I liked. I was about to say Keds when he asked, "Do you like PF Flyers?"

I couldn't believe my ears cause I only knew one kid who had PF Flyers, and her father was a doctor. There was no way Grandma could afford those. He saw me with my mouth open, and he started'a laugh. Then he asked me what size I was, and before I could answer, he went over to get this foot measuring thing. He took my penny loafers off, and I was sure glad that I didn't have any holes in my socks that day. He asked me'ta stand up and put my foot in the measuring thing. I put my right foot in, and then my left. He said, "Six and a half."

Then I said to myself, "Six and a half?" I been wearin' 6s. That's what the Keds from Cheap John's were. No wonder my feet hurt. Not only was I wearin' two left feet but shoes that were too small for me. Even the penny loafers were a size 6. He brought over two shoeboxes, both size 6.5. He opened the first box and took out a pair'a white PF Flyers with a red circle and white P.F. logo inside the circle. They were what they called high-tops, goin' up to the ankle like the baby training shoes and Grandma's old lady shoes, except they were gorgeous. What we called groovy. They laced all the way up, and the toe part was white rubber. The other box had red ones with a white circle and red P.F. logo. They had white laces. He asked me which ones I liked best. I didn't answer but couldn't stop lookin' at the red ones. I never saw anything so beautiful in my life!

He laughed again and held the red ones out in front'a me like he was givin' me a present. Then one by one, he put my feet up on a little stool so he could try the sneakers on me. I felt like Cinderella and kept turnin' around to see if the evil stepsisters were there. He laced them up really tight then told me'ta get up and walk around in'em to make sure they fit right and were comfortable. If he only knew what I was walkin' in just two days before! It was like goin' from walkin' on glass to walkin' on air. There was a mirror that went from the floor to the ceiling, and he told me'ta take a look to see if I liked how they looked. I didn't even recognize myself. I couldn't believe it! They were so cool I was almost scared'ta wear'em, and how could I play outside in'em? I was scared'ta get'em dirty!

So he said, "Whad'dy'ya think, little lady? Is it a sale?" I turned around to see if there was a lady in the store, but he said, "I'm talking to you. They look great on you. How do they feel?"

I wanted'a say like walkin' on a cloud, but that sounded so corny. I thought about the PF Flyers commercial on TV, where they say, "Wear PF Flyers and run faster!" I wondered if they really did make you run faster and imagined myself like a superhero goin' so fast and jumpin' so high that I left the ground and started'ta fly. I'd be my neighborhood's very own Supergirl, stoppin' kids from gettin' hit by cars and catchin' crooks who stole old lady's pocketbooks!

I was still staring in the mirror when Grandma said, "So you like-a da-sneak-a or no?"

I said, "Yeah Grandma, they're so beautiful!"

Then she asked the salesman, "How much-a?"

And I thought to myself, *Oh no, I knew it was too good to be true! No way can she afford them. They have'ta be way too much money!*

The salesman told Grandma that they were twenty-five dollars, and my eyes opened wide as my mouth dropped to the floor. I thought, *Great, he might as well have said that they cost a million dollars!*

Then Grandma did what she did best. Put on a show. It was what they called bargaining with the salesman, and it was her specialty. At first, I got scared when she stood up and said to me, "Mi-ke-lee, come on-a, lets-a go. Forget-a 'bout-a. We go another store-a!" Then I remembered how she use'ta do the same thing when I went shoppin' with her and my mother on Delancey Street in the Lower East Side'a Manhattan. She'd make believe she was walkin' outta the store til they begged her'ta come back in. She always ended up gettin' everything for half the price, and she talked them into givin' her a free gift too!

We started'a take a few steps outta the store when, of course, the salesman said, "Fannie, wait. Where are you going? You've been a wonderful customer for so many years. I'm sure that we can work something out. Please, come back in and sit down!" Grandma looked over at me and just gave me that look'a hers when she winks her eye and makes a sly smile, as if to say, "Watch-a this-a. Look e learn-a!"

She walked back in but didn't sit down. She had'da be standin' for her speech. Then she said, "I come-a this-a store a twenty-five-a years-a. I spend a lotta money." When she said the word money, she started rubbin' her fingertips together and did it right in his face. He started'a apologize, but she cut him off, raisin' both her hands up in the air like she was under arrest. Then she said, "No talk-a. I'm-a no finish. You think-a I'm-a stupida, born-a yesterday? I'm-a old-a ma I gotta my sensa." When she said this, she tapped her pointer finger against her brain. And I was sure it was a big one cause she was one shrewd businesswoman. No wonder Grandpa called her his lawyer!

She wasn't done yet. "You gotta nice-a house-a in-a Long Islanda, yeah? Who you think-a help-a you buy this-a house-a? Eehhh? I no can-a hear you. She tilted her head to the side with her hand cupped by her ear to be extra dramatic. Talk-a louder. Me, that's-a who! You wanna be a business-a man-a, you gotta be smart-a! The kid-a needa sneak-a. I pay fifteen dollar-a, e that's-a it-a! This-a or you no see me in-a this-a storea again-a! Capeesha?" (That meant "Do you understand, you dumbbell?") As they say in showbiz, she had'em eatin' outta her hands. I got the sneakers for fifteen dollars, and she even got a pair'a white Grandma shoes. They weren't free, of course, but pretty cheap for Red Cross Shoes.

When Grandma sat down to try on her shoes and the salesman put her feet on the stool, I realized why they called the store Red Cross. It wasn't cause they helped sick and poor people all around the world but cause Grandma had crisscrossed toes. I never noticed'em before, but they were all on top'a each other like they were fightin'a see who was gonna get inside'a the shoes first. They were all red from bangin' into each other and were what they called hammertoes. They didn't look like hammers but looked like somebody hit'em with one.

The salesman shook both our hands, then grandma led me outta the door. I looked back at the salesman. He was all sweaty, his white shirt all stickin' outta his pants, and he looked like he needed a nap or what I heard called "a good stiff drink"!

Grandma carried her new white shoes in her shoebox, and I carried my old penny loafers in mine. Of course, I was wearin' my brand-new, sparklin' clean red PF Flyers, and I felt like I was in a fairy tale. I even thought I could pick up Grandma and fly us all the way home. Talk about superpowers! I wondered if Red Cross Shoes was really named after Grandma. After all, she did spend so much money in there over the years and could'a owned it! We walked home nice and slow and didn't even worry if we were late for dinner. After all, who was gonna pick a fight with Grandma? Nobody!

I couldn't wait to show Cassie and the kids my new sneakers and hoped they were still out. I was watchin' every step I took, careful not to step on gum, or you know what, when Grandma said, "No be scared'a walk-a the sneak-a. They no glass-a. It's okay you gett-a dirty. We wash-a!" I thanked Grandma for the sneakers and just knew it was gonna be a great summer! Years later, I'd thank Grandma for somethin' else. Along with a lotta other things, I inherited her crisscross toes and ended up buyin' myself a lotta pairs'a shoes at her special shoe store, even the ones I use'ta call claw-hoppers!

CHAPTER 23

Lessons Learned

Everybody loved my brand-new bloodred PF Flyers—well, except for my mother, maybe. She didn't come out and say she didn't like 'em but just looked at 'em then rolled her eyes the way she always did whenever I did somethin' she didn't like. All she said was "I thought that you didn't want red sneakers cause they made you look like Dorothy from *The Wizard of Oz*!" Then I thought'ta myself, *No, Ma, I didn't want red Keds from Cheap John's that were either too big or too small just like Goldilocks and the Three Bears or one red and one white sneaker like a candy cane or two left feet like a bad dancer. What I wanted were these, the ones that Grandma bought me. The ones that fit just right, and the ones that nobody was gonna make fun'a me wearin'.* But I didn't say that cause I knew it sounded mean and didn't wanna hurt my mother's feelings.

Just like she could read my mind, she said to me, "I hope you know, Mikey, that I really wasn't gonna make you wear those two left feet all summer. Just a few days, so you could realize we don't have a money tree in the backyard!"

I said, "I know, Ma, and I do appreciate everything you buy me, but Grandma wanted'a buy me these cause I got a good report card, and I really do like them!"

Without even realizing it, I was using somethin' they called reverse psychology (whatever that is) on my mother cause I knew she felt guilty and a little jealous'a Grandma. Grandma never said she was buyin' me the sneakers cause'a my good report card, but my mother didn't have'ta know that. If it made her feel a little better, what the heck, right? Grandma always said, "You catch more flies with honey!" whatever that meant. But I think it had somethin' ta do with makin' my mother happy by sayin' something nice to her instead'a somethin' nasty that would'a hurt her feelings. That way, everybody was happy. She wasn't mad at Grandma, and Grandma wasn't mad at her. And best of all, nobody was mad at me, and I ended up with the best sneakers ever! Grandma said, "You gotta make-a peace in-a the house-a! Some-time-a you gotta bite-a you tongue-a so nobody fight-a! Capeesha?" I think I finally did Capeesh. I was startin'a understand all'a Grandma's silly sayin's and realized that there was a lesson'a be learned from them, broken English and all.

I never did wear the two left feet sneakers again. My mother never brought'em back'ta Cheap John's, and I don't know if she ever went back there'ta pay the money either. We just threw'em in the back'a the hall closet, where we kept the winter boots, and we never talked about them, ever again.

CHAPTER 24

Come Fly with Me?

That night, I had a hard time fallin' asleep. I was thinkin' about my new PF Flyers and how lucky I was to have'em. Even though I was excited to show 'em off to my friends, I think I was a little nervous too. I know that Grandma said not'ta worry about gettin'em dirty, but I didn't wanna ruin'em. Let's face it, I was what they called a tomboy! I even had a boy's name—Mikey! How was I gonna play jump rope; red light, green light; I eat; and especially run away from crazy Charlie without gettin'em dirty?

A couple'a days ago, my biggest problem was havin'a wear two left feet. Now I had an even bigger problem. It was the start'a summer, I had brand-new sneakers that most kids would die for, I could outrun almost any boy in the neighborhood, and I was a tomboy who was scared'a go out and play! I tossed and turned for a long time, tryin' not'ta wake up Phylo since, of course, we had'da share a bed. Another one'a my problems! I thought about my dilemma as the Beach Boys sang "In My Room" and remembered somethin' Sister Margaret Ann once told us about President Roosevelt. He said, "The only thing to fear is fear itself." Now I'm not a stupid kid, but at the time, couldn't figure out what that meant, and I'm sure that I didn't care. But now starin' up at the cracks in the ceiling and listenin' to Phylo roll and crash into the wall all night long, I started'a figure it out. I think it meant that worryin' about somethin' and all the things that could go wrong were worse than the actual thing itself—that you had'da just try somethin', and that's it! Whatever happens, happens!

I finally fell asleep and dreamed that I could fly. Now this wasn't the first or the last dream about flyin', but I definitely started havin'em a lot more often after that night.

Everybody knew I was a weird kid. I even knew that I was a weird kid. So when I started believin' that I could really fly, nobody should'a been surprised. Right? Wrong! I couldn't tell anybody about the magic of the PF Flyers and how they made me run faster and jump higher. But mostly, I couldn't let anybody know about the special powers they gave me.

When I was a kid, I used'ta slide down the banisters from one floor to the other. Big deal, right? Other kids did it too, except that when I stepped onto the landing, I thought I could take a giant step out into the air and just fly down to the next floor. It was more like floatin' or glidin' like I was weightless. Told ya I was weird! I also thought that if I ran fast enough I could jump up and peddle my feet in the air like I was ridin' a bike and keep myself up there for about ten seconds til I touched back down to the ground. Each time I ran and jumped, I went higher and higher til I glided down the block on top'a the cars.

So now, with the PF Flyers, I was sure that I could fly for real! After all, didn't the commercial say "Run faster, jump higher?" Their name even had the word Flyer right in it! Maybe this was a sign from God that I should become the neighborhood superhero. God musta known that we sure could use one with all the crazy characters we had on our block, and who was better than me? I already was a fast runner and honest (a Catholic schoolgirl and a Girl Scout). Everybody could trust me to help protect the neighborhood from criminals and do whatever I could for everybody. After all, didn't I always help old ladies across the street and go to the store for Mrs. Maluchi and carry her groceries up the three flights even though she only gave me a nickel?

But I was gettin' way ahead'a myself since I didn't know if I could really fly yet. Was I brave enough to test my theory by tryin'a fly down the staircase? And what if it didn't work? Would I break my neck or just die of embarrassment? And when I ran down the block in my sparklin' new red PF Flyers, goin' as fast as I possibly could before I jumped up into the sky, would my feet take me up, up, and away, or would I just end up fallin' on my stupid fat face? Would the kids all laugh at me and the old ladies say, "What's wrong with her? I knew she was nuts!"

I had'a lot'ta figure out. In the meantime, nobody could know what was goin' on, not even Cassie, and it was gonna be hard keepin' a secret from her. I knew she wouldn't laugh at me, but before I told her anythin', I had'da know for sure if my PF Flyers really gave me superpowers or if this was just another one'a my lame-brained ideas! Then I thought'a somethin'—the rich girl around the corner who lived in the apartment house. She was the only one I ever saw wearin' white PF Flyers, and I wondered if they gave her powers. If they did, I'm sure we woulda all heard about it. Even though I didn't know her'ta talk to, news like that would travel fast. I mean, how many girls did you see flyin' around, anyway? Wouldn't it be on the front page'a the news, and then wouldn't every girl in the world be wearin'em so that they could be the next Supergirl? Maybe that's why they're so expensive. Cause'a their magic! And only the few people in the world who could afford'em knew about it! But then, do the people who make'em know about it? And the man in the shoe store who sold'em to Grandma and me? Did he know they were special? Is that why he was smilin' so big when he brought the box out? And what about Grandma?

Oh my God! Did she know too? Did she plan for me ta'get these special sneakers cause she wanted me'ta fulfill some kind'a plan? Was it a gypsy thing? Somethin'a do with Michelina and the curse? Was I chosen to lift it from our family forever with the help'a these red sneakers? And what about my mother? Did she plan ta'get me the two left feet just so Grandma would have an excuse to get me the PF Flyers?

Suddenly, my head was spinnin' faster than a top or Sandy on her Hula-Hoop, and I felt like I was gonna barf like I just got off the tilt-a-whirl! What was supposed'ta be the beginning of a fun and exciting summer, was turnin' out to be exciting, all right, but not in a fun way! Was I part of a big suspenseful plot or just goin' crazy? One way or another, I was gonna get to the bottom'a this. If Nancy Drew could do it, so could I. I calmed down and decided I'd find a way'ta talk to the girl around the corner. Mary, in the apartment house on my block, went to the same public school as her. I'd find out her name but would have'ta make somethin' up about why I wanted'a talk'ta her. What could I tell Mary? I know. That I liked the girl's haircut and wanted'a know where she got it cut. Then I hoped that Mary wouldn't gimme the answer herself cause she was such good friends with her and knew everythin' about her. Boy, this spy stuff was more complicated than I thought! How did Nancy Drew do it? Or the Hardy Boys? I started'a miss the two left feet sneakers!

CHAPTER 25

Up, Up, and Away

(And Old Sicilian Men)

My mother was in the kitchen, makin' my favorite breakfast. Pancakes. The sweet smell'a maple syrup swirled together with melted butter traveled in waves down the hallway and around the bend into my bedroom—well, Sammy and Phylo's bedroom too. Don't even get me started on that one. I had'da share a double bed with Phylo, and was just happy that I got'ta be on the outside and she was the one bangin' her head on the wall all night long (probably why she was so flaky). There was a small dresser next'a my head that I sometimes banged into, especially on the nights when I dreamed'a flyin'. Then I'd usually wake up with a big egg on my head. Sammy's little twin-size bed was next'a the dresser that the three of us shared. Wow! I never even knew we were so poor! Compared'ta some'a my friends, we weren't so bad cause the Irish kids had seven kids in a room. I wondered what size lumps were on their heads?

Everybody was in the kitchen eatin'—well, everybody but me. Even though it was Tuesday, it felt like a Saturday or Sunday mornin' cause there wasn't any school. It felt nice to know that everybody was sittin' and eatin' together, even Grandma was there. She loved pancakes too and put orange marmalade on them. Grandpa hated pancakes and called them Medicana food (American). Instead, he had two raw eggs every mornin' in a glass'a vermouth. He just slurped it down, and every time I saw it, I thought I'd gag. But I guess it worked okay for him cause he lived to be pretty old and strong too.

It was already ten in the morning, and I was still in bed with the covers up over my head like a clam in a shell even though I was sweatin' like a pig. One'a the things my mother hated most was havin'ta call you in to eat. She only did it once, or maybe twice, if she thought you were really sick. After that, if you weren't dyin', you'd just have'ta starve'ta death! So when I heard her come runnin' in and yellin', "How many times do I have'ta call you? What, are you deaf? Are you gonna sleep all day?" I knew I'd better get up if I wanted any pancakes and especially if I wanted'a live'ta see another day! Then she said, "What's the matter? Whad'dy'ya sick? You love pancakes."

I said, "I know, Ma. I was just really tired."

Of course, I couldn't tell her that I was up most'a the night worryin' that I had superpowers cause'a my beautiful new PF Flyers that my favorite Grandma was nice enough to buy for me. And I didn't wanna tell her that I spent the rest'a the night havin' spectacular dreams'a flyin', where I flew over rooftops, rivers, and mountains. And how could I tell her that they made me so happy I never wanted'a wake up? What would she think if she knew sometimes I'd lie awake tryin'a force myself back'ta sleep so I could keep dreamin'—cause just like Bobby Darin I was a "Dream Lover"? She already thought I was weird, did I want her puttin' me in the loony bin? Now I didn't exactly know what the loony bin was, but I was sure that it wasn't a place to watch *Looney Tunes Cartoons*. It was bad enough that I already lived on Looney Lane.

So I got up outta bed and rubbed the giant lump on my head. I musta had a busy night in the land'a dream flyin'. My mother said, "You better hurry up. There's only two pancakes left. That's if Sammy didn't eat'em all. And you know I'm not makin' any more, right? The diner's closed!"

I ran inside, and lucky for me, two pancakes were still sittin' on the orange melmac plate. My mother covered them with another dish, but they were already cold. I didn't care cause all of a sudden I was starvin' and just happy that little piggy Sammy didn't eat'em on me. I saw the way he was eyein' them, his eyes all squinted through his glasses like he was Sylvester the Cat and my delicious pancakes were his little plate of nasty mice! Uggh! Yucky! Get away, Sammy! They're all mine! You had yours already, and from the mess on his face, it looked like he ate everybody else's too!

Grandma asked if I wanted her to heat the pancakes in the toaster oven (these were the days before the magic of microwaves), but I said no. They were just fine. All of a sudden I wanted'a hurry up and eat so I could go out and play in my new sneakers. None'a the kids saw'em yet, and whether or not they gave me superpowers, I'd just have'ta wait and see. I decided not'ta try flyin' down the stairs, on account'a it being too dangerous if it didn't work—not to mention, messy! Grandma just finished moppin' the hall, and I could just hear her yellin' in Sicilian if I got blood all over the carpet. Not really. She'd be upset if I got hurt. My mother and grandpa would do enough yellin' for everybody. I was just gonna try runnin' as fast as I could when there weren't too many kids out or nosy neighbors either for that matter. Then I'd test my theory of jumpin' up, up, and away! After all, what did I have'ta lose, except my life? Maybe I'd get lucky and have my namesake Michelina lookin' out for me so that I wouldn't get hurt or at least only break a leg! Make that an arm. I'd rather break an arm than a leg cause I needed my legs for runnin'. I could eat and write with one arm (if I hurt the left) but couldn't stand it if I wasn't able'ta run. Runnin' was my talent, what I was good at, and it made me feel free. Just like Fury and Mr. Ed on TV when the wild stallions got outta the gate and ran with the wind.

Like she was readin' my mind, Grandma asked me if I liked my new sneakers and if they were comfortable. I said, "Yeah, Grandma, they're great, like walkin' on a cloud!" Then I started laughin'a myself thinkin', *If my crazy theory is right, I just might be walkin' on a real cloud before I know it.*

Grandma saw me and said, "Why you laugh-a by you-self-a? Patsa!" (which means crazy) "You wanna go ou crazy housa-like-a the one-a next-a door-a?"

I said, "What? Who?"

She was annoyed, first of all, that I didn't know who or what she was talkin' about and, second of all, that I didn't understand her

English. She knew that I made fun'a her mixed up Italianish, as I called it. Actually, it was Sicilianish, which was a world apart from the broken Napolitan-ish that my father attempted. The things that came outta their mouths sometimes made your head spin. Houdini couldn't figure either one'a them out. Their childhood homes were miles apart, separated by mountains and water, but their language was light-years apart. You would never think that Italy and Sicily were on the same continent. They were that different. Imagine livin' in the same house together! No wonder I was so confused! I grew up listenin' to so much mumbo jumbo. Sentences were like a big pot'a leftovers. A couple'a pieces'a Sicilian dialect, a tablespoon'a Napolitano, and once in a while, you'd hear a proper English word sprinkled in but not too often. Neither one'a them spoke anything remotely connected to the proper Italian, and they sure as heck weren't speakin' English. No wonder everybody was always yellin' and screamin' at each other. Nobody knew what anybody else was talkin' about! When I was with my grandmother, I heard Sicilian, and when I was with my father, I heard Napolitano. Good thing that Grandpa didn't talk much. He pretty much just shrugged or yelled like my mother. Crazy house? You might say so. But it was mine, and I had'da deal with it. It's a wonder that I could walk and talk at the same time or wasn't tongue-tied! No wonder I lived on Looney Lane.

Anyway, Grandma finished tellin' me the story'a the lady who use'ta live next door that got carted off to the crazy house-a as she said it. She said that one day, her husband went out to the corner store for a quart'a milk and never came back. He left her with four small kids. "The no-good-a bum-a! The angel gonna pass-a, e take-a out-a his-a eyes-a, so he no more can-a see where-a he go!" Her words, not mine. Then, of course, for added effect, she finished off her sentence by turnin' her head and spittin' on the kitchen floor! That lady should'a gotten Fannie after her husband. She'd track him down and finish him off good! That's if the lady and her husband even existed. I never heard this story before and had a funny feelin' that she was just makin' it up to teach me a lesson or maybe it was an episode from one'a her soap operas. Either way, she made her point, by tellin' me that the lady just walked up and down the block talkin' to herself, smokin' one cigarette after another, hopin' that her husband would come home til she got carted off to the loony bin. My word, not hers. I later found out that she was talkin' about Honey Dew across the street.

Then I said, "But, Grandma, I don't smoke or have a husband and four kids."

Then she said, "No, be fresh, e you betta no smoke-a! I break-a you legs-a! Capeesh?"

I said, "Yeah, I capeesh, Grandma. I'm never gonna smoke or have a husband and four kids! Okay?"

Then she got mad cause she knew I was makin' fun'a her, and in her special way, she said, "Scimunita!" (which meant silly/stupid) "I wanna you get-a husband e kids-a, ma just-a no smoke-a e no talk-a by you self-a! Capeesh-a?"

I said "Capeesh," and she just threw her hands up in the air and said, "Okay, Basta!" (That meant enough.)

Then Grandma looked at me and asked, "You finish-a the pan-a-cak-a?"

I said that I was done, so she put my orange melmac plate in the sink with my fork to wash as she wiped her hands on her apron. Then she turned to look at me still sittin' at the table and said, "Ma, what-sa-matta? You no wanna go out-a-side-a e play? Go show you friends-a you new sneak-a. E staggione! [summer] va, [go] have-a nic-a time-a!" Then she said, "Oh, Micheli, just I wanna ask-a se you take-a Grandpa ou dendista? One o'clock-a. Okay? No forget-a. First-a, go play, then-a you come-a back-a for Grandpa."

I said, "Okay," then finally got up from my chair and went into the bedroom to get dressed. It was already goin' on eleven thirty, so I didn't have much time outside. Grandma was right about me stalling to go out. I didn't know what I was more a'scared of, findin' out that my new red PF Flyers didn't gimme superpowers at all or, worse, that they did! Then what was I gonna do? A lotta power for an eleven-year-old, and I didn't think I was ready for it.

I threw on my pink pedal pushers and the white T-shirt of Niagara Falls that my aunt Teensie brought back for me. I went into the bathroom to splash water on my face and brush my teeth then grabbed a rubber band and put my hair in a ponytail. All that was left were the sneakers. There they were on my bedroom floor, in front'a the dresser, still in the box. I took'em out of the white tissue paper, picked'em up, and just looked at'em like the way a mother might look at her newborn baby or, worse, like somebody holdin' a time bomb in their hands. I told myself I was just bein' stupid. Like Grandma said, "Scimunita!" I didn't wanna end up in the crazy house, right? So I'd better just snap out of it! I was so mad at those stupid commercials, sayin', "PF Flyers, run faster, jump higher!" But they didn't say they could make you fly, right? So where did I come up with this crazy idea, anyway? I decided to follow President Roosevelt's advice and have no fear! So I put'em on, makin' sure'ta double knot the laces. With my luck, I couldn't afford ta take chances. I'd probably just trip and break my neck before I even got ta find out if they had magic powers or not.

I ran outta the door, feelin' like I was walkin' on air. When I got to the first landing, I slid down the banister like usual. Then I ran around to the top'a the second staircase and just stood there, frozen like an ice pop, tryin'a decide what to do. Should I try it once and for all findin' out if my crazy theory was real? Or would I be a big fat chicken doomed to live the rest'a my life wonderin' what mighta been? I could just hear myself, drivin' myself Looney Tunes, talkin'a myself, "If only I took that one giant leap down the staircase, I could be flyin' with the birds right now, sleepin' on a cloud, or solving crimes in my own Brooklyn neighborhood!" My costume woulda been red and white to match my PF Flyers. Red satin like Wonder Woman with a big white "M" on my chest for Mikey. People would see me comin', get excited, and scream, "Look, here she comes. It's Super Mikey!" But now I'll never know! Then I thought'a somethin' we kids always said'ta each other when somebody dared'ya ta'do somethin'. If you were scared, they'd call you a chicken. Then your smart answer would be, "I'd rather be a live chicken than a dead duck!" That usually shut the other kid up for a while anyway. But I somehow felt that it didn't work the same when you were the one callin' yourself a chicken. It was harder cause maybe you wouldn't rather be a live chicken than a dead duck. Blabbing a wisecrack at one'a your dumb friends was easier than doin' it to yourself. Maybe you couldn't fool yourself. Then I knew what I had'da do.

I stood there teeter-tottering when, all of a sudden, the door opens, and the Italian fruit man, Mr. Guerrio, steps out. I don't know who was more scared, him or me. In his Napolitano accent, he says, "Ma, che fa?" (Meaning, "What are you doing you, stupid kid?") Then in broken English, "You wanna gett-a hurt-a? Break-a you neck-a? Ma, che e, stunada?" (Meaning, "What? Are you nuts?")

I wanted'a answer, "I been tryin'a figure that one out."

Instead, I just shrugged my shoulders and mumbled somethin' that sounded like sorry. He looked at me again, just shakin' his head, then raised his arms, showin' me the way down the stairs as if I didn't know. (I was nuts, not stupid!) So I held on to the banister, which, of course, I woulda slid down if he wasn't watchin' me and slowly started climbin' down the stairs like the little lady that I wasn't, takin' baby steps so he'd have nothin' bad to report to Grandpa Mike. At least I hoped he didn't.

Grandpa was the landlord, and everybody was a'scared'a him. He wasn't really mean but just acted that way so people respected him. Mr. Guerrio owned the fruit and vegetable market around the corner, where Grandma and my mother sometimes shopped on Saturdays. Of course, they always dragged me along. Now I was surprised that they didn't give Grandma free stuff, bein' that she was the landlady and all. They weren't scared'a her (they didn't know how tough she could be), but they did respect her.

As soon as they saw us comin', Mr. Guerrio and his wife would say, "Bon giorno, Senora Fannie, come stai?" (Meaning "Good day, Mrs. Fannie, how are you?") They'd scurry over to her like little mice, so attentive, holdin' her elbow, as they led her across the store towards the ripest tomatoes, the juiciest plums like she was the queen of England or somethin'! Well, maybe just the queen'a our neighborhood. They acted like everything was shipped in especially for her.

"The best-a orange-a from-a California, the best-a limon-a from-a Sicilia!"

Yeah, right! Who were they foolin'? Not Fannie, that's for sure! But still, they played the game. Fannie played too. I can't believe that she was a genius at gettin' the best bargain everywhere she went, just like with me in the shoe store but kept buyin' fruit and vegetables in their store even though they weren't givin' her any big bargains at all. Matter'a fact, she probably coulda gotten stuff cheaper at the other store down the avenue. So why did we go there? For respect. They respected her as the landlord, and she respected them as good business owners. They didn't cheat her, wouldn't even try cause they knew she'd never stand for it, not from them or anybody else. Still, they weren't throwing bags'a free stuff at us either! Sometimes they'd hand me a peach, which, of course, I couldn't eat cause I got chills touching the fuzz. But they didn't know that, and they'd throw in a couple'a extra grapes or bananas, but they didn't give it away. Grandma said that they were good tenants, paid their rent on time, and didn't cause any trouble, and that was worth more than savin' a few pennies. She also said, "You catch-a more flies-a with-a honey! Better to keep-a the peace-a!" Like they say, "Keep your friends close and your enemies closer!" Now nobody's sayin' the Guerrio's were our enemies, but Fannie figured, you never know, and why take chances? They mighta been shrewd business people, but they were no match for Fannie! Told'ya she was shrewd!

Mr. Guerrio followed me down the stairs, always keeping two steps behind until we finally made it down to the first-floor hallway. I passed in front'a the big gold-framed mirror above the mahogany table with the fake flowers and gave myself a quick glance, thinkin', "Is that the face of a chicken or somebody who's just been saved by a nosy fruit man?" Again, I didn't know. He followed me out through the door into the vestibule where the mailboxes were and opened the door to the street. I stood on the top step, then he turned to me and said, "Guarda!" (Be careful!)

I said, "Okay," and watched him walk away. I just stood on the stoop for a couple'a minutes, leanin' against the railing, wonderin' if this was my lucky day or not!

I looked around to see if any kids were out and I was surprised that there weren't that many. Of course, Sandy was down the block with her best friend, the Hula-Hoop, twirlin' herself into a frenzy. The Maynor cousins, Tommy and Jay, were playin' stoopball, and

Jimmy Cassey was ridin' his little sister's pink bike that was so small for him, every time his knees hit the handlebars, he fell off. Guess I'm not the only kid on the block with bike problems. Cassie wasn't out, not Lukas and Leja, not even crazy Charlie. This was definitely a good time for plan B. I'd run down the block in the opposite direction of the kids, towards the apartment house, and test out my theory of up, up, and away! I had'da remind myself that it was gettin' late. I wasted a lotta time in the hallway with Mr. Guerrio, and I had'da be back to take Grandpa to the dentist. Boy, people really made it hard for a kid to test out a theory!

I came down from the stoop and stood in the middle'a the sidewalk like somebody steppin' their foot into a pool for the first time, scared'a how cold the water was gonna be. I decided I better start runnin' before I got chicken skins. I bent down to retie my laces and reminded myself'a those runners in the Olympics that sprint (I think that's what they call it) before they take off to run. They bend over, touch one toe, and stretch the other leg all the way back. I don't know what it did, but I was sure it couldn't help you'ta fly. Anyway, I would'a looked pretty stupid tryin' it right now. I was tryin'a keep people from noticing me, not show'em how weird I was—if they didn't already know! I saw my father do that sprint move, but that's another story I have'ta remember to tell later.

I looked ahead, the coast was clear, so like a plane on a runway, I made a run for it! I started runnin' slow at first, past the Logan house next door, where the kids usually played cowboys and Indians in the gate. But lucky so far, they weren't out. Goin' a little faster, I passed Josie and Nancy's house, a mother-and-daughter team that usually fought with Mrs. Logan. But it looked like they were at peace for today. I started pickin' up speed as I came in front'a the apartment house, hopin' I didn't see Eddie, the Jewish boy who use'ta like me—or his mother! Ever since she called me a shiksa and my mother put a *malocchio* on her, I ducked every time I saw her. Lucky so far, nobody was comin' in or outta the building. I was gettin' closer to the corner and knew that if I was gonna try my up, up, and away thing, I was gonna have'ta get ready to jump up pretty soon. I started pumping my legs up higher and harder, my knees comin' almost up to my chest, and my arms were swingin' like a monkey in the zoo, and my PF Flyers were workin' hard too. They felt soft and cushiony, but I knew that they were strong and powerful too! I looked down at my beautiful red-and-white beauties and softly whispered to them, "Don't fail me now!" I felt like a jockey on a racehorse. I remembered seein' how excited my father got watchin' the races on TV on Saturdays. He even took me to the track at Aqueduct once with my Uncle Mike. They said I was their lucky charm, better than a rabbit's foot, lettin' me pick a number and rub the dollar bills between my fingertips for good luck. I always picked my lucky number two. He's the one that always made me win at the Earl's Saturday races. I won Colorforms and even Twister. Anyway, my father and uncle were so excited, jumpin' up and down, screamin' for their horse, the one I picked, and lucky for them and me that they won, or I woulda had not one, but two crazy men cursin' at me in broken Napolitan-ish!

Anyway, I felt that same thrill right now. The only difference was, I didn't know if I was the horse, the jockey, or just the crazy kid, and the only one bettin' on me was me! I closed my eyes, took a slow deep breath, and saw myself runnin' in a big green field like Laura on *Little House on the Prairie*, except it was me, half girl, half horse. I silently and slowly counted to three then jumped up as high and powerful as I could! With my eyes closed tight, I tried the up, up, and away thing, pushin' my feet up, pedalin' as fast as I could on my imaginary bike! When I hit the ground and opened my eyes, who did I see standin' there right in front'a me but Angela Turso's grandfather, the one who wore the suspenders and smoked those ginny stinker cigars—oh yeah, and the one who talked to my Grandpa Mike. What was it with me and these old Italian men today? Why were they all gettin' in the way'a me achievin' my dream? Or was it Michelina again, my namesake, lookin' out for me by doin' her gypsy magic from the grave ta'keep me from killin' myself? Was she puttin' the old Italian men in my path on purpose? Was it her way'a sayin', "Stupida, Scimunita forget-a-bout-a! These-a just-a shoes-a, that's-a it-a! Basta! [Enough!] You no-canna fly! Patsa! (Crazy)!"

The old man just gave me a look as I sat on the sidewalk, rubbin' my knees. The same look he gave me when I was up their house so

Angela's father could pierce my ears with the ice cubes. I was still pullin' the strings with the vaseline. One hand snapped his suspenders as the other smoked his ginny stinker cigar. It was more like a stump, like the stick a dynamite that exploded in the Road Runner's mouth. Then he took his hand off the suspenders and started scratchin' his head while squintin' at me like the sun was in his eyes. I could tell he was tryin'a figure out what he was gonna tell Grandpa. Between him and the fruit man, it was gonna be a crazy and loud night tonight! I could hear him yellin' already! I wasn't bleedin' since I landed on my butt with my feet tucked under me, like an Indian in a teepee. If I only had the peace pipe to smoke with Grandpa! Now I didn't really do anythin' wrong, right? And shouldn't get into trouble, right? All I did was fall while runnin', right? It could happen to anybody! But he saw what I did, jumpin' up like on a pogo stick, ridin' my imaginary bike in the air. And I knew that he knew from the way he kept lookin' at me and scratchin' his head. And he didn't really ask me if I was okay. All he said was, "Che eh, patsa?" (What? Are you nuts?) The scary part was that he really thought I was nuts! Patsa! Get it? I was sure gonna get it from my grandfather, and worse, I was startin' to think maybe they were right! What if I was nuts (*patsa*)? Let's face it! Two attempts at flyin' in one day, in one hour, and I failed both times! What other kinda proof was I lookin' for? My theory was wrong—end of story! Over and out! I was gettin' this hairbrained idea outta my head once and for all! What did I need?

For Grandma ta hit me over the head with her big black cast-iron fryin' pan that she used for meatballs? Or for Michelina ta'fly down, scoop me up, and shake me like a rag doll? No, I have enough proof, I thought. It was time'ta give up. Just like in the war movies, I was wavin' the white flag, even if it meant that President Roosevelt was gonna be mad at me. (If he was still alive?) At least I tried. And I wasn't scared either! And I'd rather have President Roosevelt mad at me than Grandpa kill me!

Grandpa! I almost forgot. I had'da take him to the dentist! What time was it anyway? The old man had a watch on, so I asked him what time it was. First in English, and when he didn't answer, I tried Sicilianish. "Che ora, eh?" I asked.

He rolled up the sleeve of his plaid shirt then squinted at his watch and said, "E luna meno un quarto." ("A quarter to one.")

I jumped up so fast I scared him. I screamed, "A quarter to one, oh my God, Grandpa's gonna kill me!"

Then he said, still scratching his head, "Ma, I no say nothing-a yet-a!"

He thought I had nothin'ta worry about, but I knew better! I sprinted away, back towards my house like somebody who never fell off a horse. I ran as fast as my PF Flyers could carry me, and all the while I could hear him, "Patsa! Patsa!"

CHAPTER 26

Ou Dentista!

I didn't waste time goin' into my house, just ran right into Grandma's. But it didn't matter cause I could hear Grandpa's feet pounding the linoleum from out in the hallway, like a hundred elephant stumps echoing in my ears. Time to face the music. My only hope was that the two nosy old men didn't get to him yet. I was in enough trouble just being late. I knocked on the door and could hear Grandma telling Grandpa in Sicilianish to calm down, stop yellin', that I was there. It wasn't workin' cause now I didn't just hear his elephant stumps but his lion roars too! She opened the door and just motioned to me the way Italian people do when they cup both their hands close to their face and just wave them like crazy. Then she scurried me in, shushing me with her pointer finger, touchin' her nose. She knew if I said anything, it woulda made it worse. Always wise! Grandpa stood there, lookin' like he was all ready'ta go, wearin' his brown shoes and brown pants with the cuffs on the bottom and his brown and tan flannel shirt. He wore his tan button-down sweater with the pockets in front and, of course, his old brown hat that tipped down in the front. He was all ready, except for one thing. He had'da let me have it first. He started tappin' his gold watch at me while yellin', "Stupida, ma you know-a che ora eh?" (Stupid, don't you know what time it is?) Half English, half Sicilianish. This was bad! "I gotta go dendist-a!" (Dentist.) Grandma tried to calm him down by sayin' if he stopped yellin', we could hurry up and get there on time (my translation). Now I just thought about how slow Grandpa walked and knew there was no way in heck we'd make it in five minutes, not even if I carried him and ran with my PF Flyers! Grandpa kinda rocked back and forth when he walked, side to side. Each time he shifted his weight from one foot to the other, he tipped over like the song about "I'm a Little Teapot." This was gonna take a while. Well, at least he stopped yellin', and we were out on the sidewalk. No time ta'stop and talk'ta nosy neighbors today, and I was hopin' I didn't see any'a my friends either. He'd have another fit if I stopped to say hello or even waved at somebody. I hoped the dentist waited for us and didn't take another patient first.

Grandpa was seventy-three, and this was his first dentist appointment! I couldn't believe it. I wondered if he still had his baby teeth but didn't think so. He had a really bad cavity and was in pain for a long time. He was tough, strong like a bear, and I never heard him complain of any kinda pain before. So for him to go and get his first tooth pulled ever, I knew he had'da be in a lotta pain. When we were little and had a loose baby tooth, my uncle Meno would take some string, tie it to the tooth, and pull until it fell out. I guess Grandpa was too old for that. Anyway, I'm sure my uncle woulda been scared'a Grandpa givin' him a big smack!

So I held onto Grandpa's arm, and we walked as fast as we could without him tipping over, and luckily, we didn't bump into anybody. Well, not until we got around the corner, past Red Cross Shoes, where Grandma bought my PF Flyers, and right across the street from Cheap John's, where my mother stole my two left feet Keds—I mean, accidentally walked away with. We were almost ready'ta cross the street when who do I see comin' at us but Mary's friend, the girl who lived in the apartment house around the corner, the one and only other kid in the neighborhood that I ever saw wearin' PF Flyers. I let go'a Grandpa's arm and just stood there lookin' at her with my mouth open. This was the chance I was waitin' for. I had'da talk'ta her. But how?

I couldn't remember her name, and she didn't know who I was. It wasn't like there was a PF Flyers fan club and we all knew each other. I remembered that I was gonna ask her where she got her haircut for an excuse to talk about the sneakers. But now that I looked at her hair, there was no way in heck I'd ever have a haircut like that, even if I was just pretending. She had one'a those page boys that flipped under at the bangs and all the way around her head, almost like a lampshade. She looked like Trixie from the *Honeymooners*! I had'da get her attention, so I just yelled, "Hey! Aren't you Mary's friend?"

She looked over at me, givin' me one'a those "Are you talkin'a me?" looks and then looked behind her to see if I was talkin'a somebody else. I started'a smell the smoke comin' outta Grandpa's ears but just asked her again.

"You're Mary's friend, right?" I said. "From around the corner. She's my friend too. I saw you with her once."

I knew I had'da do this fast before Mt. Etna erupted all over Liberty Avenue, so I just asked her, "How'da'ya like your PF Flyers?"

She looked at me weird (like I wasn't used'ta that by now) then looked down at her feet like she forgot what shoes she was wearin'.

All she said was, "They're comfortable" while givin' me one'a those, "Take a picture, it'll last longer" looks.

Then I thought 'ta myself, *Wow! Rich, dumb haircut, and boring! How can Mary stand her? Maybe she was smart. I didn't think so.*

Then Grandpa grabbed my arm and yelled, "Ou Den-dista!"

I said, "I know, Grandpa. Just one more minute, okay? It's important."

What could be more important than him gettin' to *ou den-dista* to pull out his very first tooth? It's not like I could tell him that I had'da find out if her PF Flyers gave her superpowers cause if they did, I'd tell her to fly Grandpa to the dentist. I was gonna tell him it was somethin'ta' do with homework but remembered it was summer. Either way, he just wanted to go and now!

I just blurted out, "No, I mean, do'ya think they make you run faster and jump higher like the TV commercial says?"

I didn't say anythin' about flyin' or superpowers cause I figured her face would'a given her away with a sly, crooked smile if she did have powers. Instead, she just looked at me like I had two heads and I didn't know who was gonna kill who first—Grandpa killin' me or me killin' her! Now the lava was spewing, and he started doin' his crazy jump up and down on one foot routine that he did whenever he got mad. He threw his hands up in the air and just screamed, "Stupida, Ou Den-distal!"

I grabbed onto Grandpa's arm again and started walkin' away from her when she said, "I don't run or jump. I have asthma. I just wear these because I have flat feet and need good support shoes."

If I didn't know any better, I woulda thought I was talkin'a Grandma or one'a her lady friends. I thought, *Wow, what an old lady! If anybody could'a used superpowers, it would'a been her!* No way could it be her! But then I thought'a somethin' else. I saw those spy movies on TV with my mother where somebody tries'ta cover up who they really are by actin' totally different. What if that's what she was doin'? Makin' believe she was a boring, doofy old lady so I wouldn't know her true identity! If she was, then she was the best actress in the world and deserved the Academy Award!

I decided that she wasn't anything but a boring, doofy girl, and if somebody in the world had superpowers from wearing PF Flyers, it wasn't her! It should be me. At least anybody but her! I walked away from her, told Grandpa I was sorry cause I really was, and told myself I wasn't gonna think about her or flyin' ever again! At least I wasn't gonna think about her. That's for sure!

Grandpa and me made it to the dentist about ten minutes late, a pretty big miracle, considering everything that happened. Our dentist's name was Dennis Duniff, but everybody called him Denny Dunny. It was a big joke in the neighborhood cause almost everybody went'ta him. All the kids and grown-ups too. We laughed cause his name was what they called a real tongue twister, and we used'ta have a contest to see who could say it faster and longer than anybody else. We did it until our jaws hurt or we got outta breath, and it sounded like somethin' on a Chinese menu. Other people thought we were talkin' Martian.

The hallway was dark and scary, and we had'da climb a narrow, winding staircase up'ta the second floor. There was one yellow light bulb in the ceiling, and it hurt my eyes. Grandpa was behind me, on account'a it takin' him longer to climb the stairs, and I could hear him mumbling in Sicilian. The door to his office was mahogany wood with one'a those old-fashioned frosted glass doors in little white octagons. The floor was tiled in little black-and-white octagons too. The sign on his door said "Dr. Dennis, Duniff, Dentist," not Denny Dunny. I sort'a laughed to myself when I saw his name cause I was thinkin'a how all the kids made fun'a it, but Grandpa didn't think it was funny and was still mad at me for makin' him late. So I opened the door and held it open for Grandpa so that he could go in before me. I was tryin'a show him as much respect as I could to get on his good side, which wasn't very easy for anybody to do, and some people thought that Grandpa didn't have a good side. But I knew better. He was a softy underneath. He just wanted things done right or "Giusta Giusta!" as he would say.

Anyway, we walked into the waitin' room, and it was empty, except for the furniture—I mean, it was full'a dark green leather couches and chairs and mahogany tables full'a magazines that I'd never read, not an *Archie* comic book or Teen magazine in the bunch, only *Life* and *Time* with pictures'a bloody soldiers or starvin' children from Africa on the cover. How depressing! Didn't he know that kids saw these? Not very smart'a him, if you ask me. As if goin'ta the dentist wasn't depressing enough! What did he wanna' do? Scare the heck outta us til we ran screamin' outta the door? Not too good for business, if you ask me. Okay, so he had a weird name and wasn't too smart. What else could be wrong with him? Not much, right? Wrong!

So Denny Dunny opens the door and comes into the waitin' room. We didn't even get a chance'ta sit down. I was scared he was gonna tell us that we had'da leave cause we were late, but instead, he just said, "Mike, come on in."

I got scared cause I thought he was gonna say Mikey. Now I loved Grandpa and would do almost anything for him, but I wasn't gonna trade places with him and sit in that dentist chair. To me, it was the worst torture on earth!

Denny Dunny looked at me and said, "You can come in too, Mikey, if you want to come in with your grandfather."

He knew my name cause I was goin' there ever since I was little but he never met Grandpa before and didn't know if he spoke English or not. Denny Dunny wore a white jacket with a high collar in front like a chef, and it had buttons down the front. He had on white pants and shoes to match, and he looked like Ben Casey from TV, except Ben Casey was cute. He had white hair with black in it, what they called salt and pepper, and it stuck straight up in the air like he just put his finger in a socket. And he had holes in his face, probably from pickin' his pimples when he was a teenager. I couldn't picture him ever bein' a teenager. It's what they called crater face.

But the weirdest thing about Denny Dunny was that he smoked cigarettes right in his office. You'd be sittin' in the scary big black chair, surrounded by all the machines and hoses, with the big glaring yellow light in your eyes blindin' you like a prisoner being tortured to talk or else, when Denny Dunny would walk over'ta you with a cigarette hangin' outta his mouth. And if you were a kid like me, with a crazy imagination, who watched one too many spy stories on *The Late Late Show* or *Million Dollar* movie on a Saturday night with your mother and grandmother, you might be scared that he was comin' over to burn you with his cigarette! But of course, that never happened. Everything else was scary enough. As soon as he came over and clipped that white paper bib around your neck, he'd finally take the cigarette outta his mouth, which was just danglin' there like a droopy branch on a tree. Then he'd take one long last drag and suck it in like he was snorin' before he put it in an ashtray sittin' on the counter. When I think about it now, I don't know how he got away with it! It's a wonder that he wasn't arrested or that we didn't all blow up in flames! Maybe there was a shortage'a dentists, or maybe we were all just too dumb'ta know any better. I don't know.

Then he started coughin', and I was worried he was gonna keel over or somethin', and I just hoped that if he did, I wouldn't be strapped in or anything so that I could escape. Not a very comforting position ta'be in—or safe for that matter. It kinda made'ya understand what it musta felt like to be in the electric chair. But that's just me. Maybe I'm exaggerating cause'a my deep fear'a dentists, but my friends were all a'scared'a him too, and we wondered how our parents could let us go there. Maybe that was their way'a punishin' us. Anyway, he always washed his hands, though. He kept goin' over ta'the sink ta'wash his hands over and over. But nothin' could get the cigarette smell off'a his hands or the yellow stains off'a his fingertips. And they didn't wear gloves in those days, so he'd put his bare cigarette-smellin' fingers in your mouth, and you thought you were gonna gag! Then as if all that wasn't enough, he played Frank Sinatra and Dean Martin music, which I didn't like at the time. Come on, I was eleven years old and wanted the Beatles, the Ronettes, or even Chubby Checker! But no such luck! And the worst part was that he started singin' too! But he couldn't, not'ta save his life. It was my life I was worried about—me and Grandpa and every other kid and grown-up stupid enough'ta come here! If he wasn't smokin', he was tryin'a sing and sounded like a dyin' cat while doin' it. I wondered if Grandpa's wine could'a helped him the way it did my father's friend Sammy but then realized that not only would he be smokin', singin', and dancin' but drunk too! His office would be a regular Copacabana! He put the hose in your mouth and stuffed it full'a gauze pads so you couldn't scream then he started singin' and dancin' around the room. I didn't know if I was at the dentist or *The Lawrence Welk Show*!

So that's why I was so scared about Grandpa. I knew what'ta expect from Denny Dunny, but this was Grandpa's first time at any dentist, ever, in his whole life, and I felt sorry for him that it had'da be the looniest dentist on earth Dr Death!

Denny Dunny asked me'ta come into the room, so I did—for Grandpa. I watched as he put Grandpa in the chair and lowered his head and shined the big yellow light in his face. He tied the bib around his neck, and I wanted'a cry. Here was Grandpa, a big bear of a man who wasn't scared'a anything or anybody, but Denny Dunny was treatin' him like a little baby! I felt so bad for him. I heard Denny Dunny say, "Now open wide, Mike, this won't hurt a bit," and I wanted'a yell out, "Liar!" But I didn't. Instead, I did what any Catholic schoolgirl who loved her grandfather would do. I blessed myself, makin' the sign'a the cross, and started'a pray. Now at this exact moment, Denny Dunny was singin' one'a his Frank Sinatra "doobie-doobie-doos" and turned around to do a little soft shoe when he saw me. Good thing that he didn't have his smelly hands in Grandpa's mouth cause he started cracking up, laughin' like a hyena. I guess he wasn't Catholic. He started wavin' and clappin' his hands up over his head like he was at a Frank Sinatra concert, and Grandpa turned around in the chair, yankin' the hose outta his mouth and the gauze too. Now Grandpa didn't see me prayin' cause I stopped when stupid Denny Dunny started laughin' at me, and I silently promised myself, right then and there, that I'd never come back here ever again, even if all my teeth fell out!

So Grandpa said, "Ma, wa happa?" (What happened?), and the dumb dentist tells him that I was prayin'. Then Grandpa started laughin' too but in a good way. I guess he was happy that I was worried about him. He still didn't realize that there was so much to be worried about since he didn't see Denny Dunny's full crazy act yet.

Then the dentist from hell told my grandpa, "Your granddaughter was prayin' for you cause she didn't want you to have any pain."

He still chuckled like an idiot, as I thought to myself, *No, I was prayin' for him cause you're his dentist*!

Grandpa smiled at me as Denny Dunny said, "You're a lucky man, Mike, to have a granddaughter that cares about you so much!"

I'd bet my brand-new pink Spaldeen ball that he didn't have a granddaughter or anybody who would pray for him!

Then I realized that the worst thing about Denny Dunny wasn't that he had a weird name like a Chinese restaurant or that he smelled like cigarettes or even that he couldn't sing or dance. The worst thing about him was that he was mean!

I wanted'a drag Grandpa outta there, but he nodded at me as if to say that he loved me too then just turned back around in the chair like nothin' happened. I guess his tooth hurt him so much that he just wanted it pulled out no matter what. Then I wished that my uncle Meno woulda pulled it with the string like he did to us kids. But Grandpa was a grown-up, and this was his choice.

That's when Denny Dunny says, "I think you'd better go back in the waiting room, Mikey. I'll bring your grandpa out as soon as I'm done. Don't worry. It won't take too long, and he'll be fine."

Now he was tryin'a act all nice, makin' believe like he cared about Grandpa and me, but I knew better. He was Dracula! All he needed was the black cape and the fangs! I said okay and went back into the empty waitin' room. Now I figured out why it was so empty. Maybe all the other people in the neighborhood were finally startin'a realize that it wasn't worth riskin' your life to come to this Dracula! Maybe. Maybe not.

The floor in the waitin' room was dark green oilcloth to match the furniture and so shiny that I could see myself in it. So I paced back and forth in my brand-new red PF Flyers like Ricky on *I Love Lucy* when she was in the hospital having little Ricky. My new sneakers might'a had magic powers, but maybe not. Either way, I listened to them squeak with every footstep on the shiny green floor as I kept on pacin', and yeah, even prayin'. Maybe Denny Dunny could stop me from prayin' in there, but not out here. After all, it was still a free country, right? The Russians or Japs didn't capture us yet, and the president said we should pray at home and in school, whether Catholic or public. So that meant I could even pray in a dumb, cigarette-smellin', bad-singin' dentist's office. Let him try and stop me!

As I waited for Grandpa, I looked into the big mirror hangin' over the green couch. It was kinda like the mirror in our hallway without all the gold trim. I looked at myself up close and thought that I seemed older somehow. I can't explain it like I was growin' up and startin'a realize the things I believed in and the things that I didn't—the things that were important ta'me and the things that weren't. I was kinda proud'a myself cause I knew that I stood up for myself by prayin' for Grandpa even though stupid Denny Dunny thought it was silly. I knew I had a long way'ta go but felt like I was turnin' into who I was supposed'ta be.

Grandpa came outta the door, holdin' the side'a his face, and I could see bloody gauze in his mouth. He was holdin' a little plastic bag with a picture'a teeth and a toothbrush on it that had more clean gauze in it. Denny Dunny smiled his fake smile at me and said, "See, Mikey, I told you he'd be okay. You were praying for nothing."

Then I surprised myself even more than the two'a them by answering out loud, "Prayin' is never for nothin'. It can't hurt, and it might help!"

Denny Dunny tilted his head at me as he raised his eyebrows and opened his mouth. He couldn't believe that I answered him back. Grandpa just smiled at me as he took the prescription for antibiotics from the wacky dentist's hand.

Then Denny Dunny said to me, "Make sure he takes all those, Mikey. That was a real nasty tooth we pulled," as if Grandpa couldn't take care'a himself or understand English. And we didn't pull the tooth. He did. And the only thing nastier than the tooth was him. And the only reason Grandpa needed antibiotics was cause Denny Dunny had his yucky, cigarette-smellin' fingers in his mouth.

Grandpa and me took our time walkin' home. It wasn't as if I had big plans today anyway and was still tryin'a forget about the fiasco with the doofy apartment-house girl. I couldn't believe the way I ran after her. No way could she have superpowers. I didn't even think she was human. I looped my arm through Grandpa's and held onto him as he did his famous teeter-totter walk all the way home. He was goin' slower than usual. He didn't complain, but I knew he was in a lotta pain cause he'd stop every once in a while to take a breath and spit his bloody gauze out. At first, he waited til we came to a garbage can to spit out the gauze and replace it with a fresh one from the bag he was carryin', but by the second block, he looked for a garbage can and didn't see one, so he just started spittin' them into the street, tryin'a get'em down the sewer. I took the bag from him and just started handin' him the clean gauze every time I saw him walk over to the curb and spit. It's weird, but I wasn't even embarrassed and didn't care if my friends saw me with him either. He was my grandpa, and I felt bad for him. That's it.

I tried'a take his mind off'a the pain by askin' him, "Grandpa, you wanna buy some soup from the Chinese restaurant?" cause I knew he wouldn't be able'ta eat real food.

Then he answered, "No, Grandma make-a real-a chicken-a soup-a. No this-a junk-a Chink-a soup-a!" (His words, not mine.) So after what seemed like forever, we made it home, and sure enough, Grandma made her famous chicken soup with orzo pasta, carrots, onions, celery, fresh herbs, and a little tomato sauce. Mmmm! You didn't have'ta have a tooth pulled to love that although this was usually a meal we only had on cold winter nights—Monday nights'ta be exact. But this was one'a those times when it was okay to change the normal routine, and who said you couldn't eat soup in summer anyway? It wasn't a law, right? We all had homemade chicken soup that night, and I think it was the best ever. And by the next day, Grandpa was feelin' better. He kept takin' all the antibiotics even though he never took medicine. He said pills were poison and that his homemade wine was medicine—that and his glass'a vermouth every morning with the two raw eggs. He swore that was the reason he lived to this age without ever goin' to the doctor or dentist up til now. Well, he did go to the doctor when he had malaria after he fought in the war. He was in Tripoli, in Africa, and was really sick when he came home. I remember him havin' a relapse once when we were up the country in Marlboro. He was in bed with chills and fever and shakin' all over. But he never talks about that or the bullet hole in his leg. Nobody does. To us, he is, was, and will always be just Grandpa. The man who is as strong as a horse or a superhero.

Grandpa never did go back to Denny Dunny for his checkup. He said it was a waste'a time and money. He knew he was better, so why did he have'ta go see, "This-a jack-ass-a Den-dista!" (His words.) He was right, as usual, and I never went back there again either. My mother asked me why, and I just said that I didn't like him and wanted'a go someplace else.

Suzie down the block who I went to Girl Scouts with said that her dentist was in the neighborhood and that he was nice. His name was Dr. Lechter. So my mother switched me over'ta him for my next checkup. He dressed pretty much the same as Denny Dunny, but he didn't smoke and put his smelly smoky hands in your mouth. He didn't try'ta sing like Frank Sinatra and dance around the room either. Actually, he was boring, and that was good. He was just a regular, normal dentist who cleaned your teeth and fixed your cavities. I still hated goin' there and still got scared every time he sat me in the big black chair and tied that paper bib around my neck. But I wasn't scared the room was gonna go on fire or that I'd get burned with a cigarette, so I was happy. I told Cassie about him, and she switched too. Then so did a lotta the other kids. We kinda missed makin' fun'a Denny Dunny, but it wasn't worth the risk. We still had our whole lives ahead'a us, and we were pretty sure we'd find new and more interesting people to make fun'a.

CHAPTER 27

Cinderella and Charlie the Prince

Every Saturday was always the same old story in our house. After breakfast, I'd go out to play for a while but not before my mother told me for the millionth time that I had'da go food shoppin' with her and Grandma after lunch. "Don't forget!" she'd say. "Don't make me have'ta call you from the window or, worse, have'ta come out on the stoop. You know how mad I get when I gotta stop cleanin' the house right in the middle'a somethin' just'ta come out and stop you from doin' your dumb jump rope or that crazy ring-a-levio. So if you don't wanna be embarrassed, be ready! Understand?"

Then I'd just say, "Okay, Ma, I won't forget. Twelve thirty, right?"

Then she'd yell back at me, "Not a minute later!" as I flew outta the door.

I didn't wear a watch, so I had'da hope that one'a the other kids had one. I had a watch that my mother bought me for Christmas when I was ten but hated wearin' it cause it had a pink band with a picture'a Cinderella on the face when she was runnin' down the steps from the ball cause she was late.

Now she really needed a watch! Funny! Anyway, it made me feel like a baby. So I made sure'ta be home on the dot before she started askin' me, "Why aren't you wearin' your watch? I paid a lotta money for it, you know! If you don't like it, your sister Phylo will wear it. She'll appreciate it!"

Then I'd think'ta myself, *What does she need a watch for, anyway? Phylo doesn't even go outside. All she does is watch her dumb cartoons.* But of course, I didn't say that. I said, "I'm sorry, Ma, I love the watch." (Lie! I'd have'ta go'ta confession next Saturday.) I was scared'ta say the next part but always said it anyway. "I just can't find it today."

Then I'd duck as she started screamin' and yellin', "So you're not only late but absentminded too? Whadd'ya mean you can't find it? You'd lose your head if it wasn't attached. That's the last expensive gift me and your father buy you til you learn'ta take care'a things!"

This was the last thing I wanted'a hear.

Lucky for me, Crazy Charlie was out wearin' his decoder ring, carryin' his magnifying glass, and best of all, wearin' his big black watch with all the dials on it. When he wasn't drivin' his light-blue Cadillac, he was an undercover spy! I was in front'a Cassie's house playin' jump rope with Cassie, Sandy, and a couple'a the Flan girls. We were doing All In Together Girls when Tina down the block came over and asked if we did double Dutch. She had two ropes in her hand and just came back from her friend's house in the Projects, on Linden Boulevard, where they played double Dutch every Saturday morning. She said they had teams and competitions. She went to public school and just moved on the block. None of us knew how'ta play, and she was just about'ta show us when I looked over at Charlie and saw his dumb watch.

I yelled out, "Charlie, what time is it?"

And wise guy that he was, answered me, "Do you want the time in Tokyo or London?"

Losin' my patience for his shenanigans, I just yelled, "Charlie, do'ya know what country we're in?"

And he said, "Sure do, my dear Mikey. We're in the good old US of A, where I'm proud to be of service in the good old secret service. Agent Charlie at your service, ma'am!"

Then I just screamed at him, "Don't call me ma'am! Who says that? Unless you're workin' behind the counter at Key Food servin' my grandma Fannie! What time is it here, Charlie? In the good ole' US of A? Right now, on this block in Brooklyn, New York? Understand?"

I guess he figured out in that numbskull brain'a his that I was in a hurry and not in the mood for him today, so he answered, "It's twelve twenty-two and thirty-six seconds, Eastern Standard Time."

Then just like Cinderella, without the glass slippers or the Prince, I ran away as fast as my new red PF Flyers could take me. I didn't say goodbye, and I didn't try'ta fly. I just about gave up on that up, up, and away idea, especially after the last fiasco when I fell flat on my face in front'a the old man with the ginny-stinker cigar. I could still hear him callin' me "Patsa!" as I ran away. I was late that day too. Maybe I really should wear a watch!

I ran til I reached my stoop, all the while listenin' to Charlie rant and rave, "Where 'ya goin'? Was it somethin' I said? Are you mad at me? You asked me for the time, right? I thought you said New York time. Perhaps it was Paris or Rome." Then he yells out, "I'm forever at your service, my lady. Your humble servant!"

I climbed up the steps, laughin'ta myself, thinkin', *Wow! Charlie is even wackier than I thought! First, he thinks he's a spy. Then he's my Prince. Well, there are two things I know for sure. I'm not Cinderella, and Charlie is definitely not a Prince. Not in this fairy tale. That's another story.* As I opened the door to the vestibule, I could hear somebody's radio blastin' "He's a Rebel" by the Crystals!

CHAPTER 28

Saturday Rituals

My mother and grandma were sittin' in Grandma's livin' room, or parlor as she called it. Grandma was in her usual spot on the gold couch with the plastic covers, leanin' against one side, pillow behind her back, legs crossed, hangin' over the side, touchin' the gold coffee table. My mother was sittin' in the red velvet armchair opposite her, the only piece'a furniture in the room besides the table that wasn't covered in plastic. Lucky her! It was Grandpa's chair cause as he told Grandma, "I'm-a no gonna sit-a this-a chair-a cu plastic-a stick-a my cuolo [butt] every time-a I sit down-a. Like-a in-a the showroom-a. Cuesta e mia casa!" (This is my house!) Then a big bunch'a Sicilian curse words would follow. The table next'ta the red chair was a white marble with a gigantic lamp on it that was a statue of some queen from someplace. It was so big I thought it was alive! The same queen sat with her king in a giant picture hangin' over the couch. I don't know who they were, but they were everywhere, watchin' every move I made, and they were scary! Grandma's furniture was just like she was—loud and flashy but in a good way. Everybody knew when she was comin'. The more gold the furniture had, the richer she felt.

Anyway, my mother was really happy that I made it home in time. She looked at the gold clock on the gold coffee table, and it said twelve twenty-five, New York time. I came flyin' in so fast that I slammed the door, and Grandma yelled at me, "Why you run a lik-a bull-a, you wanna break-a the door-a?" I said sorry. They were watchin' American Bandstand with Dick Clark, and I started laughin'. The guys and girls on the show were doin' the jerk and dancin'ta "My Boyfriend's Back" by the Angels. After the song was over, he'd go over'ta some'a the dancers with his microphone and ask them how they'd rate the song from a one to a ten. They always said the same thing, givin' it an eight or nine cause it had a good beat and was easy'ta dance to. It was so silly cause it didn't look like it was so easy for them to dance to. Most'a them couldn't even dance. If I was on the show dancin'ta that song, I would'a been doin' the dog or the monkey cause everybody knew that's what'ya did to that song. What a bunch'a dumbbells! But I was only eleven, and they were at least fifteen or sixteen, so what did I know, right? I guess I'd just have'ta wait a few years to show'em the right way'ta do it, but just my luck, the show would probably be off the air by then. I didn't wanna be on that dumb show anyway.

My mother asked if I liked that song, and I said, "Yeah, it's one'a my favorites." Then like she was readin' my mind, said, "You dance better than those girls, Mikey. When you get older, you can go on the show and really show'em the right way'ta dance." Then she asked me if I still did the twist and the mashed patāda's, and I said, "Not to that song, Ma." My mother was a good dancer and loved doin' the Lindy Hop. Once in a while, she'd go dancin' with my father to a nightclub like the Copa, where he use'ta work. They'd get all dressed up, and if Grandma didn't watch us, Mrs. Spatini did. But they didn't go out too often, and I think she missed it. So she gets up off the red chair and says, "Come on, Mikey, show me how'ta dance to this song."

By that time, the song was over, and the dumb dancers were givin' their rating of eight or nine. I wish that just once somebody would tell the truth givin' a song a one or a two cause "it's too slow and boring" or somethin' like that. But that would'a never happened. They musta told'em, "If you wanna be on the show, you gotta say all the songs are great even if you hate'em." Now I really didn't wanna be on the show cause I couldn't lie. They started playin' "Louie Louie" by the Kingsman. It was a crazy song, and nobody knew what it meant, but it made'ya wanna dance.

Then my mother screamed, "I love this one. Come on, let's dance."

She grabbed my hand and started doin' the twist, so I told her, "No, not like that. Do this!"

I started doin' the jerk cause that was the time'ta do it and not when those dumbbells were dancing to "My Boyfriend's Back." She started laughin' and asked me the name'a the dance. When I said the jerk, she laughed even louder and copied my every move. "The jerk," she said. "Oh, you mean just like those jerks on TV. We could teach them somethin', can't we, Mikey?" My mother could be so much fun sometimes, just like hangin' out with one'a my girlfriends!

So before'ya know it, my mother and me start dancin' all around Grandma's livin' room as Grandma laughed hysterically on the couch, sayin', "Basta, Io peesha tutta cosa!" (That means, "Enough, I'm peeing everything!")

Then my mother tries'ta get Grandma up off'a the couch, sayin', "Come on, Ma, it's good for your circulation. Better than the polka! Tell her Mikey."

As we're laughin' like hyenas, I said, "Come on, Grandma, try it. Make believe it's *The Lawrence Welk Show*!"

It's a good thing that the song was almost over cause we were so loud I was scared Mr. Guerio upstairs was gonna call the cops. He was probably workin' in the fruit store, anyway. Besides, Grandma was the landlord, so we had nothin'a worry about, except for Grandpa, that is. He slammed the door louder than I did, and by the time he walked into the livin' room, Grandma was almost on the floor. She was laughin' so hard and probably lettin' out a little pee too and with the plastic couch covers slid all the way off'a the couch. If my mother and me weren't singin' and dancin', he probably would'a thought she was havin' that heart attack she talked about every day. Between the TV blastin' and us laughin', he had one'a his fits. He started screamin' and pullin' his hair out first. Then he went into the crazy jumpin' dance he did that looked like he was stompin' grapes or killin' bugs. He looked like he wanted'a kill us when he screamed at me and my mother, "Che eh patsa?" (What? Are you nuts?) We stopped dancin', and just gave each other a quick look that said, "Eeehhlll!" We ran over'ta help Grandma off'a floor, and she was still laughin'. Grandpa started screamin' again cause he thought she was cryin'. We tried'a get her back on the couch, but she kept slidin' off cause the plastic covers were wet with pee. I looked over at the TV real fast ta'see the dancers ratin' "Louie Louie." I thought'ta myself, *If they said that it didn't have a good beat and you couldn't dance to it, then they were nuts and liars and for sure couldn't dance cause not only me and my mother but even my old grandmother wanted'a dance to it.*

Grandpa caught me lookin' at the TV again instead'a tryin'a help Grandma up, so he started cursing in Sicilianish again and stomped over to shut the television off.

Then Grandma said, "No, Mike-a, leave-a lone-a the show. I like-a. Come on-a, Mike-a, you wanna dance-a?"

Then she started laughin' and peein' all over again while me and my mother just covered our mouths, tryin' not'ta laugh out loud.

But Grandpa started again, "Bunch-a crazy family! Mother and daughter. Patsa!"

We finally got Grandma off'a the floor, and my mother walked her into the bathroom to wash up and change her underwear. Grandpa was still yellin' that we were jumpin' around like a bunch'a patsa's instead'a doing the *speeza* (grocery shopping) like we were supposed'ta.

Then my mother looked at me and said, "Wow, Mikey, I can't believe I was havin' so much fun I forgot about the food shoppin'!"

I said, "I'm glad'ya had fun, Ma. So did I."

Then she asked what "Louie Louie" was about, and I said, "Nobody knows, Ma. It's a big mystery. But it has a great beat, and it's easy'ta dance to."

Then she looked up at me with one'a those *I Love Lucy* crooked smiles and said, "The jerk, right?"

And I said, "Yeah, Ma, the jerk."

She laughed a little and said, "I give it a ten!"

Then I said, "So did I til Grandpa came in. Then it became a zero, real fast!"

We both started laughin' again til suddenly, just as fast as it started, she jumped back into reality, turnin' from a teenager into a

TWO LEFT FEET

grown-up again. It was like she turned a switch on and off. Playtime was over, and my mother was back. Like she was makin' up for lost time, she sprang into action, wearin' her invisible Mommy Cape. "Well, wha'ddy'ya waitin' for? Christmas?" she said. "Go get the shoppin' cart, and I'll see if Grandma's done puttin' on her powder and rouge. I swear she thinks she's Mae West! We're only goin' to the A&P for God's sake. Who does she think she's gonna meet there, Lawrence Welk?"

We both laughed out loud, and I said, "Grandma doesn't like Lawrence Welk anymore, Ma. Now she likes Liberace."

Then my mother started'a say somethin', and all of a sudden, she was laughin' so hard and snortin' like a pig. This was somethin' that always happened ta'her, kind'a like an epileptic fit, when she thought her jokes were so funny, she cracked herself up and couldn't get a word out. The only thing'ya could do when this happened was'ta just wait til she stopped snortin', caught her breath, and spit the joke out like a pit caught in her throat. It was like waitin' for somebody who stuttered to tell a story. By the time they finished it, you forgot what it was about in the first place. And the other thing was, it was a shame but her jokes left her hysterical and everybody else just standin' around with their eyebrows crinkled and mouths wide open.

So I was surprised when she finally said, "Well, I don't think Lawrence Welk or Liberace are gonna be at the A&P, but maybe if we tell her they are, she'll hurry up and get the hell—I mean heck—outa the bathroom so we could get this dumb food shoppin' over with already!"

I said, "Good one, Ma!" and meant it. Maybe her jokes were finally gettin' better.

Then my mother said, "Come on before there's no food left! Grandpa's gonna have a fit if they're all outta broccoli rabe. You know how he gets if he doesn't have fresh vegetables!" Then she was screamin' at me like it was my fault my grandmother thought she was the queen'a Brooklyn, sayin', "And forget about that crazy fruit man upstairs! He charges an arm and a leg. Who does he think he is, Al

Capone? Grandma only makes an appearance there cause she thinks she's the queen'a the neighborhood."

"Of Brooklyn," I said.

"What?" she screamed at me.

"The queen'a Brooklyn," I said. "Not just the neighborhood."

"Who cares!" my mother screamed in my ear. "Neighborhood, Brooklyn, the whole"—she started'a say goddamned but stopped—"darn world! What's the difference? If she doesn't get outta that bathroom soon, Grandpa's gonna blow the roof off'a this house like the big bad wolf, and we're all gonna starve'ta death!"

Then I said, "Ma, wha'ddy'ya yellin' at me for? Grandma's the one who's still in the bathroom."

My mother calmed down for a second and said, "You're right, Mikey. It's not your fault, but I can't yell at her. She's my mother!" She didn't say it, but I knew that meant, "So don't you ever get any big ideas about yellin' at me!" Then she started snortin' again, and after a few seconds, she hiccupped it out. She held onto the chair for support cause she was laughin' so hard. Then she said, "Imagine her wedding day? It musta taken her a week to get ready! I'm surprised Grandpa didn't change his mind and run the heck outta there!"

Now we were both laughin' out loud again. Her jokes really were gettin' better!

Then I said, "Nobody runs out on the queen'a Brooklyn, Ma. She would'a put a *malocchio* on him!"

We were still laughin' when, all of a sudden, Grandma came walkin' outta the bathroom. She was all dolled up in her navy-blue and white polka-dot dress, tan Red Cross shoes with the straps, and tan pocketbook to match hangin' over her arm. And of course, her face was covered in powder (or *provelia* as she called it) with little red circles'a rouge on each cheek. From the looks'a her, nobody would'a guessed that just a couple'a minutes ago, she was on the parlor floor covered in pee. Both of us knew to never tell a living soul about that, or it would'a been the last thing we ever did. Grandma would'a killed us. She had too much pride and a reputation to uphold as a well-dressed, important lady on the block. She was a landlady!

Then Grandma said, "Stop!" We thought she was mad cause she heard us callin' her queen or that she wanted'a remind us to never tell about her peeing herself, but that wasn't it. She said, "You forgett-a what-a day is it-a today? This-a Saturday, no? Where we go-a Saturday night-a?" Then with a twinkle in her blue eyes that always shined like stars, she said, "Ma, who we gotta go make-a ou visita sta sera (tonight)? Last-a week-a we see Zia Rosalia. Maybe tonight-a Zia Immaculata, no, what-a you say-a?" If food shoppin' was part'a our Saturday ritual, then visiting *gumadas* and *gumbadas* was part'a our Saturday night one. Every Saturday night!

So my mother said, "But, Ma, we're late. What about the broccoli rabe? Papa's gonna go nuts if he doesn't get any!"

And of course, Grandma said, "Forget-a 'bout-a ou broccoli rabe. Eh, no worry 'bout-a Grandpa. I take-a care-a. He do-a what-a I say-a. No forget-a. I getta the broccoli rabe from a Questa Scimunitu [the dumbbell] upstairs, Mr. Guerrio. I pay a few cents-a more-a, ma [but] I getta fresh-a stuff-a. No forgett-a, I'm-a the lanlor! [landlord]"

And the queen, I wanted'a say but didn't.

So my mother leaned the shoppin' cart back against the wall as we once again went into the parlor to sit on the plastic-covered furniture! We sat and waited as Grandma got out her little black phone book. I loosened the laces on my new red PF Flyers cause I wanted'a get comfortable—well, as comfortable as you could get when your butt was stuck'ta plastic. I knew this was gonna take a while. We were watchin' a woman on a mission. She was lickin' her pointer finger, turnin' the pages, sayin' more'ta herself than to us, "No, forget-a 'bout-a Gumada Antoinett-a. She gotta big-a mouth-a. She say-a my Zeppole e heavy like-a lead-a! Putana! My Zepole e lighta lik-a feather, they can-a fly away! They the best-a in-a the west-a! Maybe we better go someplace-a close-a tonight-a. Already it's-a late-a!"

I wanted'a say, "That's for sure, Grandma" but didn't.

I just sat with my mother as Grandma licked her finger and turned the pages. I looked at the clock—four fifteen. Then I thought ta'myself, "We're never gettin' dinner tonight!" Then I wished I'd eaten more pancakes that morning. I was just glad that I wasn't wearin' shorts, or I would'a had'da peel my thighs off'a the chair. Just like waitin' for her'ta come outta the bathroom, you couldn't rush her when she was pickin' *gumadas* to visit. We just sat and waited til her eeny-meeny-miny-moe was over and hoped that the store would still be open.

After what seemed like an eternity, Grandma announced that we were gonna visit Gumada Tina and Gumbada Gaspano. They were Grandma and Grandpa's oldest friends from the old country, and in fact, Gumada Tina was the matchmaker who set Grandma and Grandpa up. I guess she knew what she was doin' cause even though they argued like cats and dogs, Grandma and Grandpa were a perfect match. She told him what'ta do, and he listened. Whenever somebody asked Grandpa a question, he'd point to Grandma and say, "Speak to my lawyer!" I guess that's why they were still married after forty-five years. In those days, nobody got divorced. When they said "'Till death do us part," they meant it. You could get away with killin' your spouse, but you couldn't divorce'em. It was a sin. End of story. You just had'da suffer and hope that one'a you died young. But Grandma and Grandpa really loved each other and couldn't live without each other. All their bickering was just the silly game they played.

So Grandma yelled out'ta Grandpa, "Mike-a, get-a bottle-a wine-a from-a the cellar, e forget-a 'bout-a watch-a *Red-a Skelton-a* tonight. We gonna go see ou gumada!"

Then Grandpa yelled from the kitchen, "Eh, this-a crazy gypsy-a familia, all the time-a gotta go-a galavanting-a! Bunch a vagabond-a!"

It wasn't that Grandpa hated visitin' so much as he hated missin' his favorite TV show *Red Skelton Show*. At least he knew that at Gumbada Gaspano's house, he'd get to watch his favorite show with his favorite friend. The two'a them would laugh like two kids bein' tickled on the belly whenever they watched Red Skelton's crazy shenanigans. They especially cracked up at "Gertrude and Heathcliff," which was supposed'ta be two giant birds talkin'ta each other.

Grandma pulled Grandpa's dress clothes outta the closet, the ones he always wore for visitin'. His white shirt, brown pants, and brown tie were always ironed and ready'ta go just like a costume.

Then she turned around and yelled at me and my mother, "Come on-a, lets-a go. What-a you wait-a for, Chris-amiss-a?"

I wanted'a say, "We been waitin' for you all day, Grandma. First, so you could doll yourself up for the A&P, and then so you could decide who we were gonna visit tonight!" But of course, I didn't say a word. I just grabbed the shoppin' cart and carried it back into the hallway while Grandma made a quick call'ta Gumada Tina to say we were comin' over tonight. It was funny, but Grandma just figured that everybody would be home just waitin' for a surprise visit from the queen'a Brooklyn. She usually didn't call but this time, she did. She'd just say, "They old-a, where they gonna go?" She was old and always gallivanting all over. There were some people we always had'da call first, like Grandma's cousin Pete and his wife, Frances. Their sons were in a band and always practiced on Saturday nights in the basement. Grandma couldn't stand the drumming and sat holdin' her head all night long. They all had'da scream over the music to hear each other talk, so Grandma would only go there if the band was practicing at some other kid's house. She'd say, "I no gonna go deaf-a just a to make-a visit-a! Forget-a 'bout-a. They come-a my house-a se they wanna see me, or I no see them-a no more! That's all! Basta!" (Enough.)

We also had'da call Grandma's Gumada Margie and her husband, Joe, cause they were younger than Grandma and Grandpa and were always goin' to nightclubs, drinkin' and dancin'. Margie had gigantic boobs, much bigger than Lilly's. If Lilly had eggplants, then Margie had watermelons! Grandma would always make fun'a them and call 'em melons as she laughed while motioning with her hands.

"Tene duo meloni!" (She's got two melons!) she'd say. Margie always laughed along with Grandma and was a great sport about the whole thing. I guess you can't go through life carryin' giant watermelons on your chest without havin' a sense'a humor. Margie would slap Grandma on the shoulder then lift her giant watermelons with her two hands while she made silly faces. Whenever she did this, she made a giant line down the middle that they called cleavage, and I imagined what the Grand Canyon musta looked like. Now when Lilly and Vicky did their crazy show for me and Cassie, it was disgusting. But this was somehow funny. Maybe cause I was with my family, and my grandmother, of all people, thought it was hysterical. Still, I was kinda embarrassed cause it looked like a fat baby's butt! And Margie and Grandma were the only two laughin'. My mother just rolled her eyes. I tried'ta look away, and I saw Sammy coverin' his mouth to hide his giggles. Phylo was just too dumb'ta notice what was goin' on. Grandpa didn't like it though and looked embarrassed. His face was turnin' red, and it wasn't from the wine either.

Then her husband, Joe, would say, "Margie, stop it! What's wrong with you? Can't you see that there are kids here? That's it. No more wine for you!" Then he said, "Mike, whaddy'ya put in this wine? Dynamite?"

I wanted'a say, "It's the grapes," but kept my mouth shut. Then I remembered my father's friend Sammy and what Grandpa's wine did to him. Maybe Margie was allergic too. After all, she was very blond, and I don't know if she was even Italian. Matter'a fact, she did look German, and I was glad that she at least wasn't singin' like Caruso or, worse, yodeling! Grandma and Margie finally calmed down, but not til Grandma announced that she peed her pants a little. She was doin' a lotta that lately! Now Grandpa was really mad and took the wine bottle off'a the table. He put it on the floor by his feet, and I just hoped they didn't have a dog or cat with a liking for red wine!

After that night, we didn't visit them much anymore, and if we did, we never brought wine, especially not Grandpa's wine! I was startin'a think that he musta just created a lethal batch and not since the days'a Sammy had we seen such an outbreak. So far, Margie had the worst reaction, so as they say in the medical field, "I don't think we have an epidemic yet, folks!" But we had'da keep an eye on who drank the wine and how it hit'em. I suddenly felt like a scientist. Of course, I didn't tell anybody else about my theory. They already thought I was nuts, and I was still tryin'a get over the whole flyin' thing!

We finally did get to the A&P that day, but it was so late it was almost dark out by the time we got home. They were outta broccoli rabe and almost everythin' else too. My mother bought cold cuts so we could have Italian bread sandwiches when we got home with tomato and mozzarella salad. On the way home, as I lugged the cart'a groceries up and down the curbs (cause, after all, that's what I was there for), I realized that I was starvin', and each time we stopped to cross a street, I started rummaging through the bags to open the bag'a Oreo cookies.

My mother yelled, "Wha'ddy'ya doin'? You're gonna spill all the bags into the street, and anyway, you're gonna spoil your dinner!"

"What dinner?" I wanted'a say. Was there gonna be a big surprise feast waitin' for us when we got home that I didn't know about, or were we just havin' cold-cut sandwiches cause we wasted all day waitin' for Grandma? And to top it off, now I had'da go visitin' old *gumadas* on a Saturday night! Wow! Wasn't my life so much fun! I wondered how old I had'da be ta'stop this stupid ritual? I was eleven years old for Pete's sake! Some kids my age were allowed'a go'ta the movies on Saturday nights with a group'a kids or have sleepovers but not me! My father was scared'ta even let me roller skate! I'd better face it. There was no way I was gonna grow up! Not halfway normal, anyway! I'd never be able'ta go on a date, and if I did, my father would'a been sittin' right between us, passin' the popcorn. Then he'd say, "Watch out-a, no eat-a too fast-a, you gonna chok-a! Eh no drink-a e talk-a the same-a time-a, you gonna choka!" I was doomed. Maybe I could still become a nun. I'd ask Sammy since he had connections in that department.

So we lugged (I mean I lugged) the shoppin' cart to the German bakery, where we got Grandpa's favorite, apple crumb cake. It's the least we could do since not only did he have'ta wear a tie and dress shirt instead'a his favorite tan plaid and not be able'ta watch his favorite *Red Skelton Show* from the comfort of his red velvet chair without the plastic covers, but the icing on the cake was that he'd have'ta eat salami on Italian bread with tomato and mozzarella salad instead'a his usual Saturday night meal'a steak, mashed patāda's, and corn. And I, for one, didn't wanna be there when Mt. Michelangelo erupted! The only good part was that we were visitin' his best friend, Gaspano.

One'a the best parts about goin'ta Tina and Gaspano's house was that it was close enough'ta walk to, about ten or twelve blocks.

This wasn't very far since we were use'ta walkin' all over cause we didn't have a car. My uncle Meno was the only one with a car, and he always took us to the drive-in movies Upstate but he'd never go visitin' unless my aunt Teensie went too, and then we had the problem'a fittin' all of us in the car. I remember how we packed the car full'a people when we went up'ta the country, and it was like a circus car full'a clowns! I don't know how we didn't get arrested. And anyway, we were all smaller then, even Grandma put on a few pounds although I'd never tell her. So we always walked to their house, huddled together, like a little pack'a mice crowdin' the sidewalk. I always walked arm in arm with Grandma so I could help her across Atlantic Avenue before we were all crushed like roadkill. My mother held on to Phylo, draggin' her along, cause she was always whinin' about somethin'. Grandpa and Sammy always walked behind, as if to protect all the womenfolk. (Yeah right, big joke. Not Sammy, that's for sure!) Sammy was the first one'ta run from danger—we all knew that, especially me! Anyway, he couldn't see two feet in front'a him, even with his Coke bottle eyeglasses on, so Grandpa was there to hold up Sammy more than the other way around. I always carried the apple crumb cake in the white bakery box in my free hand, and of course, Grandpa always carried the bottle'a wine. He wouldn't trust anybody else with it. And anyway, God forbid, it ever fell and smashed on the ground, leaving a trail'a wine bloodstains all over the sidewalk! I didn't want that blood on my hands or any other part'a me. That's for sure! That's what I say! Grandpa made it, so let him be responsible for it. End of story!

The bad thing about goin'a Gumada Tina and Gumbada Gaspano's house was that they had Dobermans. Two'a them! Their names were Lisa and Debbie. Two sweet names, right? Wrong! They should'a been called Fang and Killer cause they had pointed ears that went straight up to the sky and razor-sharp fangs. All they did was snarl and drool at'ya like you were Saturday night's steak dinner! (the one we didn't get'ta have cause we were here with them). We'd climb up to their porch and knock on the kitchen window, so as not'ta alarm the dogs with the dinner bell! But we couldn't hide. *Gumada* or her daughter Santa would look out the window while shushing the Dobermans away, as if ta'say, "No, it's not the delivery boy with your dinner."

Then Grandma would yell, "Getta this-a dog-a outa here, se no, I go home-a!" And she meant it! We had enough experience goin' there ta'learn our lesson. We use'ta just ring the bell, and before you could get your foot in the door, it was in one'a the Doberman's mouths! I ruined so many shoes that way. We'd all be pushin' somebody else to the front, sayin', "I rang the bell last time. Now it's your turn!"

Of course, chicken skin Sammy never had a turn and he'd hide all the way in the back, behind Grandma. So Santa would bring the dogs to a back bedroom, and Grandma made sure that she locked them in. Then we'd hear them bangin' and scratchin' on the door all night, not'ta mention howlin' like wolves, tryin'a get out. I wished that she would'a just thrown some raw steaks into the room, like into a lion's cage, just to shut'em up. Why couldn't they get it into their dumb heads that we weren't dinner? I knew that if the devil were a dog, he'd be a Doberman! All they did was growl and drool all over the place, saliva drippin' down'ta the floor. They weren't the kinda dogs you could pet and cuddle, not even to their owners. At least I never saw it!

Gumada Tina was short and skinny with short straight white hair and a stubbly chin that scratched when she kissed you. I once saw her shavin' it with an electric shaver just like a man. Maybe she needed a better razor or had'da go to the barbershop with the red-and-white-striped pole so he could shave her with the brush and that whipped cream stuff. But I think that was just for men. Gumbada was a cute, chubby man with a round face. He had white hair too and always wore suspenders on his pants so they came high above his waist. He'd sit in his rocking chair as Grandpa sat on the couch opposite him. Then they both drank Grandpa's bloodred wine and laughed like hyenas at Red Skelton's zany antics. Meanwhile, my mother and grandma sat at the kitchen table havin' coffee and apple crumb cake. Grandma made sure'ta save some for Grandpa. He didn't want any now cause he was too busy gettin' drunk with his best friend, but she knew for sure that he'd want some later. Sammy and Phylo just sat at the table, bored outta their minds, or went into the livin' room to watch TV with Grandpa.

Santa had a daughter named Gia who was my age. She had a room full'a toys, next'ta the room that the Dobermans were in. It was kinda scary cause you could hear'em bangin' on the wall, and I was a'scared they were gonna break in. Her room was full'a suitcases that had tons'a Barbie dolls in'em and tons more full'a Barbie clothes. There were billions'a outfits like Barbie was takin' a permanent trip around the world! That Barbie had more clothes than anybody I knew, real or fake! There were suitcases full'a shiny silvery dresses with shoes and pocketbooks to match. There were gold dresses, fur coats, business suits, casual wear, and beachwear. Then there was a whole Barbie world to go with it. Her dream car, dream house, swimming pool, even a motorcycle! And of course, cause no princess is complete without her prince, real or imaginary, there was her dreamboat—Ken!

Now everybody knew that I hated playin' with dolls and especially Barbies, but this Barbie was somethin' else! She had her own world! Now Santa was a dressmaker, just like my mother, and I'm sure she made most'a these outfits for Gia, and I knew that if I wanted, my mother woulda made'em for me, too, but I'd never be caught dead playin' with Barbies in my house or with my regular friends! No way! But somehow it was okay here with Gia cause I was isolated, away from Cassie and the other kids. It was weird, like you did some things with some people that you wouldn't do with anybody else and even acted different dependin' on who you were with. Maybe we chose different friends in the first place cause they brought out a part of us we shared in common with only them. Confusing! All I knew was that I wasn't embarrassed to play Barbies with Gia even though I wouldn't be caught dead doin' it with anybody else. Cross my heart and hope'ta die!

Then I laughed out loud ta'myself as Gia put Barbie and Ken in the dream car. It was a convertible, and Barbie had one'a those long silk scarves around her head and neck, like the movie stars from the old movies. It was so the wind wouldn't blow her perfect hairdo out'a place cause Ken would be drivin' way too fast with the top-down.

And of course, the music would be blastin'. Probably a Beach Boys song like "Surfer Girl" when Ken would grab Barbies hand as he looked over at her to tell her that she was the most beautiful girl in the world! A real livin' doll! Haha!

Wow! I could see how this Barbie stuff could really get your imagination goin'! But I couldn't do it all the time. Once in a while when I came over ta' play with Gia was plenty for me. Then I imagined Barbie as a real, live person and saw her walkin' down the block, past us kids playin' a game'a freeze tag or I eat. She'd be walkin' tall and straight like a runway model but not conceited like that Flan girl across the street, who thought she was so great but not even pretty! No, Barbie would have it all, not just tons'a clothes, sports cars, dream houses, and dreamboat boyfriends. She'd be beautiful, smart, kind, and fun! She'd catch the ball for us if we dropped it and toss it over. She'd stop'ta say hi and even help carry old Maluchi's groceries up for her. She'd be a real girl with a good heart and not a stuck-up, conceited witch, or else, I'd never be able'ta play with her again! I couldn't stand her or, worse, ever face myself without wantin'a throw up every time I looked in the mirror! Yeah, playin' with Barbie once in a while was good enough for me and more than I could stand. It was my secret—me and Gia's. That was our special friend bond. Barbies, who knew?

On the walk home from *gumada's* house that night, I held Grandma's hand like always, as my free hand rubbed my chin where *gumada's* beard scratched it. When we got to Atlantic Avenue, Grandma grabbed my arm really hard and started singin' "I Wanna Hold Your Hand" by the Beatles. It was her favorite song lately. We started laughin' so hard while dodgin' traffic, and I hoped she wasn't peein' her pants again, but mostly, I hoped the both of us weren't gonna end up as roadkill!

CHAPTER 29

Street Fight

(Summer in the City and a Can of Lysol)

It was a Friday afternoon, and I was bored outta my mind. Summer just started, and there wasn't a hint of a fight in the air. The weatherman said we just hit the ninety-degree mark, so I thought there'd at least be some sparks flyin' around, but no. It was like a western ghost town, where all the cowboys disappear into thin air, except they at least left behind the smoky smell'a sizzling guns, so there'd be no doubt in anybody's mind that somethin' big just happened there. Summer heat brought out the savage beast on my block, and the Fourth'a July was the official opening day for fight season. It was like the flags went up, race cars were on the track, and the horses were outta the startin' gate. It wasn't called Looney Lane for nothin'!

The Fourth'a July was just a few days away, and it always sparked more than just fireworks on our block. Other blocks had arguments and even hissy fits, but we had in the ring, all-out, pullin' hair, scratchin' faces, fistfightin' brawls. And we loved it. And nobody ever got knocked out in our ring either. They just kept gettin' up for more or waited for two new replacements to come in. Of course, we never had a shortage'a crazy neighbors who couldn't wait for their turn'ta get back at somebody with a bloody nose. Our prize was bein' able'ta live on the most exciting block in Brooklyn, maybe all'a New York City. Fights on other blocks were the sparklers on the Fourth'a July while we were the Roman candles, ash cans, and M-80s. We always put on the best show, Fourth'a July and every other day too. But as they say in the movies, "All's quiet on the western front" (whatever that meant) and somethin' about "the calm before the storm" (whoever said that). Well, all this calm and quiet was makin' me nuts, and I felt like Dorothy waitin' for the big twister to scoop me up and fly me'ta Oz. When we finally erupted, everybody was gonna know about it, just like Grandpa and Vesuvius.

My grandma Fannie was a bloodhound when it came'ta sniffin' out a fight and could smell one brewin' from a mile away. She'd stop whatever she was doin', tilt her head up'ta the ceiling, then her nostrils would flare out like a fan. One night, while cookin' steak in the electric fryin' pan she kept on her white kitchen table, she threw the salt-and-pepper shakers down and yelled out to Grandpa, "I gotta go-a. Mike-a, watch-a the steak-a no burn-a!" He thought she was finally havin' that heart attack, but instead, she ran out to the stoop. What she smelled burnin' wasn't well-done steak but rare human flesh in the middle of a juicy fight.

The bloodhound was never wrong. Less than a minute after she flew outta the door, we'd hear her notorious ring. She pressed her finger on the buzzer so long and hard you'd think Jack the Ripper had his hand around her throat. It was like the time Sammy and me were chased by Rock and Roll. I pressed on the buzzer like crazy, except my father didn't answer cause he was cookin'. Well, we all knew Grandma's ring by now, and even Grandpa unplugged the electric fryin' pan ta'run out onto the stoop. We all stopped whatever we were doin' and ran like mice into a cheese factory. Grandma had one foot on the top step'a the stoop and one foot in the vestibule as she pressed with all her might like she knew the answer to the million-dollar question on the TV game show. Then we'd all hear her scream, "Ou Show, Ou Show Che!" (That meant "There's a great show goin' on out here and you're missin' it!") Of course, she never let go'a her foothold on the best seat in the house. (Okay, we were standin'.) She liked bein' on the top step under the red awning so she could laugh as hard as she could (and maybe even let out a little pee) without anybody seein' her.

Tonight's fight was a new episode in the ongoing saga of Mrs. O'Flannagan versus Mrs. Ferrari, better known as Bunny Hop and the Crow, or like a football game, the Shamrocks versus the Meatballs. Mrs. O'Flannagan had long straggly gray hair and wore dark red lipstick. It wasn't as red as Rosalie's, and it didn't go all the way up'ta her nose either but looked so red cause her face was so white, bein' Irish and all. Besides, she wore a'lotta powder on her face, not *provelia* like Grandma's but real white like baby powder, and she kinda looked like Bette Davis in *What Ever Happened to Baby Jane.* She'd stand on her stoop with the Kelly Green door and wall of climbin' ivy behind her and put her hands on her hips like she was gettin' ready'ta sing the "I'm a Little Teapot" song or "I'm Writing a Letter to Daddy" from the Bette Davis movie.

In the other corner of the ring was Mrs. Ferrari, alias the Crow. Now she not only looked like a crow with short straight black hair and a beak of a nose but cacawed like one too whenever she laughed, but I really don't know who gave her the title. She hung her elbows over the white metal fence in front'a her small white house while cupping her chin between her hands to hold her head up. It almost looked like her head might fall off and roll away if her hands let go. Mrs. Ferrari was a good fighter cause she always stayed calm and, as they say, never lost her cool. She'd call Mrs. O'Flannagan and everybody else all kinda names, all the while smilin', as she jiggled her head back and forth between her hands like those dolls in the back window of cars that wobbled back and forth or like a crow peckin' at a farmer's cornfield.

So the Crow started the round off by yellin' across the street, "There was an old Irish woman who lived in a green shoe and had so many brats she didn't know what to do!" Then, of course, she started cacawing out loud (like the Crow that she was). She was so proud a herself that she did that thing where you blow into your cupped hand and then rub your fingertips on your shoulder. Then she yelled out, "Top that, you Mick!" I think she fought with so many people cause she was so annoying, and no matter what, you couldn't get her mad. She just kept on smilin' and shakin' her propped up head back and forth. She was silently sayin', "Na, na, na, na, na!" And that drove people nuts!

So Bunny Hop yelled back, "Welfare bum! Welfare bum!" cause there was a rumor that the Ferraris were gettin' relief. Now I thought that was mean and what they called hittin' below the belt. It wasn't fair fightin' and not funny. Even Grandma stopped laughin'. It was time'ta put somebody else into the ring cause I saw a few other families on the block carryin' home big blocks'a American cheese and boxes'a powdered milk. Some people were poor, and it wasn't their fault if they didn't have enough money for food. Then I wondered if we didn't live in Grandma's house, maybe we woulda been on relief too? I suddenly felt bad for her and wanted'a punch Bunny Hop right in her Bette Davis face.

But like they say in boxing, Mrs. Ferrari was the Comeback Kid, and nothin' could rattle her. So she comes back with "At least my kids eat. The last time your kids saw a piece'a meat, they were at the zoo. How'da they like those Wonder Bread and sugar sandwiches anyway?" This was startin'a get juicy. We were all huddled on the stoop, laughin' our heads off, and I'm just glad that we got'ta eat dinner first. This was one'a those Saturday nights when we didn't go visitin' *gumadas*. Maybe we were finally runnin' outta people to visit. Anyway, Grandma and Grandpa wanted'a eat steak on the electric fryin' pan in their own house that night instead'a together cause it was also one'a those rare Saturday nights when my father wasn't workin'. He was cookin' my mother's favorite tripe in marinara sauce, and the rest'a us wanted'a steer clear'a that one, even Grandma and Grandpa. Good thing that us kids had hot dogs and French fries before the show started. But I felt bad for Grandpa, and I wondered if his steak turned'ta leather yet. Grandma, as usual, was havin' too much fun'ta think about eatin' now and would probably just make a patāda's-and-egg sandwich later or maybe toasted waffles with ice cream. But I could hear Grandpa's stomach rumbling from the bottom step and felt like goin' inside ta'make jiffy pop popcorn on the stove, but I didn't wanna miss the show cause I knew the good part was comin'. My father was in the house watchin' his favorite, Abbott and Costello, and didn't wanna watch the fights unless they were on TV.

So Mrs. Flan was gettin' all nervous now and started twirlin' her Bette Davis curls as she yelled out, "Well, at least I gotta husband!"

Again, below the belt. I'm not sure what happened'ta the Crow's husband, but I'm sure it wasn't her fault and definitely not Bunny Hop's business. So like a tennis match, the ball kept flyin' back and forth across the street. And it was definitely a hardball.

So Mrs. Ferrari yelled back, "Oh, is that what you call that sci-munito" (jerk—and I couldn't believe she knew Grandma's word) "that I see leavin' your house every morning at 5:00 a.m.? I thought he was the milkman or the Wonder Bread delivery guy. Oh, that's right, he has'ta make the doughnuts. Or is it chocolate candy? All those sweets, no wonder your girls all have a spare tire around the middle!"

Now all the Flan kids were in the gate, tryin'a cheer their mother on for morale cause she was losin' fast.

"Come on, Ma," they said. "Let's get her. There's more of us than them!"

"We're the fightin' Irish, remember?"

That last remark about the spare tires really got'em mad, and their faces were beet red. Now, all the Ferrari kids were in their gate, and it started'a look like a scene from *West Side Story*. I guess the Flans would'a been the Jets and the Ferraris would'a been the Sharks cause Italians are closer to Puerto Ricans than Irish.

Meanwhile, the woman next door'ta the Flans comes out on her stoop and started yellin' at Bunny Hop, "Leave the poor woman alone! It's not her fault she don't got a husband. She's probably better off without the no-good bum anyway!"

Turned out, her name was Honey, and they all called her Honey Dew. She's the one that Grandma was talkin' about who walked around talkin'a herself cause her husband went out for a quart'a milk and never came back. I guess she was back from the crazy house after all.

So Bunny Hop yelled, "Shut up, Honey Dew! I wasn't even fightin' with you. Mind your own business. Why don't'ya go eat a piece'a melon or go out lookin' for your husband?"

Now Honey Dew, who was much younger than Bunny Hop, decided'a jump into the ring, leavin' the Crow'ta sit out the next round. She climbed over the black wrought-iron fence separating her house from Bunny Hops and onto their stoop. Now we all started cheerin', even the Crow and her kids. By now, almost everybody on the block was out, and it looked like it was gonna be a good show after all.

The Flan's one son Timmy came out and stepped in front'a his mother, sayin', "Get back in your house, Cantaloupe!"

The girls all giggled as Mrs. Flan patted him on the back.

"Who you callin' a cantaloupe, you little Irish rug rat!" she said. "I'll mop the streets with your moppy little towhead. Better yet, mop your house. God knows it hasn't been cleaned since the potato famine!"

"Good one," said the Crow. "One point for you, Honey Dew! Pull her Betty Davis's hair out!" said the Crow to Honey Dew.

Bunny screamed back across the street, "Ha! You're the big old Crow! Everybody on the block knows that. That's why they chase you with scarecrows!"

Then as cool as a cucumber, the Crow yelled back, "Well, I'd rather be called a Crow than look like an old hag!"

The Ferrari kids started cheerin' and jumpin' up and down in the gate just as Bunny Hop started'a cry. I felt like there shoulda been cheerleaders in the middle'a the street wavin' their pom-poms up and down while girls walked around sellin' popcorn and peanuts.

Just as Honey Dew was about'ta pull out Bunny Hop's Baby Jane hair from her whimperin' head, Mr. Flan comes outta the house and said, "What's goin' on here? Why is my Bunny Hop cryin'? Get back into your own gate, Honey Dew, and leave us alone!"

Then Honey Dew said to Mr. Flan, "Oh, I'm so scared! My hands are shakin'. Yes, Mr. Candy Man!" Then she started laughin' so hard like a hyena crackin' herself up. She started bangin' her foot on the ground and grabbin' her sides. She was doublin' over laughin'.

The Crow jumped in again, sayin', "Go ahead, Honey Dew, punch her!"

So Honey Dew yelled over at the Crow, "Why don't you punch her, big mouth?"

And the Crow answered back, still smilin', "My pleasure, Honey Dew, and I'll even punch you too while I'm at it!"

So the Crow started goin' outta her gate and across the street when Josie and Nancy next door ta'her came out, yellin', "Go back in your house you, Old Crow, and stop fightin' with everybody! We all want peace and quiet!"

Meanwhile, we're on our stoop, thinkin', *No, we don't! We wanna see a fight!*

Then Grandma yelled out loud to Josie and Nancy, "Go back-a you house-a e mind-a you business-a! We wanna see ou show!"

Then Grandpa gave Grandma one'a his looks as she just shooed him away.

The Crow's oldest son, Junior, tried'ta stop her from goin' across to the Flan's house by grabbin' her arm, sayin', "Don't, Ma, it's not worth it!"

So Bunny Hop, who finally stopped whimpering like a puppy, yelled out, "That's right, listen ta'ya juvenile delinquent son. I guess he learned some manners in reform school after all. I heard what he did to that puppy!"

So Junior said, "Never mind, Ma, I changed my mind. Go get her. Sic 'em, Fido!"

So the Crow started chargin' across the street, and everybody on the block was out now, cheerin' like a bullfight. "I wouldn't talk about dogs if I were you, Mrs. Shamrock," said the Crow. "Your big Irish dog is leavin' his stinky duty all over this street, and I saw him do it right in front'a my gate!"

"Well, that was a special delivery present just for you," said Bunny Hop. "It's probably the only one you'll ever get too!" Now Bunny felt like she just got a punch in, but the Crow was cacawing again.

She charged into the Flan's gate, and nobody could hold her back. It was like the dam broke, and the floodgates opened. The bull was in the ring, and she saw red!

Everybody in the crowd was yellin', "Ole and Toro!"

She ran up the Flan's stoop two steps at a time and ran smack into Mr. Flan's face. He was tall and skinny with reddish-brown hair just like their Irish Setter. He put his hands on the Crow's shoulders, tryin'ta hold her back, as he said, "Remove yourself from this house! You have no powers here!"

Then her son Junior yelled, "Get your hands off'a my mother, you no good Mick!"

So she turned around and answered, "Don't worry, I got this son!"

All of a sudden, the Crow reached up and pulled Mr. Flan's hair off'a his head! He had a wig for men. I think it's called a toupee. Who knew? I guess she did. That's for sure cause she started cacawing like a crow again while yellin', "The jig is up, Irish boy, and so is your phony hair! You couldn't fool me, carrot top! Why don't'ya give it ta'ya little woman? Everybody knows she could use a new hairdo. Maybe then she can finally get that Bette Davis mop off'a her head!"

Then Bunny Hop started cryin' her eyes out again while Mr. Flan covered his head like he was naked in public. The Crow dangled the wig in front'a his face, screamin', "Come and get it if'ya really want it. All'ya gotta do is catch me!"

She started runnin' outta the gate and down the block, wavin' the wig or toupee over her head, all the while smilin' her calm and evil smile. Mr. Flan started chasin' her but couldn't catch her. She was really fast, weavin' and dodgin' between cars, so I looked ta'see if she was wearin' PF Flyers! Nope, they were Keds. Funny! Now the whole block was hysterical, and everybody on my stoop was pee'in themselves. There was even a little puddle on the bottom step. Then all the Flan kids tried'a help their father catch the Crow as he kept runnin' while holdin' his bald head. So the Ferrari kids started chasin' the Flan kids, and there were so many people runnin' down the block it looked like a marathon. All the while, the Crow was wavin' Mr. Flan's toupee over her head like the flag of a losin' country surrenderin' in battle. But the Crow sure wasn't surrenderin'. She was winnin' this war by a mile, bobbin' and weavin' like the best-prize fighter in the ring. Now she was yellin', "Cacaw! Cacaw!" right out loud, and her cacawing laugh even started'a sound like a real crow. The Flan kids were all chasin' her with scarecrows.

Still, Bunny Hop balled her eyes out on the stoop, twirlin' her Bette Davis curls with her fingertips. Meanwhile, Honey Dew just sat on the Flan's stoop, laughin' hysterically in her own puddle'a pee. Nobody would dare call the cops. We were havin' too much fun.

All of a sudden, Bunny Hop's other neighbor, to her left, came out screamin', "What's all the noise? Some people are tryin'a sleep!"

It was only seven o'clock. Who goes'ta bed that early, except babies and maybe the milkman. Lena Sorento was an old lady but younger than Grandma. She never had kids and always yelled at everybody to get away from her stoop. She always sent Sammy and sometimes me ta'the store for her, and it was always for the same thing: three or four giant spray cans'a Lysol. I could never figure out what she did with so much Lysol til, one time, Sammy musta been at the rectory hangin' out with the priests, and she called my mother on the phone ta'ask if I could go'ta the store for her. I got up'ta her stoop and rang the bell. There was no answer, so I kept ringin'. I looked into the glass window, past the vestibule, and into her hallway ta'see if she was comin'. I was about to walk away, thinkin' maybe she changed her mind or went out herself when I couldn't believe what I saw. There she was, on the hallway floor, crawlin' on her belly like a reptile. She was wavin' one arm in the air as she paddled the other in her imaginary ocean while screamin', "Wait, don't go! I'm comin'!"

I couldn't believe my eyes and wondered if I should go get help cause she was really sick or somethin'. She was sick, all right! I don't know how she reached up'ta turn the doorknob and open the vestibule door, but she did. That's when I saw all the empty beer cans lyin' all over the floor in front'a her apartment. Then she was tryin'a get'ta her knees, in front'a the mailboxes, and I thought she was gonna ring all the bells for help but didn't. She just kept screamin', "Don't go. Gimme' a minute."

She was floppin' all over the vestibule floor like a beached whale and lookin' up at me through the glass like I had a giant net ta'save her. She kept tryin'a jump up to reach the doorknob and then fallin' back down on her face again. It was like watchin' a seal at the aquarium, except nobody I knew would pay for this show. She finally got the doorknob and screamed, "Turn and push!"

I did, and the door flew open, sendin' her flyin' as she held on'ta the doorknob for dear life. Then like nothin' happened, she said, "Come in, Larry's sister," like she was invitin' me in for a glass'a lemonade.

Sammy was goin'ta the store for her for a long time now, but she never got his name right and called him Larry. I was so shocked. I just said, "Who's Larry?"

And she said, "What? How am I supposed'ta know? Don't get me more confused before I forget what you're here for!"

Then she pulled a ten-dollar bill outta her cleavage and stretched her arm up'ta give it ta'me. Then she told me, "Get four cans'a Lysol spray, the big ones, and a candy bar for yourself. You got that, honey?"

I told her I got it, and she asked if I needed a list. I shook my head no and felt like I was in *The Twilight Zone*.

Then she asked, "Where's Larry today? In school?"

First of all, I had no idea who Larry was, and who goes'ta school in the summer unless you're a real dumbbell?

Again, I said, "Who's Larry?"

And she said, "You're startin' that business again? Whad'dy'ya stupid or somethin'? Larry, your brother!"

So I said, "Oh, you mean Sammy!"

And she said, "Who's Sammy?"

So I just said, "I better go before the store closes."

Then I thought about how she'd open the door when I got back and asked if she could push the rug under it so I could get back in.

She said, "Hey, you're not such a dumbbell after all, are'ya, kid? What's your name anyway?"

She should'a known my name by now too, but I just said, "Mikey."

Then, of course, she said, "Who's Mikey?"

I felt like I was watchin' Abbott and Costello but answered anyway. "I'm Mikey," I said.

Then she told me, "Hey, are you playin' games with me today cause I don't got time for this, kid."

So I told her I wasn't playin' games with her and that my name really was Mikey, short for Michelina.

Then she said, "What, is your mother a comedian? Or does she just hate you?"

I can't believe that I thought about it for a minute before answerin', "No, she's not a comedian, and she doesn't hate me either."

Now I was startin'a think that she wasn't just an old drunk but mean too and didn't even wanna tell anybody that she couldn't get off'a the floor. It would'a deserved her right to keep lyin' there in her beer-and-pee mixture. No wonder she needed so many cans'a Lysol spray.

Then she said, "Sorry kid, tough break. No girl should have'ta go through life with a name like that." I just told her that I liked my name, both'a them. And I meant it. She just made a face and said, "Yeah right! And I'm the queen'a Sheba!"

Now I knew my grandmother was the queen'a Brooklyn, but I didn't know who the queen'a Sheba was. I just knew that it wasn't her. The only thing she was the queen of was the hallway. Anyway, I didn't even know where Sheba was or if it was even a real place, but if I had magic powers, I'd send her there right now. Maybe Charlie could give her a ride there on his magic carpet.

So anyway, I just left her lyin' on the vestibule floor and shoved her yucky ten-dollar bill into my pocket. I didn't wanna touch it cause it was all covered in her cleavage sweat. I wanted'a barf. I was walkin' away when she yelled, "I'll just wait here til'ya get back." As if she had a choice!

I wasn't wastin' any time callin' the fire department or whoever it was that picked old drunken ladies off'a the floor. I didn't even stop ta'tell my mother. Anyway, I had a feelin' this wasn't her first time crawlin' like a bug. I thought for sure Sammy would'a told me or my mother if he'd seen it unless he kept his mouth shut cause he didn't wanna give up her big quarter tip and candy bar. Maybe that's how Sammy kept his pockets full'a Bazooka bubble gum cause I sure as heck wasn't buyin' him any. I decided ta'tell my mother when I got back and did. Sure enough, she was still there on the floor when I got back. I thought maybe somebody else in the building would'a found her and helped her up, but I guess they were fed up with her shenanigans already. And what about her husband? Where was he? Maybe he was fed up with her too unless he was lyin' on the floor inside her apartment. What if he was worse than she was? I didn't think so cause I saw him comin' home from work at night, and he wasn't wobbly or anything. He walked straight and said hello.

Anyway, I gave her the bag with the four giant cans'a Lysol spray, and she gave me a quarter and a candy bar. Well, I bought my own candy bar like she said. I got a Nestle's Crunch Bar. She said, "Thanks, and goodbye, Larry's sister with the boy's name!"

I said "See ya!" and didn't bother ta'wait and see how she was gonna get back into her cage.

She didn't ask for help, and I didn't offer. Maybe it was mean, but I just wanted'a get away from her. I told my mother about it, and she couldn't believe it. She said she knew that she drank but didn't know she was that bad or she'd never let me and Sammy go'ta the store for her. Then came the good part. My mother went after Sammy. He was back from the rectory and playin' with his baseball cards. I hoped he said a'lotta prayers today cause he was gonna need'em when my mother got through with him.

She said, "How long have you been goin'ta the store for Lena Sorento?"

He just played dumb (okay, he really was dumb) and said, "What?"

She said, "Whad'dy'ya deaf? Get the wax outta your ears. You been goin'ta the store for her for a long time. Whad'dy'ya buy her?"

He looked at me then back at my mother while squinting his eyes and twistin' his mouth like he always did whenever he got caught lyin'. He said Lysol, and my mother said, "Just Lysol?" He shrugged his shoulders, and she said, "Didn't ya think it was weird that she wanted so many cans'a Lysol every week?" He didn't answer, so she said, "Tell me the truth. Did you ever see her lyin' on the floor?"

He said, "I guess so."

She said, "I guess so? Whad'dy'ya mean I guess so? How many times? And you never told me! Sammy, I'm gonna break your legs!"

My father ran in screamin', "Wha happa?"

And Grandma said, "Leeva the kid alone!" shielding Sammy with her body.

Who knows how many years Lena Sorento spent on the hallway floor or who bought her Lysol before me and Sammy, but it sure wasn't gonna be us anymore. That's for sure. My mother went over there that day and rang her bell, but of course, she didn't answer. She had beer and Lysol, and I guess that's all she needed. She did stop her the next time she saw her on the stoop when she wasn't drunk and told her that we couldn't go'ta the store for her anymore. That's all she said.

So when we saw her come out on'ta the stoop in the middle'a the fight between Bunny Hop and the Crow, my mother said, "Oh my God!"

And Grandma said, "Umbriagga!" (That meant the drunk.)

We didn't know what she was gonna do or in what condition she was gonna be in. Well, she was swayin' back and forth like she was seasick, so I knew the show was about ta'get even better. So Lena yelled to the Crow, "Come on, ya'old Crow, give the old guy his rug back!"

I figured she meant his toupee. She sounded like she had marbles in her mouth too, like when *I Love Lucy* did the vitameatavegamin routine.

Then Honey Dew yelled, "Shut up, Lena, and mind your own business. Go back to your house. There's a beer can with your name on it!"

So Lena yelled back, "Look, Honey Dew, it's your husband comin' up the block. He finally came back with that quart'a milk. He musta gone'ta milk the cow himself! Haha!"

So Honey Dew yelled, "You crazy old drunk. I'm gonna get you!"

She got off Bunny Hop's stoop and climbed over the railing onto Lena's stoop. She charged up the steps and went to pull Lena's hair out. I guess this was a hairpulling kinda day. Now we were all wonderin' if she wore a wig too. Lena was wearin' one'a those summer cotton housedresses that Grandma wore—fitted at the waist then flarin' out like a fan to just below the knee. Well, she saw Honey Dew comin' towards her like a tiger let loose from the zoo, so she put her hands up to block her and wobbled backward a few steps to the top railing. Then she turned her head around really fast so Honey wouldn't punch her in the face when I couldn't believe what happened next! The railing came up'ta her thighs, and she lost her grip on it and started'a fall over the top. It happened so fast, and Honey Dew couldn't stop it, even if she wanted to (and of course she didn't want to). Lena tried'ta regain her balance (if she ever had any) but teeter-tottered like a drunken duck before goin' overboard. Okay, so she wasn't a duck, but she sure was drunk!

Then a summer breeze musta flown by cause just as she went flyin' over the railing, her summer cotton dress flew up over her head like a parachute. And the craziest part was that she wasn't wearin' any bloomers! We couldn't believe it, and at first, I really wasn't exactly sure what I was lookin' at. Let's face it, how many real-life adult human butts had I seen in my life? Okay, I admit the one time I climbed up on top'a the toilet seat in the bathroom and almost broke my neck tryin'a turn around so I could see in the mirror how big mine actually was. And there was the time when I was ten when Cassie and me went into her bathroom together (I don't know where her mother was), and on the count'a ten said, "I'll show you mine if you show me yours!" Dumb kids, I know, but I went'ta confession for it. But this was the real thing, and we just stood there with our mouths open, peein' our pants, as Lena Sorento's full moon fell from the sky. Just like humpty-dumpty, she had a big fall over the railing and bounced like a giant rubber ball on every step until her sore red butt landed at the cellar door. It reminded me of the song "The morning sun shining like a red rubber ball."

Well, everybody was in front'a Lena's gate now, and Mr. Marino down the block, who was a police officer, pushed his way through the crowd ta'see if she was all right.

He said, "Somebody call an ambulance!

Well, I didn't see anybody goin' into the house ta'call, and I'm ashamed'ta admit that we didn't either cause we wanted'a see what happened next. These were the days before cellphones, so we all just stood there in our own little rivers'a pee. At least we stopped laughin'!

Mr. Marino yelled out again, "Call an ambulance!"

Then I saw his wife, Marie, run into the house ta'call. She just came out ta'see what all the commotion was about when she heard her husband yellin'.

She ran into her house, yellin', "What's wrong with you, people? You'd rather stand and watch a show than help somebody who might be dyin'!"

Then I felt really bad cause I didn't want Lena Sorento ta'die and not just cause I'd miss laughin' at her or gettin' her stupid quarter tip and chocolate bar either. I didn't want anybody ta'die. I was Catholic! I thought we were just havin' fun, but it didn't feel like fun anymore, not for any of us.

The ambulance showed up a couple'a minutes later. We saw its flashin' red lights as it came screamin' down the block. They pulled up in front'a Lena's house and two men in blue uniforms jumped out. They ran around'ta the back, opened the doors, and came runnin' out with a white stretcher. Even Bunny Hop and the Crow looked scared, and I think Honey Dew was prayin'.

Mr. Marino yelled again, "Get outta the way! Give'em room!"

The sidewalk and the middle'a the street were packed with kids on bikes and roller skates, tryin'a see over the grown-ups' heads. Cars were beepin' cause they couldn't get through. We were blockin' traffic. Only Mr. Marino and his wife were in the gate. They were talkin'ta the ambulance workers as he told everybody else ta'get outta the way. Everybody was stretchin' their necks ta'see when, all of a sudden, we saw them carry Lena up the cellar steps on the stretcher. She had a thing around her neck they called a collar, not like a dog but big and all the way around, ta'keep her from movin' it in case it was broken. Everybody was askin', "Is she dead?" "Is she all right?" We didn't see her movin' or talkin', so we didn't know. She was covered in a white sheet that went up'ta her chest so at least her butt was covered, and we were glad that the sheet wasn't over her head cause that woulda meant she was dead. Sammy was still on the stoop, squintin' and bitin' his nails like crazy. I was surprised that Grandma and Grandpa were still on the stoop too, but me and my mother were in the middle'a the street like everybody else.

Nobody knew where her husband was, so Mr. and Mrs. Marino went in the ambulance with her so she wouldn't have'ta go'ta the hospital alone. As Grandma woulda said, "Alone-a like a dogg-a!" We saw them open the back door'a the ambulance and turn the siren on when, all of a sudden, we heard her screamin', "What's that damned noise? Are you people nuts? Can't'ya see I'm tryin'a sleep here? Hey, get'ya hands off'a me, mister. I'll call the cops! Who'da'ya think ya'playin' with? Ya'sister?"

That's right. Lena Sorento was back and not dead after all. We all sighed and started laughin' again!

CHAPTER 30

Norman and the Magic Radio

There was a guy who lived on the block, and his name was Norman. He was a lot older than me, a teenager, maybe sixteen or seventeen, and he lived next door'ta Cassie. Cassie's sisters were about his age, and they always teased him cause there was a song named "Norman" from the fifties, and they sang it ta'him every time they saw him. I guess he was what they called "slow," but I remember some mean kids callin' him retard, and I always felt so bad for him that I wanted'a run up'ta them and punch'em in the face, but I never did. They were usually older, teenaged boys that hung out at the ice-cream parlor and probably in the L&L gang anyway, so I was scared they'd beat me up or at least pull my ponytails.

Norman just sat on his stoop with his blond crew cut hairdo and round roly-poly cheeks, lookin' like an overstuffed porcupine, mindin' his own business, never botherin' anybody. He wore gigantic dungaree overalls with suspenders that were so big on him he coulda fit another Norman inside. And his pants were always cuffed up twice at the ankles like he was tryin'a run from a flood. He always wore a red-and-blue plaid flannel shirt with a white undershirt showin' through, even in the hot summer. So I guess'ya could say that poor old Norman was a target for all the mean boys, bored kids, and even the nice teenaged girls in the neighborhood. Like our own private mascot, he sat on the stoop with his wide, silly grin, happy as a clam cause Norman had the one thing he needed in the world. His transistor radio, AM and FM. And it was almost like he had

TWO LEFT FEET

ESP or somethin' cause he always knew just the right station ta'play whenever you were passin' by. If it was music that you wanted'a hear, he'd always be playin' your favorite song just as you walked by. And the song that was playin' always fit the occasion, like the time we hit a record-breaking 102 degrees and he was miraculously playin' "Heat Wave" by Martha and the Vandellas as I ran by him ta'throw myself under the hydrant, or as we called it the johnny pump! Then there was the time when it was Leja's eleventh birthday and she was outside wearin' one'a those doofy birthday corsages with the candy on them. Eleven was gumdrops cause I had one for my eleventh birthday that my mother bought me ta'wear to school. Everybody wore them to school, but it was really stupid'ta wear one out in the street in the middle'a summer pinned to your tank top. Anyway, she didn't even have a birthday party. She just wanted'a be a show-off so all the boys would know it was her birthday. She came off'a the stoop, already eatin' the green gumdrop from the corsage, which was so cheesy and gross! Nobody ate them. They were just for show! Anyway, she was bein' a big show-off, twirlin' her Vermont Maid braids around her fingertips as she skipped down the block til Charlie saw her with the gumdrop corsage. Then all heck broke loose!

He yelled, "Hey, guys, look! It's Leja's birthday. Let's give her the birthday punches! Me first!"

Before you knew it, Leja was in the middle of a circle, in front'a Cassie's house, surrounded by Charlie and his pack'a wolves. She was so nervous she was down'ta the last gumdrop. The yucky white one. All the boys were screamin', "Yeah, my turn!"

She squealed like a little pig for her big brother Lukas. But he couldn't save her now cause she forgot that he was away Upstate at Lithuanian camp for the week. I hoped he was learnin' self-defense cause she was gonna let him have it when he got home.

Leja kept screamin' like a banshee, takin' a while for it'ta sink through those thick braids'a hers that her personal superhero Lukas wasn't comin'a rescue her this time. All the while, Charlie the Ringmaster belted out Leja's birthday punches in full swing. And he wasn't takin' it easy on her either just cause she was a girl. He swung full fist right into the circle of her upper right arm, over her smallpox vaccine scar. He was havin' lots'a fun doin' it too, yellin' at the top'a his lungs, "One, two." Of course, he didn't stop at eleven, makin' sure'ta give her the extra punch for good luck. I looked over at Charlie and thought ta'myself, *I think he's a juvenile delinquent, whatever that is, and if any kid ever needed a psychiatrist, it had'da be him*! Of course, I didn't know anybody who ever went to a psychiatrist and wasn't even sure what they did, but I did hear my mother once talkin' about a character on Grandma's soap opera, sayin', "She's nuts and needs a psychiatrist!" I never saw her doin' anything half as bad as Charlie, so I figured he really needed one!

Charlie was yellin', "Okay, guys, who wants'ta be next?" when Mr. Connor came out, and he yelled right back, sayin', "Hey, whaddy'ya guys doin'? Leave that girl alone!"

Guess she had a superhero after all. Then he told Dylan and Ryan ta'get up in the house and that it was lunchtime. Probably sugar sandwiches again. So the boys spread out from the circle like a bunch'a mice, lickin' their chops, bellies full from their shared hunk'a cheese. And there was Leja, just like the line from "The Farmer in the Dell" ("The cheese stands alone"), her mouth was wide open, but nothin' came out. Her empty corsage, a sad reminder of the gumdrops she ate by herself, instead'a shared candy with friends, was evidence of what had'da be the saddest birthday in history. I thought about laughin' but felt sorry for her, and as she whimpered away like a little puppy, rubbin' her arm, all you could hear, loud and clear, was the song playin' on Norman's radio "It's My Party [And I'll Cry If I Want To]" by Leslie Gore. Okay, so she didn't have a party, but it was her birthday, and she sure as heck was cryin'! That's for sure. How did Norman do it? I was startin'a think that Norman wasn't so "slow" at all cause it looked like he was pullin' the wool over all of our eyes. Maybe we were the "slow" ones, and he was a genius or a witch! Coincidence? I don't know. I thought he definitely was some kinda magician.

Norman did other tricks with his magic radio too. If you were wonderin' about tomorrow's weather and if the heat spell was gonna break, all'ya had'da do was pass by Norman, and just like that, his FM music would switch to AM. Then you'd hear the familiar tune startin' every important newscast (da-da-da-da-dum), meanin' you're hearin' it here first, people. "This just in! In case you were wonderin' if the temperature was gonna drop below one hundred degrees tomorrow. Sorry, folks! No such luck. Looks like another day under the johnny pump, kids!"

I couldn't believe it. His radio was talkin'ta me! There was gonna be TV shows with a talkin' horse, "Mr. Ed," and a talkin' car, "My Mother the Car," but could there be a talkin' radio? And this wasn't a TV show. It was real life—my crazy life! Then I wondered if Norman and his radio only performed for me or if I was the only one'ta notice it. But what about Leja's "It's My Party"? Everybody heard that! I hoped this wasn't like the whole PF Flyers flyin' thing, where everybody includin' me thought I was nuts! (Patsa!) I'd just have'ta wait before I said anything. Get more evidence like Nancy Drew. But I just remembered about the time I was walkin' down the block with my father. We were in a hurry cause he couldn't wait'ta get home ta'see the soccer game. Everybody knows how Italians are about soccer! It's baseball, football, and the Fourth'a July all rolled into one. He was holdin' my arm, pullin' me along, as we passed in front'a Norman on his stoop, and of course, there he sat, wearin' his big grin and oversized overalls, playin' his transistor radio. We heard "Walk Like a Man" by the Four Seasons. Then my father started cursin' in Napolitano cause Italy was playin' Brazil, and the Italians hated the Brazilians. Said that they were sissies, or as my father called'em "Sissy-Mare." All of a sudden, we heard Norman's radio switch to AM with that familiar tune again, and the announcer came on. "For all of you soccer fans out there, Italy is beatin' the tar outta Brazil!" So my father started jumpin' up and down, twirlin' me around, doin' the "tarantella" right in the middle'a the sidewalk! He started runnin', pullin' me along like a dog on a leash when the radio switched'ta "I Will Follow Him" by the Chiffons.

I asked my father if he thought it was weird that the radio gave the soccer report just as we passed by, and he just said, "Ma, che si patsa?" (What? Are you crazy?) Everybody kept askin' me that. He just kept screamin' "Italy!" as he ran in the door although he later told me about another time when he was comin' home from work and couldn't wait'ta find out who won the eighth race at Aqueduct cause he pretty much bet all our food money for the week (he made me promise not'ta tell my mother this part), and he was scared my mother was gonna kill him. My father was up'ta his one hundredth Hail Mary when he got up'ta Norman's house, and he said he remembered that the radio all of a sudden gave the racing report. When he found out he won a bundle and we weren't goin' hungry that week after all, he sprinted up the stoop and gave Norman a giant hug. That musta been really funny cause my father was skinny and Norman was like a big bear next'ta him. He said he put his hands in his pockets ta'give Norman a tip, but they were empty. He spent it all at the track. But if I knew my father, he'd be back there the next day, givin' Norman a couple'a bucks to say thanks. He was always givin' his money away. Norman just laughed and laughed as my father walked away, happy as a clam. His hands were in his empty pockets, but he was singin' his favorite song, "Volare" by Bobby Rydel, compliments'a Norman and his radio, of course!

Well, I couldn't believe he never told me that before. Now I knew for sure and had all the proof I needed that Norman's radio wasn't just a regular radio, and Norman wasn't just a regular guy. I just didn't know what, if anything, I could do or say about it yet.

Anyway, back'ta Leja again. Just as Leslie Gore finished singin' "It's My Party," guess who comes out on the stoop? Winston! He was comin' out ta'give us his surprise Pied Piper snack'a the day. I couldn't believe that Winston and Norman lived in the same building, and as far as interesting characters go, this building even topped Cassie's. So Winston started blowin' his crazy, imaginary horn with his cupped hands, the way he always did, to let all the kids on the block know that it was snack time—Winston-style! Of course, all the boys who just finished givin' Leja her birthday punches came runnin' back ta'see what crazy concoction Winston came up with that day. Then I saw kids runnin' all the way down the block and across the street too, like hungry little mice runnin' from a burnin' building.

I couldn't believe my eyes when I saw that it was a cake. Not a real birthday cake with candles on top but pretty close. It was chocolate with chocolate frosting and looked homemade in a big rectangular aluminum pan. I looked over at Leja still rubbin' her arm, and I had an idea. I yelled out to Winston, "Hey, today's her birthday!"

So he said, "Well then, I guess that means this little lady gets the first piece as the guest of honor!"

Charlie made a face cause he was already up there, rubbin' his grimy hands together and droolin' like a wolf.

Then Winston asked, "What's your name, sweetie?"

She mumbled under her breath, "It's Leja…"

Then Winston, who always gave the first snack—whatever it was—to Norman, said, "How about we all sing 'Happy Birthday' to Leja?"

So we did—all of us—even mean old Charlie. He'd do anything for a piece'a chocolate cake. Mr. Connor stayed with Ryan and Dylan cause I guess chocolate cake was better than sugar sandwiches or whatever else they were gonna have for lunch. I was there with Sammy and Cassie, the Flan girls, Sandy Matone, and almost every other kid on the block. Everybody but Lukas.

It was almost like a real birthday party. Mr. Connor, who smoked, put a match on top so Leja could blow it out. We all sang so loud Mrs. Maluchi started yellin' outta her window in that accent'a hers, "Vat you peoples doink?" and all the dogs started barkin'.

I wondered what she wished for as she blew out the match, and I had a feelin' that besides wishin' her brother Lukas was there and that all the boys would stop givin' her birthday punches, she wished for a real birthday party next year for her twelfth. Then I wondered if she was gonna wear a candy corsage next year too cause twelve years old was Tootsie Rolls, and I could just picture that gooey, sticky, hot chocolaty mess drippin' all over her in the heat. Maybe her parents would give her a real birthday party next year, in her house, like we all had with balloons and those dumb cardboard hats with the elastic chokin' your neck. I knew I was too old for that now, but maybe Leja would'a liked it since she never had it before. Maybe she should skip the dumb hats. I'd be so embarrassed and wouldn't be caught dead wearin' one'a those hats again! I could tell that Leja was really happy we sang "Happy Birthday" and that she loved blowin' out her fake birthday candle no matter what she wished for. Of course, Norman sang the loudest, grinnin' ear to ear, and I saw Winston cut him a slightly bigger piece'a cake than the rest'a us.

What a team! Norman and Winston. Like Batman and Robin. Who knew? I think they did—right down'ta the music and the cake. I don't know how they did it, but they were definitely workin' some kinda magic, just like Santa Claus and the Easter Bunny. Either'ya still believe or'ya don't. And I do. I think they knew Leja needed a birthday party and somehow, in their strange way, made it happen.

I realized that looks could be deceiving and that the so-called "slow" people and "weirdos" on the block could turn out'ta be the kindest neighbors you'd ever meet and that sometimes people did nice things just cause they were nice. The cake was delicious and plenty for everybody. Winston even gave Leja a piece'ta bring home for Lukas. As we all walked away, the radio was still playin', "Happy, Happy Birthday, Baby," but Cassie and me stood in front'a her house a couple'a minutes, talkin' about how it turned out'ta be a good birthday for Leja, after all. She went in, and we waved goodbye as I started walkin' home. I looked back at Norman and Winston who were cleanin' up the paper plates and plastic forks off'a the stoop and heard the Chiffons singin' "He's So Fine." I think they were singin' about both'a them.

CHAPTER 31

Mrs. Spatini

(Your Meatballs or Your Life)

It was February 1964, and the weatherman said one for the record books. Just a week before, it was Alaska, and we were able'ta go out and have snowball fights, build igloos, or forts as we called'em, but today, it was Antarctica, a frozen tundra, five below, and with the arctic wind chill a whoppin' fifteen below. We couldn't stay outside in the snow all day til our mothers dragged us in by our scarves ta'dry our gloves and two pairs'a socks on the radiator in hopes that all our toes were still there. So I sat at the kitchen table, drinkin' hot chocolate, and embarrassed ta'say, wearin' my pajamas with the feet from when I was little. I wasn't little anymore and could barely squeeze my butt into'em, but they were warm. I had yellow, Sammy had blue, and Phylo had pink. I was watchin' the icicles hangin' on the fire escape, hopin' there wouldn't be a fire cause I didn't wanna freeze my overstuffed butt out there and remembered the day I saw a dead deer hangin' from the fire escape across the yard. It's somethin' I never forgot and, at first, couldn't figure out what it was. I wondered if it froze out there but didn't remember it bein' winter, and anyway, why would a live deer just be hangin' out on the fire escape?

I heard the steam hissin' from the radiator like a teapot, but the house was a meat locker even though my grandparents were the landlords. I guess it was even colder upstairs cause Bobby was bangin' on the pipes. So there was nothin' ta'do but stay in and daydream about summer, and it was only gonna take a couple'a more pancakes with butter and syrup before my yellow pajamas with the feet burst a seam and got tossed in the garbage. If I had'da watch one more cartoon with Sammy and Phylo, I was gonna beat Sammy over the head with Grandma Fannie's black cast-iron fryin' pan just like Moe did'ta Larry and Curly on *The Three Stooges* and push Phylo off a cliff just like Road Runner and Wile E. Coyote. I was stuck with'em for better or worse, and I knew there was a lot more worse than better. So I asked my mother if Cassie could come over, and she said, "Her mother's not gonna let her outta the house in this blizzard. Whaddy'ya nuts? The wind's gonna blow the both'a'ya to Ozone Park. Do you wanna end up there?" (Like that was a fate worse than death.)

I wanted'a say, "No, Ma. Bein' trapped with those two is a fate worse than death" but didn't.

"Why can't'ya just play with your brother and sister?" she said, and this time, I did answer, "Have'ya met them?"

She just threw me her look.

Cassie ate over a lot, sometimes even slept over. We were the two chubsters on the block from when we were little, and everybody pinched our fat rosy cheeks. We had history. We had twinkies. Tonight my mother was makin' macaroni with peas, Cassie's favorite. Bein' Irish, Cassie only had spaghetti and meatballs sometimes, which she called pisgetti and mighta come outta a can or had ketchup on top like the other Americans, but I'm not sure. What I did know was she never had real meatballs like Lucy's unless she ate by my house. Her mother made real great German pork chops with sauerkraut and real caraway seeds, and that was my favorite at her house, but it looked like we weren't gonna be eatin' over each other's house til the thaw. My mother had a routine. Monday was always a soup night. Tuesday and Wednesday were either chicken or meatloaf. Thursday was linguine with marinara sauce. Friday was fish or go'ta hell. Saturday was either hamburgers or steak, and of course, Sunday was the real sauce that she stirred all day with the wooden spoon along with her world-famous meatballs handed down from my namesake, Michelina, the witch. In summer, when the windows were open, the aroma traveled through the neighborhood, and every nose—human and animal—followed the scent, hopin' for a taste'a a meatball right outta the fryin' pan.

My mother's biggest fan and follower was Mrs. Spatini who would barter with my mother to babysit us for meatballs. Now I was eleven and a half and already babysittin' a'lotta kids on the block, but ever since the Phylo and the whiskey fiasco, my mother didn't trust me with her two precious babies! Come on, how could they get any worse?

She just said, "If the other mothers on the block are stupid enough to trust you with their kids and pay you for it too, then good luck to them! I just hope they lock their liquor cabinet!"

"Thanks, Ma, for the vote'a confidence," I wanted'a say. "It was just one mistake!"

Next Saturday night, my parents, along with Grandma and Grandpa and my aunt and uncle, were all goin'a Gracie and Joe's fortieth weddin' anniversary at the Knights'a Columbus, so Mrs. Spatini was up'ta bat, and I had a feelin' she was gonna strike out! She was kinda like Grandma Connie, old and kinda blind but with a cane and without the hunchback and brown tooth. Last week, when it was Alaska out instead'a Antarctica, I went to the ice-cream parlor with Angela Turso ta'sit in the back like big shots and have egg creams. We were listenin' ta Hey Paula by Paul and Paula on the Juke Box wonderin' if they were twins and why they wanted'a marry each other? Gross! We both wore our ski jackets with the fur hoods, mine white and hers black. We also wore our Eskimo hats that all the girls were wearin'. They were round like helmets in white fur with two furry white pom-poms danglin' on strings tied around your neck. She was the one that told me the Beatles were makin' their premiere performance on *The Ed Sullivan Show* Saturday night, and we were all so excited and couldn't wait!

Meanwhile, Mrs. Spatini woulda adopted us for Lucy's meatball recipe, but of course, she didn't have one. She played it by ear the way she did the piano, a little'a this, a little'a that, just waitin' for the spirit'a Michelina ta'show up and lead the way. That's all she needed—Michelina and Grandma's black cast-iron fryin' pan ta'create her magic. Saturday night, Mrs. Spatini showed up, cane in one hand, Tupperware container in the other, and a baby bib tied around her neck. Of course, my mother greeted her at the door with a couple'a meatballs right outta the fryin' pan to hold her over, a little down payment on a job she signed up for against her better judgment, but meatballs were meatballs after all! Considerin' the fact that she was practically blind and couldn't tell us apart, leavin' us alone with her was probably the closest Lucy came'ta child abuse, and she called me a bad babysitter? At least I could see! But I guess my mother and father really needed a night out, so we never told them the way she chased us with her cane, swingin' aimlessly til she hit her target, which was usually one'a our heads. Anyway, we had way more fun than she was mean cause we would rearrange the furniture when she wasn't lookin' (which didn't matter anyway cause she couldn't see). She'd swing at us with her cane, and we'd dodge her and push a chair in the way so she'd trip and land on the couch, cursin' her head off in Italian. Boy! Funny how cursin' always sounded funnier in Italian! We made sure she landed on the couch and not the floor or, God forbid, the coffee table. We weren't animals!

We had so much fun on those nights and didn't complain when she was babysittin' cause we knew we were in for a night'a fun and games. I gotta admit that I was the ringleader in all the shenanigans, maybe cause I was the oldest or just cause I had the crazier sense'a humor, but my brother and sister weren't complainin', and Mrs. Spatini wasn't talkin'. We had her over a barrel (literally on one occasion). We didn't know it then, but it was a little game called blackmail. If you tell on us, we'll tell that you peed your pants on the couch cause you couldn't make it to the bathroom in time. (Maybe we had her tied up. I don't remember.) It's all kind'a a blur. Anyway, we saw it as an equal trade. Everybody got what they wanted. My parents got'ta go out for a couple'a hours (and probably got drunk), we got'ta have some fun with a feeble old lady, and Mrs. Spatini was up'ta her chin in Lucy's magic meatballs. All was right with the world. So what if we got the occasional lump on our heads? It was worth it. I think Mrs. Spatini would'a even said that her broken hip was worth it cause she had fun too. After one'a us fell or got hit, she started laughin' like crazy and musta really missed bein' a kid. It was an accident. We weren't juvenile delinquents—well, at least I wasn't.

Okay, so like I said before, it was the night the Beatles were makin' their debut on Ed Sullivan, and there was no way in heck that I was gonna miss history in the makin' cause my mother left me with an old lady who wanted'a watch *The Lawrence Welk Show*. Lawrence Welk! And she couldn't even see the Lennon Sisters singin' in a cloud'a bubbles either. I guess she really liked the corny music. We were dumb kids, and even we knew that night was gonna be life-altering for generations ta'come. Old lady cry or not, it was three against one, and I could still get my brother and sister ta'do what I wanted.

Anyway, the world was still tryin'a recover from another life-altering event that happened just three months before in November 1963. It was also a day that I'd never be able'ta forget. President Kennedy was assassinated on Friday, November 22, 1963, when we were all called outta our classrooms ta'silently walk in single file across the street and around the corner ta'the church where the nuns were dabbin' at their eyes with a white handkerchief they pulled outta their black habit pocket. We sat there not knowin' what was goin' on til Father Camera came out, and in the middle aisle in front'a the altar, he dropped down onto one knee, his long black Dracula cape flowin' out all around him. We got scared and thought he finally died of a double exposure! Then he just said, "Our president has been shot!" All the nuns cried while they held their rosary beads, and some'a the kids cried too. The rest'a us were too in shock. They let us go home. It was very sad and somber, not a sound. Then for days, all we saw on TV were the pictures'a him when he got shot in the black car, Jackie in her pillbox hat, covered in his blood, and then his funeral with Caroline and Little John standin' there.

Only three months passed and the world was different. We needed somethin' happy ta'lift our spirits. We needed the Beatles. I needed the Beatles!

When she refused'ta bargain with me, even after I promised'ta hand deliver a month's supply'a meatballs ta'her door every week, (I didn't know who was makin' them all), I knew I was up against a tough old broad. Desperate times called for desperate measures, so I concocted a plan to lure her into the bathroom by sayin' the water was overflowin' in the toilet. (I don't know how she was gonna fix it, anyway. A blind plumber?) When she hobbled into the bathroom with her cane, cursin' in Italian, we were right behind her, and as soon as she got into the bathroom, we locked her in. Now I'm not too proud'a this fact, and I was gonna make sure she didn't get hurt. What could happen? She could sit on the toilet, and if she got thirsty, there was water from the faucet. If she could see, I would'a slipped a magazine under the door, but just like Grandma Connie, I wasn't sure if she could read. Anyway, it was only an hour show. At first, we raised the volume on the TV ta'drown out her screams cause I didn't want the neighbors ta'call the cops, thinkin' we were killin' her. Now I know this sounds terrible, and it was a long time ago, so maybe it didn't really go down exactly like this, but in my defense, we were kids, it was good clean fun, and mostly, it was the Beatles!

So the Beatles finally came on, and their first song was "All My Loving." Ed's audience was goin' wild while I just stood there half listenin' to them and half listenin' to Mrs. Spatini in the bathroom havin' her own concert. She was singin' "Where Did Our Love Go" by the Supremes, and I was kinda impressed that she even knew that song, besides bein' relieved she was singin' instead'a crying, which was a good sign. I knew right away that John was always gonna be my favorite as Mrs. Spatini banged on the bathroom door. Their second number was "I Saw Her Standing There" while Mrs. Spatini did her version of "Talk to Me" by Little Willie John. I gotta say she was pretty good, and I'd have'ta compliment her later.

Well, Sammy was pacing the floor like he always did whenever he got scared, and bitin' his nails 'til they bled. So he was really scared. I kept walkin' over'ta the bathroom door durin' commercials ta'ask if she was okay and tellin' her that it was almost over like gettin' a tooth pulled. I'm really not mean, like I said, and I wished that they would'a done all three songs in a row, but stupid Ed had'da space it out, better for ratings, I guess, ta'make sure people stayed tuned for the whole show. Anyway, we were at the home stretch, and they were singin' "'Til There Was You" while Mrs. Spatini, keepin' toe to toe, belted out that silly song "Hello Muddah, Hello Fadduh." I started'a laugh and couldn't believe that she knew a song like that and didn't even wait for the Beatles ta'take their final bows, shakin' their floppy heads. I shut the TV and ran'ta open the bathroom door. She got up from the toilet, shakin' her cane in the air, sayin' she was gonna let us have it (at least she was still alive) when she tripped over the stupid bathroom rug. (My mother always said one'a us would break our necks on that thing.) I was just prayin' it wasn't her! So I kinda caught her to block her fall so she didn't crack her head on the bathtub, but she landed on her side between the bathroom and the parlor in the doorframe between two worlds. I started wonderin' what world I was gonna end up in when my mother got home. Phylo started screamin', and I had'da slap her just like Scarlett O'Hara did to the maid in *Gone with the Wind*. Sammy needed a fix'a Bazooka bubble gum ta'calm his nerves, so he was popping away. I felt so bad all of a sudden and knew I'd have a lot ta'say in confession next Saturday if I lived that long. Her old lady bun was all lopsided, and it's a good thing that she was screamin' so I knew she wasn't dead.

    I lifted her head off the floor and gave her some water. She wasn't cryin' or screamin' anymore, and that's when I got scared. Lucky for us, my parents got home soon after (guess, it was a boring party), and my mother didn't waste any time askin' what happened. She just shot me her look before dialing 911. I couldn't help myself but started singin' "I'm Sorry" by Brenda Lee as my mother who was put on hold with the 911 operator sang "Don't Hang Up" by the Orlons. Well, if nothin' else, we were a musical family. The EMT showed up and got her on a stretcher, sayin', "Looks like you broke your hip there, little lady. Might need a new one," as Mrs. Spatini in a soft little voice sang "Don't Make Me Over" by Dionne Warwick. My mother asked them what hospital they were takin' her to and what street it was on when the EMT guy, who was kinda cute, just belted out "Meet Me on South Street" by the Orlons. Guess he came from a musical family too, and it looked like the Orlons were pretty popular tonight in this crazy concert'a ours. As they carried her downstairs on the stretcher, I heard Mrs. Spatini, a trooper till the end who didn't wanna end our little game, start singin' "I Will Follow Him" by Little Peggy March.

I went with my mother to visit her in the hospital, and I brought her flowers, pink carnations. I wanted'a bring her blue snowballs from Grandma's yard, but it was the dead'a winter. My mother brought meatballs, which lit up Mrs. Spatini's face like a kid on Christmas morning. I suddenly saw her as a big kid who was a whole lotta fun and probably the first one'ta be picked on any team and knew that if we'd been kids together, we would'a been good friends. She was just trapped in an old lady's body. My mother never bothered'ta punish me and didn't even ask what happened cause she saw how much I was punishin' myself. Mrs. Spatini never told on us, and it wasn't just for the meatballs either. She was our friend, and I carry the guilt with me til this day. We'd go back to visit her again and again in rehab on my insistence, and Mrs. Spatini would just smile at me as if ta'say she'd take our secret to her grave, which thankfully didn't happen for a few more years.

In June 1964, the World's Fair came to Flushing Meadow Park in Queens, New York, and my family all took the bus there. It was amazing and probably another attempt to raise the country's spirits after President Kennedy's death. On my visits to Mrs. Spatini, I'd tell her about all the exhibits, and she was thrilled, especially about *The Pieta* by Michelangelo at the Vatican Pavilion. I told her how it was enclosed in a big glass case and surrounded by guards. I told her about the Unisphere, the Boat Ride, and Tomorrow Land, where they had rides into the future. She especially loved hearin' about the Disney ride It's a Small World and all the different foods from around the world. I told her how much I loved the Belgian waffles with whipped cream and strawberries and could see her mouth waterin' like she was really there tastin' them.

She never babysat for us again and not cause she didn't wanna, but she just couldn't climb the stairs and ended up movin' in with her daughter in Richmond Hill where there weren't any stairs and they had a wheelchair ramp for her. Seein' her in a wheelchair gave me a deep pang'a remorse. She knew how I felt, and I knew that she knew, so we had a silent understandin' that lasted til her death a year and a half later when I was thirteen. On those visits, I always brought flowers, Grandma's blue and purple snowballs from the garden if it was summer, and of course, my mother brought her meatballs. What else? They said she died peacefully in her sleep, the best way'ta go, so I've heard. Til this day, whenever I smell my mother's world-famous meatballs comin' outta the fryin' pan, I think'a Mrs. Spatini and how much she was willin'a sacrifice just to eat'em.

CHAPTER 32

Black Jack Gum

It was another hot summer day, one for the record books, as they say. The kind'a day where you could fry an egg on the sidewalk and thought you were gonna melt as soon as you stepped outside. The kind'a day where you thought, *This must be what it feels like to be walkin' on the sun* (if anyone ever could)! Norman's radio didn't lie about the heat wave cause it was stickin' around like glue or a bad cold you couldn't get rid'da, and I felt like a fly on flypaper just like up the country when my hair kept gettin' stuck in the ooey-gooey mess! Now I know that Norman's magic radio said that today was gonna be another day for the johnny pump, and that's where most'a the kids were, shovin' and pushin' each other under the thundering gush'a water like a bunch'a hoodlums, just like Mugzy and Satch from the Bowery Boys or Alfalfa and Spanky from *The Little Rascals*.

But not Cassie. Lucky dog! She was goin'a her uncle's house on Long Island, and he had a big built-in swimmin' pool. She invited me once last summer but not today. Maybe her family had a rule where you could only bring a friend once, or maybe they just didn't like me cause I was Italian or, as the Irish said it, "Eye-talian." Then I wondered if she brought Sandy Matone today and if she was the lucky little guest'a the day. Then I chuckled to myself, thinkin', *She'll never be back there either cause just like me, she's Eye-talian too*!

I was tryin'a remember if I did anythin' wrong for her not'ta invite me again, and I couldn't come up with anythin'. I didn't barf in her brother Jimmy's brand-new light-blue convertible even though I was scared I would. Every time I felt a wave of a giant heave comin' on, I'd open my mouth and swallow big gulps'a air like I was practicin' swimmin' underwater (as if that could ever happen). But I probably just ended up lookin' like a fat goldfish cause Cassie's sister Maureen kept askin' if I was okay. So I kept shovin' piece after piece'a my Black Jack Gum into my mouth til I looked like a scared chipmunk or an old lady tryin'a gum her food cause she didn't have any teeth. (If I kept chewing all this gum, I'd be gumming my food too.) Then everybody wanted'a know who was eatin' black licorice and where the weird smell was comin' from cause her sister Colleen, in the front seat, was deathly allergic'ta anything licorice and broke out in welts.

So now everybody was lookin' at me, and I had so much gum in my mouth that I couldn't talk (probably a first) and just kept pointin' ta'my mouth. I managed'ta open my mouth enough for them ta'see the big black gooey mess oozin' outta it. Maureen kept sayin', "Oh my God!" as Colleen started coughin' and scratchin' at the same time. Then I saw Cassie, who was sittin' nex'ta me, look over and gimme one'a her looks where she turned her mouth into an upside-down smile. She just shook her head at me, sayin', "Yuck! How disgusting!" I don't know how her brother kept drivin'. Good thing there wasn't too much traffic on the highway and that we were almost there cause he had'da pull over to exit so we could get to a drugstore right away. Jimmy didn't have the top-down up til then cause although it was summer, it was a windy day. But as soon as he could pull over to the side, he put the top-down on his dream car, the one that dumb Charlie played with in his imagination every day as he ran up and down the curb with his stick.

Everybody was screamin' for me'ta spit the gum into the street, but I was gaggin', tryin'a get it all outta my mouth. I guess I had a small mouth for a big mouth. Jimmy went into the drugstore ta'get Colleen Benadryl, an allergy pill, and some itch cream, and Maureen, who wanted'a become a nurse, tried'a pry wads'a gum outta my mouth with her eyebrow tweezers. Cassie kept givin' me that upside-down smile'a hers, shakin' her head like she was Mother Superior. I was waitin' for her ta'start clickin' her tongue like a cricket (tsk, tsk), and if she started wavin' her pointer finger in my face, I was really gonna let her have it—once and for all. She had that way about her sometimes, what you'd call a know-it-all.

I finally got all the gum outta my mouth, the giant black mound lyin' in the street like a dead rat. Colleen was sittin' in the car, swallowin' her pills with the bottle'a Coke that Jimmy bought her, as Maureen inspected her body for giant welts. I took a tissue from the tissue box ta'wipe some'a the black goo off'a my brand-new pink tank top, and we all got back in the car. Maureen didn't notice that her headband was all lopsided, makin' her look a little like a drunken princess. Not that she was drunk or a princess, but she was really pretty. She didn't realize that when Jimmy put the top-down so that Colleen could breathe, all the wind messed up her beautiful blond beehive hairdo, and her bobby pins were all over the floor. Not even a hundred cans'a Aqua Net hairspray could help her now, and it was all my fault. I think I felt worse for her than I did for Colleen cause Colleen was feelin' better and didn't stop breathin' or have giant welts on her body after all.

We started drivin' again, and Jimmy asked me, "Why were'ya chewin' so much gum at one time anyway? Not for nothin', but I thought there was a horse in the back seat!"

Then, of course, Cassie did that big laugh'a hers, where she threw her head back, openin' her mouth so wide like she was at the dentist. She was really startin'a annoy me, and I started wonderin' why she was my best friend anyway. If she kept this up, I was gonna have'ta have it out with her once and for all.

I just shrugged my shoulders and told Jimmy, "'Cause I was nauseous and didn't wanna barf all over your new car."

Then Jimmy said, "You shoulda said somethin'. I keep saltine crackers in the glove compartment just for that reason. Cassie gets car sick all the time. You shoulda seen what she did to my old car. It had'da be condemned! Why'dd'ya think I had'da get a new one?"

Then Maureen started laughin', saying, "Oh my God! Cassie destroyed that car. It smelled so bad. Every time I had'da get in the car with her, I covered myself in the plastic apron I wear to dye my hair!"

Then Colleen started laughin' and said, "Remember the time she threw up all over poor Uncle Leo from Buffalo? I thought he was gonna die!"

Then Maureen said, "I know, and Mama never heard from him or Aunt Mae ever since! Haha!"

So Jimmy said, "Ever since that day, I never got in the car with Cassie without a can'a Lysol and a clothespin for my nose!" He opened the glove compartment, and sure enough, there was a box'a Saltine crackers, a can'a Lysol, and a plastic bag full'a clothespins.

Now everybody in the car was laughin'. Everybody but Cassie, who was still givin' me her upside-down smile. So I just looked her in the eye and said, "Yuck!"

She still wasn't smilin'. Then I tried'a inch myself away from her, gettin' nervous. It was bad enough gettin' Black Jack goo all over my new tank top, and I sure as heck didn't wanna get Cassie's yucky barf on it or anythin' else'a mine for that matter. I was gettin' nauseous just thinkin' about it and asked Jimmy if he could put the top-down again. Then like a chorus, Jimmy, Colleen, and Maureen yelled out, "Why? Are you gonna barf?"

I said, "No, it's just more fun with the top-down," hopin' they couldn't tell I was lyin'.

So he put it down, and Colleen tied her kerchief around her head, like Elizabeth Taylor in the movies, with it crisscrossed around her chin and tied in the back'a her head. Maureen, realizin' that her hair was a mess, didn't have a kerchief and started pickin' up bobby pins from the floor. She blindly twisted and tucked the bobby pins back into her beehive, which looked more like a bird's nest.

The wind felt great. It was warm and not too strong.

So I asked, "How did Cassie get cured? I mean, she's better now, right? Not barfing anymore?"

They all laughed again, and Jimmy said, "Oh, that was easy. She's not allowed ta'eat anythin' on the day of a car trip except dry toast and ginger ale, or she can't go. And in case she feels somethin' comin' on, she has a roll'a Peppermint Life Savers in her pocket at all times. Right, Cassie? Show her."

So Cassie, still with the upside-down smile like an umbrella top that lost its handle, took the Life Savers outta her pocket and held them up for me ta'see.

Then Jimmy said, "And in case we have'ta move to plan B, we're all ready to jump into action like trained fighter pilots. Right, team?"

Maureen and Colleen yelled back, "Right!"

Jimmy said, "As soon as Cassie feels the first hint of a barf comin' on, even before she pulls out the Life Savers, she pulls her whistle outta her left pocket and blows! Show her the whistle, Cassie."

So Cassie, lookin' like a sad puppy, pulled the whistle outta her left pocket and held it up for me ta'see. I felt like I was on a plane, watchin' the stewardess demonstrate the emergency drill in case of a crash.

Then Jimmy yelled out, "Emergency drill in effect!"

All of a sudden, Cassie started blowin' the whistle, and Jimmy immediately put the top-down on the car. At the same time, Colleen popped open the glove compartment, pullin' out a pack'a saltines and a barf bag. She handed them to Maureen, sittin' nex'ta Cassie, who was in the middle'a us. Maureen whipped a cold washcloth outta her bag that was inside a silver-insulated cold pack. She started wipin' down Cassie's face like it was covered in dirt while tyin'a plastic barf bag around her neck that looked like a lobster bib. Then she shoved a saltine cracker in Cassie's mouth while makin' her smell somethin' I later learned was called smellin' salts. Then Maureen pulled out a thermos'a ginger ale and gave Cassie a sip so she wouldn't choke on the cracker. Meanwhile, Colleen was pullin' out the can'a Lysol spray as she passed Maureen a plastic beauty parlor apron and a clothespin for her nose. Then she put one on herself. Jimmy didn't wear an apron cause he was drivin' but took the clothespin and grabbed some wet paper towels from Colleen just in case. Jimmy had the top-down then put a tape on. It was "The Lion Sleeps Tonight" by the Tokens, Cassie's favorite song. She fell asleep to it every night, and it calmed her down.

I couldn't believe it. These people were really organized. I felt like I was in an emergency room the way they showed it on TV on Ben Casey, and I knew that Maureen would really make a good nurse someday. We made it to their uncle's house in one piece, even me. I was sure they were gonna leave me on the side'a the road right next'ta the mountain'a Black Jack gum that I choked up like a giant fur ball. But they didn't. I promised myself ta'never chew Black Jack Gum again. Too messy. From now on, whenever I felt a barf attack comin' on, I wasn't gonna blow a whistle like Cassie, and I couldn't stand goin' all day on just saltines and ginger ale. I was just gonna start chewin' Big Red cinnamon gum and hope that I didn't end up in a car with somebody allergic to it.

CHAPTER 33

Superhero Alice and the Cement Pond

Their uncle's house was so far into the country that it could'a been another country. When she first told me that he had a fancy house with a giant yard and a built-in swimmin' pool, I didn't believe her, thinkin' she was pullin' one'a her braggin' routines again just like she did about Jimmy's new blue convertible. Well, I was wrong then, and I was wrong again cause it looked like a mansion. I couldn't believe that a regular kid like me from a poor block in messy Brooklyn could have such rich, high-class relatives.

I expected her uncle ta'come out lookin' like Jed Clampett from the Beverly Hillbillies, wearin' a floppy hat and carryin' a shotgun, sayin', "Howdy, y'all, how's about a dip in the cement pond?" But he didn't. I imagined her aunt lookin' like Granny with her gray bun and long dress, sayin', "You young-ins hungry? 'Cause I just wrestled up a big mess'a possum stew!" But Jed and Granny weren't there. I didn't see Jethro and Ellie-Mae either. Instead, her uncle Bob came out lookin' more like Daddy Warbucks from *Annie* without the bald head. He had on black fancy pants with a long silky white shirt. He wore black sandals with no socks and had silvery-white hair that was thick and shiny like he put V-05 on it. We were standin' in the backyard, and it had so many trees and beautiful flowers of every kind and color that I felt like I was in the Bronx Botanical Gardens. My mother and father took me there once after the Bronx Zoo. I

TWO LEFT FEET

thought about Grandma's little garden with her blue and purple snowballs and knew she'd love this place with roses of every color. It smelled like a flower shop. We climbed up to a patio that was cobblestoned and had two round glass tables with giant green umbrellas. There were lounge chairs all around, and to the side, I saw the pool. I couldn't believe it. The only time I ever saw a pool that big was in the Brooklyn Aquarium, where the seals did their magic show or at Cypress Pool where my mother took us swimmin' sometimes.

I looked over at Cassie and asked her if her relatives were rich like the Beverly Hillbillies. She just gave me her look again and said, "No, dumbbell! And they didn't strike oil in West Virginia either. This was my grandmother's house and my great-grandmother's too. It's what they call an heirloom, I think. My uncle Bob and aunt Mary live here now." She gave me the look again cause she knew what I was gonna say.

Then I asked her, "So how come you don't live here?"

She said, "Cause my mother had seven kids, dumbbell, and even though this house is big, it couldn't fit all of us. Anyway, I didn't wanna leave you all alone in Brooklyn, smarty-pants!"

Now I knew this couldn't be the real reason cause Cassie and her seven brothers and sisters were all cramped like sardines in her house, and for sure, they'd have a lot more room here. And that part about not wantin'a leave me in Brooklyn was bull! But I didn't wanna push it cause I saw she was gettin' in a mood. Anyway, just then, her aunt Mary came outta the house through a sliding glass door goin' onto the patio. I couldn't believe it. She looked like Donna Reed. She was wearin' a white skirt with a pleat in the front that came just above the knee and a cream-colored tank top that was tucked into the skirt and held together with a shiny brown belt. She was wearin' high heels the same exact color as her top and even had on a string'a white pearls around her neck! I felt like I was watchin' a movie or lookin' at the cover'a *Glamour* magazine. She was beautiful with light-blond hair in a French twist and looked a little like Grace Kelly who became a princess. I musta been standin' there with my mouth open cause Cassie gave me a quick jab in my side. I wanted'a yell ouch but bit my tongue cause her aunt was comin' over ta'say hi.

She hugged Cassie and her sisters then put her hand out for me to shake, sayin', "Welcome, Mikey. Hope you wore your suit."

I looked down at myself for a minute to check what I was wearin', thinkin' that she meant a real suit. Then I realized she meant a bathin' suit and mumbled like an idiot, "Oh yeah, sure, it's underneath."

Then she asked us if we were hungry and wanted'a eat first or go in the pool. Cassie said pool, and so did I. Her aunt poured us both a glass'a Coke and put out bowls'a chips and pretzels on a snack table by the pool. I was glad cause all I had for breakfast was Rice Krispies and half'a a banana. I knew Cassie musta been starvin' cause all she had was dry toast and ginger ale. Either she really wanted'a go in the pool, or she was really afraid'ta eat. Come'ta think of it, she did look a little skinnier. Her butt didn't pop out so much like she was carryin' a tray'a food on it, and her face didn't look like a full moon anymore. I'd have'ta compliment her later.

I couldn't swim, and Cassie couldn't either even though she bragged that she could every chance she got. The pool had a shallow side startin' at three feet and went to seven feet on the deep end. It even had a divin' board. For sure, I knew I wasn't goin' on that. I was wearin' my new yellow-and-white-striped two-piece bathin' suit that wasn't a bikini cause I'd never have the nerve to wear one'a those.

This was the first time I ever wore anythin' but a stretchy one-piece that I could keep pullin' down'ta cover my thunder thighs. Cassie had on her usual one-piece old lady black bathin' suit with the flary skirt on the bottom. Cassie's sisters both had great shapes and were lyin' on lounge chairs with their itty-bitty bikinis on. They were both wearin' big white sunglasses and slobberin' themselves all over with baby oil like chicken cutlets gettin' ready for the fryin' pan. Jimmy and Uncle Bob were sittin' at one'a the glass tables with the green umbrellas, drinkin' Rheingold beer outta the can and smokin' Marlboro cigarettes.

Cassie's aunt Mary said, "Go on, girls, get wet!"

Then she went back into the house through the glass slidin' doors. So we climbed into the pool, goin' down a little ladder with two steps. The deep side had a ladder with a lot more steps. Nobody else was in the pool. The water looked so clean and the color of turquoise. It was nice and cool but not cold. Cassie started walkin' through the three-foot water, swishin' her hands around like she was a guppy in a fishbowl. She was givin' me that know-it-all look'a hers then asked, "Do'ya want me'ta teach'ya how'ta swim?"

I was about to answer, "No thanks!" when I noticed that the skirt of her bathin' suit was all flared out around her.

She had her hand on her hip and looked like a teacup and saucer. I wanted'a sing the "I'm a Little Teapot" song and started giggling to myself.

She said, "What's so funny?"

Then all of a sudden, her cousin Alice came out onto the patio. I couldn't get over what she looked like and I just stopped dead in my tracks.

Alice was ten years old and looked like Howdy Doody if he was a girl. She had two bright red ponytails the color'a ketchup stickin' straight outta the sides'a her head, and they looked like real ponytails cause they were thick like horsehair. She had so many freckles on her face that if you played connect the dots, it would'a taken all day'ta make the map'a Ireland. Her arms and legs were white like milk, and she was skinny like a chicken. She had on a one-piece kelly-green bathin' suit, and looked like the Irish flag.

Alice waved hi to everybody then ran down to the deep end'a the pool. She was dippin' her toes in the water when Aunt Mary yelled out, "Alice, you forgot your swim gear!"

So her mother brought over a canvas bag and unzipped it. First, she pulled out a bathin' cap that was white and rubbery with a strap under the chin. Alice was tryin'a squeeze her big ponytails into it, but it was like tryin'a squeeze ten pounds'a mashed sweet patāda's into a little white pot.

It just wouldn't work. Her bright orange hair was poppin' out all over her face, and she had two ram horns stickin' outta the sides'a her head. Her mother finally took the pigtails out and piled one big pony on top'a her head, squishin' and squeezin' the cap on til the strap was so tight under her chin. She looked like she was gonna choke. Her cheeks were hangin' over the sides, and her head was so high up. She looked like a stuffed tomato that exploded in a pot. I didn't understand why she wasn't wearin' a bathin' cap that fit. It wasn't like this was her first day in the pool, right? Anyway, I was enjoyin' the show. Then she pulled these giant fins outta the bag and put'em on her feet. I looked over at Cassie and just shrugged my shoulders. Then Aunt Mary handed Alice a pair'a goggles that she put over her eyes, stretchin' a black elastic band up over her enormous head til it stopped at the back'a her head. Then if all this wasn't enough, her mother handed her this tube that she put in her mouth with a long hose goin' up in the air over her head. I thought I was watchin' a movie with Lloyd Bridges or *Twenty Thousand Leagues under the Sea*.

So Alice waddled over to the divin' board as we all watched the crazy show. She stood on the edge, bouncin' up and down a couple'a times like the Loch Ness Monster who just stopped by for a visit before she did a giant somersault dive into the air, glidin' headfirst into the water just like one'a the seals in the aquarium. I couldn't believe it! I never saw anybody swim like that in my life, and I wished that someday, it could be me too. Alice swam underwater with her hose stickin' up in the air, goin' from one end to the other in one clean stroke. I looked at Cassie with my mouth open, and she just looked mad cause her cousin was gettin' all the attention, and she wasn't.

Then like nothin' happened, Cassie asked me again, "Want me'ta teach'ya how'ta swim?"

I said to Cassie, "You're kiddin', right? If anybody's gonna teach me how'ta swim, it's gonna be her!"

So Cassie gives me one'a her looks and grabs onto the sidewall'a the pool, edgin' her way up into the four then five feet deep part. Now Cassie was taller than me, and I knew she could still stand in the five feet, but it didn't stop her from tryin'a be a show-off.

She said, "Watch this!" then let go'a the wall and made two giant splashes like a drownin' fish before grabbin' on again. Everybody was still watchin' Alice, who musta gone back and forth a hundred times already.

I looked at Cassie and wanted'a say, "Ya'call that swimmin'?" but just said, "Nice."

She knew I didn't mean it, so she tried it again, this time, lettin' go a little deeper in the water and tryin' for three strokes but just ended up lookin' like the ugly duckling tryin'a swim like a swan.

Alice was the swan, as weird as she looked, and when it came'ta swimmin', Cassie was the ugly duckling. So Cassie does her usual two strokes that were really big splashes but missed the third one and went underwater. She kept tryin'a reach the wall but was too far away since she had'da be a big show-off when she couldn't even swim. All of a sudden, her head started bobbin' up and down like we were playin' bobbin' for apples, and she looked like an apple cause her face was beet red.

Then she started screamin', "Help!" which sounded more like "Ulp" cause she was swallowin' water. Then I felt bad for her, and as everybody else started screamin', Alice swam up'ta her like a superhero who lived under the sea. I pictured the giant red A on her kelly-green bathin' suit, thinkin'a myself she's the weirdest-lookin' superhero I've ever seen. Alice's right arm grabbed Cassie under her armpits and used her left arm to swim over to the side. Cassie had both arms on the wall again but was coughin' like crazy. Maureen, the wannabe nurse, jumped off'a her lounge chair and started hittin' Cassie on the back like she was tryin'a burp a baby—a big baby. Colleen turned down the transistor radio in the middle'a "One Fine Day" by the Chiffons. She was in the middle'a harmonizing with Maureen when all the commotion broke out. She sang the low part, and Maureen sang the high part. When we all sang together, Cassie had the middle voice, and I had the highest. They all had good voices and reminded me'a the Lennon Sisters from Lawrence Welk. Anyway, Colleen stayed on the lounge chair, slowly turnin' into a human lobster but took her giant sunglasses off to see what was going on. I had'da laugh out loud cause she had big red circles under her eyes and looked like a raccoon. Then I thought'ta myself, *If she's so allergic to Black Jack Gum and anything licorice, she must be allergic to the sun too!* I just kept my fingers crossed and hoped she didn't start blowin' up in big welts cause one emergency at a time was enough.

I just kept thinkin'a myself that none'a this woulda happened if Cassie wasn't so busy bein' a show-off, tryin'a do her Esther Williams impersonation like she was gonna be able'ta do fancy dance moves in the middle'a the pool. Then superhero Alice sprang into action, rescuin' Cassie, like liquid lightning under the water. In two swift strokes, she was in the deep end'a the pool, one arm grabbing Cassie right under the trainin' bra part'a her bathin' suit, the other arm grabbin' onto the ladder. I couldn't believe what happened next cause Cassie wasn't a lightweight, even when she was bone-dry. Alice lifted Cassie's soakin' wet, teacup and saucer, black bathin' suit butt up the ladder with one hand. Now I knew she had'da be a superhero! I started imaginin' all the superhero possibilities the two'a us could do for the world. Me in the sky, and her in the sea! (That's if I actually had powers.) A big *if* since I practically gave up all hope of it anymore and even stopped thinkin' about it cause I was sure I was crazy and that it was a sin ta'think such things. I even thought about sayin' it in confession but wasn't sure how'ta say it, scared Father Voger would come around the other side'a the box and put a giant net over my head. And as my mother would'a said, "They'd cart me off'ta the loony bin!"

But somethin' about watchin' Alice in action made me think that it wasn't such a crazy idea after all. My mother also said, "Crazier things have happened!" I snapped back into reality when I heard Uncle Bob yellin'. He put his beer can down and ran over with Jimmy to help pull Cassie up the ladder. She stepped onto the concrete like a stray cat washed ashore, pantin' so hard like she just swam the English Channel. Her flary bathin' suit skirt hung down ta'her knees, water pourin' from her body like a broken johnny pump. There was a giant puddle on the ground around her, and it made her look like an umbrella turned inside out from a big wind. I wanted'a wring her out like she was on a clothesline.

Everybody helped her over to a chair, and Aunt Mary gave her a towel and a drink'a water. Alice climbed outta the pool too, but I was still in the water, hangin' onto the ladder. I felt bad and hoped Cassie was gonna be all right, but I still wanted'a try swimmin' and was waitin' ta'see if they were comin' back in the pool. Just then, like she was readin' my mind, Aunt Mary said, "Well, I guess that's enough swimming. I think we've had enough excitement for one day!"

And I wanted'a say, "Hey, but I didn't get'ta see if I could swim and be a superhero like Alice. That was Cassie's excitement, not mine. What a gyp!" But I didn't say that cause just like Father Voger, Aunt Mary woulda put the butterfly net over my head, and just like my mother said, "They'll cart you off'ta the loony bin!" So I climbed up the ladder and stepped onto the concrete where Cassie left her giant flood. I'd have'ta wait for another time ta'find out if I could swim like a fish the way Alice did.

CHAPTER 34

Queen for a Day

Well, I was thinkin' about Cassie and how she was in her uncle's beautiful big swimmin' pool, makin' believe she could swim while watchin' her superhero cousin Alice perform magic acts in the pool, and I guess I was feelin' kinda jealous (somethin' else to say in confession). Why didn't I have a rich uncle with a pool? All I had was the little square pool in the backyard that looked like a toy sandbox or a kitty litter box for cats. It was so small. My crazy cousin Mickey (like the mouse) dived in headfirst one time and needed stitches cause he cracked his head open. Not too smart. There was only six inches'a water in it. Grandma use'ta soak her feet in it while sittin' on the Adirondack chair and waterin' her snowballs. We had the bigger pool up in the country, but we weren't there all the time cause my uncle Meno had'da come home'ta work, so we went back and forth like gypsies.

My aunt Teensie watched a show called *Queen for a Day*, where they picked a lady outta the audience without her knowin' about it and said all kinds'a nice stuff about her, thankin' her for all the stuff she did for other people. Then they brought her up on the stage and sat her in a queen's chair and put a crown on her head. Then she'd start cryin' her eyes out, sayin' how she couldn't believe it and that she really didn't deserve it, but the host'a the show said she did, and different people started talkin' about all the good stuff she did for them. Then he'd announce her big prize. Well, if they had *Queen for a Day* for kids (*Princess for a Day*), for sure, I'd want my prize ta'be a giant built-in swimmin' pool with turquoise water and deep enough so you could jump in without crackin' your head open like a coconut. I don't know what wonderful things I could'a done to deserve such a prize, but if I was a superhero, I'm sure there would'a been tons. Oh, there I was, thinkin' about that again. I was either gonna have'ta get that crazy idea outta my head once and for all or give my PF Flyers another chance to prove they had magic powers just like Alice in the water and Norman with his radio. I mean, it could be possible, right? But after what happened in the hallway staircase with Mr. Guerrio and then with Angela Turso's grandfather, when I was tryin' the up, up, and away thing, I just didn't know if I had the guts ta'try it again. What else could I do? Go up on the roof and see if I could fly off like a bird? It did sound nuts, even ta'me. Anyway, there were always teenagers up there, like Cassie's sisters, lyin' on beach chairs, cookin' themselves like they did at their uncle's house. And then there was Joey Vento next door, who was about sixteen and had dog races on the roof where he took bets from all the neighborhood juvenile delinquents while his dogs ran and jumped from roof'ta roof. Just another crazy person on the block. Add him to the list.

Anyway, back to *Queen for a Day*. I could picture my aunt Teensie on that show cause she was always doin' stuff for everybody, and she worked really hard. She worked around the corner in Simpkins department store, and every time I went in there, I heard all the customers sayin' how nice and helpful she was. If I went in there ta'buy ink for my fountain pen or a new notebook, she'd pay for it herself, outta her pay, and tell me'ta buy some candy with my money. Whenever I went'ta her house, she was always cookin', cleanin', ironin', or washin' the bathroom floor. She was the only girl in the house, and like she said, with my uncle and three boy cousins— Mickey, Tommy, and Donny—the bathroom floor always smelled like a train station on account'a all those hoses! When she first said it, I didn't get it, but then when I started laughin' she said it all the time, probably cause she knew I was gonna laugh, especially when she started pointin' down towards her crotch whenever she said the word "hoses" while pinchin' her nose and makin' the "pee-you" face. It cracked me up every time.

My aunt Teensie did another job called homework, where she put pens together at home. One day, I heard my mother say, "I'm goin' over'ta Aunt Teensie's house ta'help her with her homework." I shook my head cause I couldn't believe my ears, then thought ta'myself, *Homework? Is Aunt Teensie goin'a college?* I didn't even know if she finished high school. Now I'm not sayin' that I thought she was dumb cause I'm not, and she wasn't. It's just that I heard a lotta other mothers that were her age sayin' they had'a drop outta school to work so they could help their families cause everybody was really poor after the war. Either that or they just got married really young. Then I thought, *If my mother's helping her with homework, it sure as heck can't be math and can only be one thing—dressmaking.* I'm not sayin' my mother's dumb either, but put it this way. When it came'ta long division, Grandpa was the one I ran'ta every time. He did math in his head faster than a calculator. I guess that's why he was a good businessman.

    I told my mother I was goin' over'ta help Aunt Teensie with her homework and then take the bus with her ta'cash in her billion-plaid stamps. That was another job she did. She collected'em at the A&P, Inkelbrinks Deli, where she bought her Camel cigarettes, no filter, and at the gas station when my uncle filled up his Plymouth Belvedere. As she said, "Ya'gotta pinch pennies ta'save a buck." And she always did. She never went'ta the A&P for groceries without all her coupons ready ta'go, and she made her own homemade Chinese food, chicken and shrimp chow mein, better than the restaurant on Liberty Avenue. My aunt was lickin' and stickin' those plaid stamps into those books since forever and was so excited cause she finally had enough ta'get the ceramic Christmas tree she wanted. I didn't have anythin' else ta'do today, so I figured I might as well go hang out with her. I didn't tell her that, of course, but my mother, spy that she was, asked, "How come you're going over'ta Aunt Teensie's on a Saturday instead'a playin' outside with your friends? Where's Cassie today?"

    I swear, sometimes I thought she could read my mind. I told her Cassie was at her uncle's house and didn't say anythin' about the pool cause I didn't wanna get her started about how maybe the reason I wasn't invited back again was cause I didn't behave like a nice young lady. I knew I shouldn'ta told her about the whole Black Jack Gum fiasco. I told my mother as convincingly as I could that I liked goin' over'ta Aunt Teensie's, that she was fun, and we always had a good time. And I meant it too. All right, maybe I'd rather be in a big built-in swimmin' pool, but as my mother would say, "Sometimes you gotta play with the cards you're dealt." These were my cards, and I was ready ta'play if my mother would just let me outta the house already. Anyway, as far as aunts go, Teensie was a good one, not like my Aunt Carmella. I'd never go hang out with her on a Saturday afternoon unless I wanted'a be punished for a sin I didn't commit. But she's another story.

Before I walked outta the door, my mother told me I had'da stop at the shoemaker first cause Grandpa needed new heels on his shoes again on account'a how he rocked back and forth when he walked. I was there every two months, and the shoemaker knew me by name. The heels were all worn out on the outsides cause that's where he put all his weight, and they looked like mini slidin' ponds. I grabbed the shoes and was outta the door before she could ask me ta'do anythin' else like throw the garbage, but my mother always had'da have the last word. She yelled out, "Have a nice time!" as the door slammed behind me.

I couldn't believe how hot it was. You could fry an egg on the sidewalk, like my mother always said. There were still tons a kids out, though. I guess none'a them had rich uncles either, and I suddenly wished we were up the country this weekend. My cousins complained that it was boring, but I loved it and never got tired'a countin' how many cars went by. Anyway, Sean Rafferty was in the middle'a the sidewalk with a bunch a kids around him. He was showin' off his yo-yo skills again and said that he was a runner-up in the yo-yo championship competition a'the world. Maybe some'a these dumbbells believed his story, but I knew it wasn't true. He was really amazing, and I'm sure he could'a beat every kid in Brooklyn, maybe all'a New York, but not the whole world! No way. Anyway, he never even went off'a the block. So how could his mother fly him off on a plane to someplace like Germany or Japan? And where would they get the money? Besides, I heard those kids in Japan were the best at yo-yo. I think they invented it. But on our little block, he was yo-yo champion'a the world, whether he had a gold medal around his skinny neck or not. I stopped ta'watch a couple'a his signature moves like Rock the Baby, where he swings the yo-yo back and forth in the air and Around the world, where he throws the string all the way out, then it comes back ta'make a full circle through the air. But my favorite one was Walk the Dog, when he throws the yo-yo out in front'a him, and it bounces backwards on the sidewalk like a dog on a leash.

Yeah, I guess'ya could add him ta'the list'a characters on the block. But I had'da get'ta the shoemaker and then to Aunt Teensie.

She was waitin' for me and makin' grilled-cheese-and-tomato sandwiches on rye bread. I loved that. Charlie was tryin'a drown his brother Nicky under the johnny pump, holdin' his head under til he gave up and Leja was sittin' on the stoop making pot holders. She'd be sittin' on the stoop tomorrow with a little sign that said, "Potholders for sale. Twenty-five cents," but she never sold any'a them cause everybody made their own or had a kid in their family who made'em for free. I used'ta make'em and lanyards too, where you braided skinny leather strips in different colors. We made key chains outta them or bookmarkers, but I never tried to sell'em. Nobody did—only Leja. She was crazy if she thought she was gonna make money at it. Good luck! She used'ta try and sell lemonade outside too. Sometimes people would buy a cup if they were dyin'a thirst, but she had'da lower her price to ten cents instead of a quarter. Maybe she could get away with it back in Lithuania but not here in Brooklyn. We were wise'ta her schemes. Anyway, Winston was usually out there every day givin' away Kool-Aid.

I started'a cross the street and heard Nicky yellin', "Stop! I give up!" and thought ta'myself, *It's just a matter'a time before Charlie ends up in jail. I just hope it's not for killin' Nicky or anybody else either.* I crossed the street and saw Millie DeFalco on her stoop with her kids. Sandy Matone was showin' off her Hula-Hoop skills, as usual, and Millie was noddin' and clappin' for her. She looked like a dog doin' tricks, and I was waitin' for Millie'ta throw her a bone! Sandy lived next door'ta Millie and always hung out there. Millie was really nice, and Cassie and me use'ta sit on her stoop and talk ta'her all the time. She was a Mom but younger than our mothers, so she seemed almost like an older girlfriend. We'd tell her stuff we could never tell our mothers, and she'd talk'ta us about all kinds'a stuff too, like how'ta do hair and makeup, boys, and even cookin' recipes. Sometimes we'd meet on her stoop after dinner and sit there, eatin' lemon ices and talkin' til our mothers called us in or the street lights came on. It was usually dark by then, and we watched all the little kids run up and down the block, tryin'a catch lightning bugs in empty jelly jars with tiny holes in'em so they wouldn't die. We had so much fun doin' it when we were little, but then, just kinda stopped. I guess we outgrew it, but still loved watchin' the flickerin' yellow lights go in and out. I missed doin' that.

Anyway, Millie had platinum-white hair, in a giant beehive, that went up so high it really looked like a beehive, and she put so much hairspray on it that it was so stiff like giant cotton candy. I wondered if she took all those bobby pins out before she went ta'sleep at night and didn't it feel itchy, and did her head get squished in the headboard? I wondered what her hair looked like after she washed it. I pictured it all wet, hangin' long, and straggly down her neck.

She woulda been at least six inches shorter and wouldn't'a looked like the Millie I knew at all. Did her kids even recognize her? I think she was a beautician, but I'm sure she couldn't'a done that big job all by herself! And how long did it take? I wondered how much money she spent on hairspray. Probably as much as Lena Sorento spent on Lysol, and I knew that had'da be a lot. I'd have'ta ask Cassie about Millie's hair. I'm sure she knew.

Millie asked, "Where's Cassie today?"

And before I could say anything, Sandy chimed in, "She's at her uncle's pool in Long Island."

I wasn't surprised that she knew where Cassie was, but I was glad that she wasn't there instead'a me. Is that mean? I don't know.

Millie just said, "Lucky her!"

I said, "I know," and Sandy didn't say anything.

Sandy was Cassie's friend, and I played with the two'a them together but only if Cassie was there. Sandy and me never really hung out with each other alone. I guess Cassie was our glue.

I said, "See ya later," and finally made it to the shoemaker.

The shoemaker smelled like glue and matches—well, not Guiseppe but his shop (although I never actually smelled him up close. I'm sure he smelled of it too). He stood inside a big wooden corral (like they kept horses in) and wore a big glass shield over his face—I guess ta'keep all the fiery sparks outta his eyes. When I walked in the door, he turned around ta'wave at me cause he heard the bell ring that sounded more like a loud buzzer. It was attached to the door, and a light went off; otherwise, he wouldn't know anybody came in cause it was so loud in there. I wondered how he wasn't deaf. Sparks were flyin' all over the place as he did his magic on somebody else's old shoes. I went to sit in another little wooden corral that had a swingin' door and felt like I was in an old saloon just like on *Gunsmoke*, except there wasn't any cowboys havin' a shootout, and nobody serving me a shot'a whiskey. He stopped drilling for a minute (or whatever you call it) and yelled over to me.

He said, "Hey, Michelina, how's Grandpa?"

He was one'a the only people who still called me Michelina. Most'a the teachers in school always called me Mikey, except, of course, Sister Margaret Ann. She did everythin' she could to annoy me, and everybody else for that matter.

He said, "Come on-a, le me see wha you gotta. Grandpa shoes again-a? Eh this-a cheap-a old man-a gotta buy a new shoes-a! Ma, eh least-a he keep-a me-a in-a business-a! No?" Then he laughed and laughed.

Guiseppe and Grandpa were good friends, and Grandpa liked'ta walk his broken shoes over himself so they could drink wine and talk about Sicily, but I guess Guiseppe was right, and Grandpa really was cheap and needed a new pair'a shoes cause the only ones he had left were his brown sandals, and he only wore them in the yard, on the stoop, or in the country. Well, at least he wasn't wearin' two left feet. I was the only one stupid enough ta'do that. Maybe Grandpa didn't buy new shoes cause he wanted a reason to keep goin' to the shoemaker. But if he was such good friends with Guiseppe, he could'a gone over just'ta talk ta' him without bringin' broken shoes. Come'ta think of it, he never came over to our house, and we never went to his, so maybe Grandpa did keep going there just'ta keep Guiseppe in business. No, he was too cheap! Anyway, Guiseppe fixed the shoes in about ten minutes.

He charged me fifty cents, put 'em in a brown paper bag, and said, "Look-a, just-a like-a new-a! Tell-a Grandpa, now-a he gott-a new-a shoes-a again-a, come-a take-a walk-a eh make-a nice-a visit-a! Arrividerci, Mikey. No be-a stranger!" He blew me a kiss as I walked outta the door.

I said, "Bye, Guiseppe!" as the buzzer sounded behind me.

I was walkin'a Aunt Teensie's house and realized that I was really hungry and heard my stomach growlin' like Tony the Tiger from Kellogg's Frosted Flakes. I was a block away from her house when who do I see but Esterina. She was another *gumada*'a Grandma's, and if Rosalie with the big red lips, who use'ta pinch my cheeks off, made me wanna duck behind a bush, Esterina made me wanna disappear like Casper the Friendly Ghost. She was that bad. She had giant warts all over her face that looked like raisins, and she was so big and round that she looked like she was hidin' two giant bed pillows under her housedress. But she wasn't. It was all her, and when she hugged you, it felt like you were smotherin' and couldn't breathe. Besides that (God forgive me, and I'll have'ta confess this on Saturday), she smelled so bad, like provolone cheese. I wanted'a hide, but it was too late. She saw me. I tried'ta take a deep breath and hold it, like Cassie's Supergirl cousin divin' underwater, but it didn't work.

I had'da say hello when she yelled out, "Hey, Michelina!" and wrapped me in between the giant puffy clouds'a her cheesy-smelling boobs.

I forgot. She was another person who called me Michelina. What was it with all these *gumadas* and *gumbadas*? I had'da find more friends my own age. I felt bad cause she was a nice lady and couldn't help it if she looked like an overstuffed Pillsbury Doughboy. I just wished she'd let go'a my head so I could breathe again. She held my head in between her two enormous hands like a coconut she wanted a crack. Then she started kissin' the top'a my head, callin' me "Bella! Bella!"

She finally let go'a my head, and I took a breath til I came face-to-face with her raisin face. I just prayed that she didn't make me kiss it!

"God, please," I said ta'myself. "I promise I'll never do another bad thing as long as I live! Just don't make me have'ta kiss her crater face!"

Well, I guess God heard me cause she let go'a me, and she took a step back ta'look at me, sayin', "Ma, you getta so big-a!"

I took a step back too just in case she tried'a kiss me. Then I said, "I gotta go, Esterina. My aunt's waitin' for me. I'll tell Grandma I saw you!"

I ran away as fast as my PF Flyers could take me before she had the chance ta'grab me again.

CHAPTER 35

Ralph Kramden

The Singing Bus Driver

Aunt Teensie buzzed me in, and I could hear Lisa, the German shepherd, barkin' from all the way down the hall. I guess they didn't have'ta worry about anybody robbin' their house, not with Lisa around. As soon as the door opened, she was nibbling my feet but not in a mean and devilish way like the Dobermans. No, Lisa was a good dog, the kinda dog you could pet without losin' a hand. She was smart too and knew if you were sick. She'd look up at you with her big puppy dog brown eyes and tilt her head, like she was sayin', "It's okay, you're gonna be all right." Then she'd cuddle you, restin' her head in your lap. Nothin' like the evil Dobermans.

Anyway, Aunt Teensie said, "What happened ta'ya? I thought you were comin' for lunch?"

I said, "It's a long story. You don't even wanna know!"

She said, "Okay," and shrugged her shoulders. I started'a tell her anyway about the shoemaker and Estherina, but she cut me off, askin' if I wanted a grilled cheese sandwich and some lemonade. I said okay, that I was hungry. Then I noticed that she looked like she was cryin', wipin' her eyes, and blowin' her nose. I asked her what was the matter and how come she was cryin', wonderin' why Lisa wasn't lickin' her face all up. Aunt Teensie started laughin', sayin', "I'm not cryin'. I'm peelin' onions for chicken chow mein. I wanna cook it now before we go ta'cash my plaid stamps." All of a sudden, she got so excited, like a kid on Christmas morning. She wiped her eyes, then said, "Come over here. I wanna show'ya somethin'." She pulled out the catalog and showed me the picture'a the ceramic Christmas tree, so happy that she finally had enough plaid stamps ta'get it. I couldn't believe how long she was waitin' ta'get that thing, probably since last Christmas. I couldn't believe her tongue didn't fall off yet from all that lickin'. She was what you called determined. She said'ta hurry up and eat my sandwich while she finished cookin' the vegetables. She'd throw the chicken in tonight cause it was already cooked from last night. She was home alone cause my cousins were out roamin' the streets (her words) and my uncle was at the track checkin' out a hot tip (also her words).

I sat on the couch, eatin' my grilled cheese with tomato on rye bread and drank my homemade lemonade while lookin' around at all the big cardboard boxes in the room.

Then I asked, "I thought I was gonna help'ya do homework?"

She said there wasn't time for that now cause she just wanted'a get'ta the plaid stamp cashin' place, that it was gettin' late, and we still had'da wait for the bus. "Besides," she said, "I better be back here before Uncle gets home. You know how he gets if he has'ta wait ta'eat! A big baby! And forget about if he loses at the track, you'll hear him screamin' from around the corner!"

I started'a laugh but realized it was true and suddenly felt bad for her. What was it with Italian men and their tempers? I promised myself that if I ever got married someday, it wouldn't be to an Italian—not an Irishman either cause they were drunks. (That's what Grandma said.)

I asked her if the boxes were done and full'a pens already put together, and she said that there was only one box left ta'do, and if we got back in time, I could help her finish before dinner. She really was a hard worker. She told me that the truck was comin'a pick up the homework tomorrow night, so it had'da be done by then. I couldn't believe that she only made a dollar for every thousand pens she made. It couldn't be legal, and if I ever became a lawyer, I'd arrest all'a them for makin' her work so hard.

We waited fifteen minutes for the bus on account'a it bein' the weekend. Up til I was seven or eight, my mother told me'ta put my head down and duck so I could sneak on the bus without payin' cause, as she said, "they got a lotta nerve makin' a six-year-old pay ta'ride the bus when the kid could just sit on their mother's lap for free!" Well, that mighta worked if you were talkin' about a normal-size six-year-old, but nothin' about me was normal, not even at six and especially not my size. My mother and grandma had'da buy my party dresses in the jumbo section of Bernard and Bo Peeps, and I was always so embarrassed when the saleslady walked over and said, "How may I help you ladies today?" Then she'd take one look at me, roll her eyes, and say, "I think we might have a little somethin' for you right over here, honey!" Then she'd lead us ta'the back'a the store where they hid the ugliest dresses on earth, and there was nothin' little about'em. I know she was just tryin'a be nice, but I bet she was really thinkin', *Let me show you where we keep the tents and baby elephant dresses. They're made from the finest material left over from last year when the circus was in town*! And there wasn't much'ta choose from, that's for sure. The reject dresses only came in pastel pink or yellow with lots'a extra crinoline slips underneath just in case'ya didn't look fat enough already, and they itched your legs and thighs like crazy. Of course, the cherry on top'a the cake was the big fat bow in the back'a the dress, strategically placed, so the world couldn't miss your already gigantic butt! It was like pin the tail on the donkey and your butt was the donkey. Thinkin' about it now, reminded me'a poor old Leonard Summers. We were so mean ta'him when his butt got stuck in his desk. I promised God that if I could get skinny, I'd never make fun'a a fat person again.

Well, I guess God heard me cause luckily, by the time I was ten, I started'a lose my baby fat. It musta been on account'a all the roller skatin' and street games I played, not'ta mention that my mother finally stopped spoon-feedin' me pastina with butter every single day. But of course, like a long-lost enemy, my baby fat would come back'ta haunt me over the years.

Anyway, one day, my mother tried'a sneak me on the bus, and the bus driver looked over at her, sayin', "C'mon, lady! I wasn't born yesterday! Who d'ya think you're foolin'? If that kid's six, I'll eat my hat!" He sounded just like Ralph Kramden from *The Honeymooners*. Well, he didn't eat his hat, but my mother's eyes darted back and forth from him to me while she was tryin'a decide who she wanted'a smack first. Him for makin' her pay, or me for bein' a jumbo. My mother held on to that quarter for dear life then looked at it in the palm'a her hand like she was sayin' goodbye ta'her last friend on earth. Then she gave the bus driver one last smirk before finally droppin' it into the coin collector. She watched it circle around, clinkin' and clackin', till it reached the bottom'a what looked like a gumball machine. Ralph Kramden tipped his hat at her. She gave him another look then grabbed my arm towards a seat in the front. I remember her mumblin' ta'herself, sayin' she was gonna make a complaint to the mayor's office, that she wasn't cheap, but it was a matter'a principle. If they could get away with this, what was gonna be next? Tell us what color socks ta'wear? People started'ta look at us, so she finally shut up. My mother definitely had her opinion on things and wasn't afraid'ta voice them, that's for sure. I laughed ta'myself, thinkin', *If my mother had been a teenager in the sixties, she would'a marched in Washington DC, protesting the Vietnam War and burnin' her bra! I bet the mayor would'a listened to her too!* As Archie Bunker use'ta say to Edith on *All in the Family*, "She was a real pip!"

    Thank God, Aunt Teensie didn't try'ta sneak me on the bus. Anyway, I was eleven. Picture me sittin' on her lap. They'd cart the two of us off'ta the loony bin for sure. She paid for both of us, and we sat down. She was so excited like a kid on Christmas morning, and I thought it was cause she was finally gonna get her ceramic Christmas tree, but then she told me she was gonna start sellin' Tupperware. She couldn't wait to have her first party where a bunch'a ladies came over for coffee and cake while learnin' how'ta "lock in freshness" with a variety'a containers in every size, shape, and color known'ta man. She said these containers even knew how to "burp," and I wondered if that meant you had'da feed'em a bottle like a baby. She said she was even thinkin'a servin' raw vegetables with dip. It was called somethin' like a cru d'etat and that she read it in the *Ladies' Home Journal*.

"Now I finally get to use my Lazy Susan!" she said, soundin' like somebody who just drank a gallon'a coffee. I knew what a Lazy Susan was cause it was the big prize she got the last time she cashed in her million-plaid stamps. It seemed like an awful lotta work for a little prize, but she was in such a good mood I didn't wanna ruin it for her. So I just said, "That's great!" but really wondered how she was gonna find the time to do all this stuff. Between her job at Simpkins, the pen homework, and all her chores at home, it woulda been when Uncle was at work or at the track (which basically was most'a the time). Either way, we knew that he expected dinner hot and ready on the table when he walked in the door, and I knew that even if she had ten jobs, she'd always make sure it happened.

All of a sudden, Aunt Teensie unzipped a big, plastic shoppin' bag that she kept her crocheting wool in. I forgot that she made hats too. They had these shiny plastic spangles hangin' from'em and came in any color combination the customer ordered. She was workin' on a black hat with white spangles and asked me how I liked it. I told her that it looked great, but my favorite one was the one she made for me last winter. It was off-white with rainbow-colored spangles and reminded me of a vanilla ice-cream cone with rainbow sprinkles. She sold a lotta them and only charged two dollars each.

Then she said, "I'm thinkin'a making matching pocketbooks to go with the hats. Wouldn't that be a good idea, Mikey?"

I said, "Sure, great," but was really thinkin', *She's gonna have'ta hire an army of elves to help her with all these jobs. Who was she? Wonder Woman?*

That's when I decided she really should be *Queen for a Day*, and I was gonna figure out how'da get her on the show. Maybe my mother could help me. She was still talkin' about who else she should invite to the Tupperware party when I looked up and noticed all the posters decorating the bus. They were advertisements, sayin', "Vote for Miss New York City Transit Authority." There were pictures'a girls hangin' all over the bus, each one grinnin' from ear to ear, silently beggin', "Please pick me!" Under each face was the girl's name, high school, and favorite after-school activity. They each wrote a sentence about themselves like "I love baton twirling more than anythin' on earth!"

or "I won't stop dancin' till I've danced'ta every Motown song ever written!" but the one that really cracked me up was "My goal is to swim the Atlantic Ocean and climb up the Eiffel Tower!" Wow! How desperate was she? And what a liar! She shoulda just said, "I plan'ta fly to the moon and, in my spare time, end hunger and find world peace!"

Each girl's picture was numbered from one'ta ten, and on the bottom'a the page was a phone number ta'call and vote for your favorite. I asked Aunt Teensie who her favorite was, so she looked up from her crochet work. Her eyes moved from picture to picture, glancin' at the interesting variety'a faces that came in almost as many shapes and colors as her spangled hats. There were blonds with blue eyes, dark-haired girls with brown eyes, white faces with freckles, and brown faces with curly hair. It looked like she was lookin' into a big box'a assorted Christmas cookies and couldn't decide which one she wanted. She finally lifted her head and said, "I like number four." I looked at number four who had long blond hair and teeth so white it looked like she brushed'em with the blue Grandma washed the clothes with. Her favorite activity was volleyball, but I didn't believe her cause she had every hair in place and I couldn't picture her puttin' it in a ponytail so she could play without it hangin' in her face. And anyway, she looked like one'a those girls who stomped her feet and had a hissy fit if she couldn't get her own way. In other words, a spoiled brat and not a team player. I definitely wasn't votin' for her!

The bus driver was playin' a transistor radio while singin' and tappin' along to "Meet Me on South Street" by the Orlons. He was havin' a ball, a party all by himself, but I hoped he was payin' attention to where he was goin' and keepin' his hands on the steerin' wheel. I didn't know where "South Street" was, and I didn't wanna end up there since I never heard'a one anywhere in New York City.

Aunt Teensie asked, "I wonder what kinda prize those girls win."

I said I didn't know, but whatever it was, I was sure it couldn't be as good as winnin' Miss America or *Queen for a Day*.

I laughed ta'myself, imagining the winner bein' called up'ta a stage in a large auditorium of people. She'd be so excited, her winnin' hands tremblin', slappin' herself in the face, not believin' her good luck. They'd put the crown on her head, which woulda been made'a miniature buses and trains. Then with black mascara streamin' down her face, her raccoon eyes woulda thanked the world for votin' for her.

Aunt Teensie asked me what I was laughin' at, and I just said, "Nothin', but I bet her prize would'a been somethin' really dumb, like a year's supply'a free bus and train rides ta'anyplace she wanted'a go in the five boroughs. She'd never have'ta worry about havin'ta sit on her mother's lap for a free ride!"

Aunt Teensie laughed out loud, crackin' herself up and she said, "Well, at least for a year anyway!"

We were still laughin' as I looked over ta'see the girl next'ta me singin' and tappin' her feet to "Da Doo Ron Ron" by the Crystals. I looked down at her feet and couldn't believe she was wearin' white PF Flyers with red logos on them. They were the opposite'a mine, red with white logos. I musta been starin' cause she was givin' me a dirty look like, "Take a picture. It'll last longer!" Next'ta me and the doofy girl in the apartment house, she was only the third kid I ever saw wearin'em. She noticed my sneakers then rolled her eyes at me in a real stuck-up look, like she was sayin', "You look so poor, how'd you ever get PF Flyers? You probably won'em in a contest for the lamest lookin' girl in your class!"

I was so embarrassed and didn't really know why. My face musta been turnin' red cause she gave me a smirk then turned her head away while flippin' her greasy brown hair with her fingers. Her hair was in a flip like Betty from *The Flintstones*, and her fat white headband was tryin'a keep the greasy bangs outta her eyes. I looked over at her and thought ta'myself, *I don't wanna be mean, and God forgive me for thinkin' it, but what a dog!* I knew I'd be in confession next Saturday but couldn't help it. I was wonderin' what she had'da be so stuck up about cause she was so mean and sure as heck not pretty, that's for sure! I knew I coulda beat her in a game'a rank out, endin' up with her ballin' her eyes out like a little girl, and as sure as my name was Mikey, short for Michelina, knew there was no way she could run fast in those PF Flyers, not even if they had wings on'em! I was wishin' that I could challenge her to a race, fair and square, and knew that just like Uncle's winnin' horse at the track, I'd beat her by a mile, leavin' her gaspin' for air in my dust.

All of a sudden, Aunt Teensie yelled out, "Come on, this is our stop. Get up!"

I grabbed onto the pole, tryin'a steady myself til the bus stopped cause Ralph Kramden was flyin', laughin' and singin' to that crazy song about "If you wanna be happy for the rest'a your life, get an ugly girl to marry you!" Everybody on the bus was laughin' and singin' too like it was somebody's birthday. The only thing missin' was the cake and balloons. We already had plenty'a clowns on the bus, especially Miss PF Flyers sittin' nex'ta me. She was tappin' her feet like crazy too, so when the bus finally stopped short, I went flyin', steppin' on her brand-new, spankin' clean white PF Flyers with the red logo.

Aunt Teensie was already headed for the front door, but I let out an "*Uugghh*!" silently mouthin', "I'm sorry!" I felt my arm bein' pulled outta the door and turned back ta' see the steam comin' outta her ears. Her face was beet red, and I wished she would'a run off the bus and chased after me. Then I'd know once and for all if she could run or not. But I couldn't believe what happened instead. We stepped onto the sidewalk, the doors'a the bus closed, and as Ralph Kramden started'a pull away, already tunin' up for his next song, I looked up, and there she was sittin' in the window seat. She was makin' that stupid face that kids did when they got mad. The one where you stick your thumbs in your ears and flap your fingers like an elephant while makin' yourself cross-eyed and stickin' your tongue out at the same time. I couldn't believe it! What a two-year-old! And she was tryin'a make me jealous'a her! Wow!

Aunt Teensie was already walkin' ahead and didn't notice what was going on. She heard me laughin'ta myself out loud and turned around, sayin', "You better stop doin' that, Mikey! It doesn't look good. People are gonna think you're crazy!" She sounded just like Grandma Fannie. I kept laughin', thinkin'a myself, *You have no idea!*

CHAPTER 36

Plaid Stamps

(Christmas in July)

The plaid stamp place was a zoo. Everybody and their mother was out. They musta been givin' stuff away. Aunt Teensie piled all her books on top'a the glass counter, waitin' for somebody ta'come and help her. I never saw so much junk in my life. There were shelves piled high with everythin' from kitchen dishes to CorningWare, and the floors were crowded with vacuum cleaners, bikes, and furniture. Some lady was lookin' at a glass coffee table, and I was sure she musta been savin' for that since the day she was born and probably had'da hire a U-Haul truck ta'carry all her books in. They had all kinds'a pictures and mirrors hangin' on the walls, and everythin' in the store had a brown cardboard price tag hangin' on it with a string. Some'a the glass cabinets were locked. Those were the ones with red velvet boxes full'a shiny gold watches and sparkling earrings, rings, and bracelets. It looked like a treasure chest, and I kept lookin' around for Captain Hook. But the scariest thing in the store was hangin' up on the wall right next'ta the cuckoo clocks. It was a giant deer's head, his big brown eyes bulgin' in surprise, screamin', "What happened?"

A saleslady finally came over, and she looked like the mother on *Father Knows Best*. She had short curly black hair with spit curls hangin' from her forehead and temples like upside-down question marks. I laughed ta'myself, thinkin', *That's how my hair looks the morning after my mother sets it in rags before I get'ta brush it out!* I made sure I wasn't laughin' out loud. She had glasses hangin' on a chain around her neck. There were little white pearls on the chain that perfectly matched the white pearls on her cardigan sweater. She was smilin' like she just won *Queen for a Day*. Either that, or she really loved her job.

She said, "Haaaa! Haaooww ya daawwn?" like she came from Minnesota or North Dakota, but I mighta been wrong. It coulda been Alabama.

Aunt Teensie had the catalog book open to page 95 and said, "I want item number A643, the ceramic Christmas tree."

She was so excited that her frosted pink fingernails tapped away on the glass countertop, and she was shufflin' her feet the way Lisa (the dog) did when she wanted'a go out to pee. The woman looked down from her glasses, which were now hangin' off the tip'a her nose, and raised her eyebrows in a very Mother Superior kinda way.

She said, "Aaww ya feelin' awwriight, ma'am?" (On second thought, it was definitely Alabama.)

Aunt Teensie, kinda embarrassed, just said, "Oh yeah, sure! I just can't wait'ta get my Christmas tree. I've been savin' for so long!"

I was thinkin', *Not to mention lickin*! She was gonna need a new tongue soon.

The lady said, "Let's see whatchya have, all righty?" She took the catalog away, scanning the page with her finger, sayin' "Hmmm" to herself while Aunt Teensie looked like her heart was jumpin' outta her chest. "Ya saaiid number A643, is thaat car-rect? Sew sar-ree, hunney, I dew ba-leeve we're all outa stock on thaat par-tic-a-laar eye-term at this time."

She never stopped smilin' for a minute, and I could hear my mother if she was there, sayin', "I'd like'ta wipe that smile right off'a her face! Why don't she talk English? What the heck's she sayin', anyway?"

But Aunt Teensie wasn't my mother. She just stood there with her mouth open, her big brown doe-shaped eyes starin' just like the deer on the wall.

At first, I thought, *Maybe she didn't hear her right.*

But then, all of a sudden, it was like she woke up from a trance, and just like the deer on the wall, she yelled out, "What happened!" Like a fighter knocked out in the ring, who just got a sudden whiff a smellin' salts, she was back and ready for action. "Whaddy'a mean you don't have it? You gotta have it. I been savin' since forever for that thing. One thousand two hundred and fifty-five plaid stamps. Right there in those five books. Personally licked by my tongue! Count 'em. Go ahead! Count 'em!" She was startin' ta'explode just like the Fourth'a July, and if I didn't know any better, I woulda thought she turned into my mother. Let's just say her Brooklyn was really showin'!

People started starin', and a security guard came walkin' over. "Is there a problem here, Wilma?" he said to the saleslady, who really did look like a Wilma.

"Well," said Wilma, "as eye was tryin' ta eggsplane ta thiis luvlee lady here"—she looked over at Aunt Teensie and batted her eyelashes—"we seem a be outa thaat par-tic-a-lar eye-term."

Now Aunt Teensie was mumblin'ta herself like a crazy lady and flappin' her arms like a plane tryin'a get off the ground. Then I saw her eyes wellin' up with pools'a water, and she pulled a flowered handkerchief outta her pocketbook to honk her nose.

The security guard, who looked like Fred Mertz from *I Love Lucy*, said, "There, there. Calm down, ma'am. Let's see what we can do for you." Then he asked, "Wilma, are you sure we don't have one lying around in the back somewhere? Can you please see what you can do 'cause this lady's falling apart out here!"

Wilma looked a little annoyed, playin' with her spit curls, but said, "Oohh-keey, Ralph, I'll try ma beest? She batted her eyes at us again and went in the back. Meanwhile, Aunt Teensie was wearin' out the carpet, pacin' back and forth, like she was waitin' for somebody ta'have a baby. I told her not'ta worry, that she'd find one in the back (I hoped). Well, at least she stopped cryin', and people stopped lookin' at us.

It felt like forever, but we saw Wilma come walkin' out. She was wearin' her *Queen for a Day* smile and carryin' a big brown box. Aunt Teensie started jumpin' up and down and clappin' her hands like a kid on the last day'a school. I even started clappin' my hands.

Wilma put the box on top'a the counter and said, "Weell, eesn't eet yer lucky daayy?"

Then just ta'make sure, Aunt Teensie said, "Take it outta the box. I wanna see it!"

Well, Wilma opened the box and gently pulled the Christmas tree out. And there it was! A perfect Christmas tree, green with all different color bulbs on it just like the picture in the catalog! Aunt Teensie wasn't satisfied yet. "Plug it in," she said. "I wanna make sure the bulbs light up!"

Then Ralph, the security guard, said, "Let me do the honors, little lady!"

He plugged it in, and all the bulbs lit up just like they were supposed'ta.

Aunt Teensie was cryin' again, but this time cause she said she was so happy. Wilma put the tree back in the box and collected the books'a stamps. She didn't even bother countin'em—not after all that. I think she couldn't wait'ta get rid'a us, but maybe I was wrong. She carefully put the box in a double shoppin' bag with two heavy handles, then Ralph put the bag in Aunt Teensie's hand. He started clappin', and so did Wilma. Then all of a sudden, everybody in the store was clappin' and cheerin' too! Then Aunt Teensie started cryin' again. Tears'a joy, she said. I couldn't believe that this ceramic Christmas tree meant so much'ta her! Then I wondered if she ever had a Christmas tree when she was little. My mother told me her mother died when she was really young.

Ralph said, "Too bad we couldn't wrap this up like a Christmas gift. Christmas in July, isn't that funny?" He looked Aunt Teensie in the eye and winked at her, sayin', "Well, Merry Christmas, young lady! Enjoy your gift!" just like Santa Claus talkin'ta a little girl!

I couldn't believe it! He even looked a little like Santa, and I coulda pictured him with the red suit on. Good thing she didn't sit on his lap, or I woulda flipped for sure! And then they'd take us all away to the loony bin!

We walked outta the store, and everybody was smilin' at us. It was just like she won *Queen for a Day* after all! I know that she couldn't'a been any happier—that's for sure!

She bought two doughy salted pretzels and two cans'a coke at the hot dog truck outside the store, and we both ate and drank while we waited for the bus. She asked me if I'd give her dancin' lessons for cousin Sally's surprise fortieth birthday party next week at the Knights'a Columbus hall on account'a her havin' two left feet. In shock, I looked at her feet, only ta'see two brown sandals, perfectly the same.

I said, "They look all right ta'me."

And she started laughin', sayin', "No, I mean I can't dance! I have no rhythm."

I said, "Of course, ya'have rhythm, you're Italian, and ya'come from Brooklyn! Anyway, I'm the only one dumb enough'ta wear two left feet!"

She said she heard that story from my mother, and I was surprised my mother wasn't too embarrassed ta'tell it. Then she said she liked my PF Flyers, and I told her Grandma Fannie bought'em for me.

Then she said, "Well, will'ya do it?"

I almost forgot what she meant then said, "Sure, what kinda dances do'ya wanna learn?"

She said, "Everything, especially cha-cha, the twist, and whatever else the kids these days are doin'."

I said, "Okay. Just let me know when."

She went to shake my hand and said, "Deal?"

And I said "Deal!"

She was the coolest aunt ever. The bus was comin', and then she said, "Oh, Mikey, don't get mad if I tell'ya somethin', okay?"

She sounded like my mother again, and I knew when somebody started a sentence with "don't get mad," it wasn't a good sign and usually ended up with somebody gettin' mad.

I said, "I won't. What?"

She said, "Well, when we were on the bus, your arms were rubbin' against mine, and I noticed ya'had bumpy skin on the tops'a your arms, like chicken skin. Did'ya ever notice it?"

I wanted'a say, "Well, I sure do now," but didn't. One more thing for me'ta worry about! That's all I needed! Well, at least I didn't have zits all over my face! Thank God!

I told her that I never noticed it, and she said, "Don't worry." *A little too late for that now*, I thought'ta myself. "A little cocoa butter will clear it right up. You'll see. Just rub it on every night before bed and after every bath. I got it from Avon. It's great. Here, feel how soft my arms are."

I felt them and said, "Nice," not knowin' what else'ta say, but thinkin'a myself, *Don't tell me you're sellin' Avon too!*

Then she said, "You know, Mikey, before'ya know it, you'll be a teenager and have a boyfriend, so'ya want your arms to be really soft." Then she winked at me and said, "Ya'know what I mean, right?"

I felt my face turn beet red and said, "Yeah, I guess I do."

We got on the bus. It wasn't Ralph Kramden but somebody else. We sat in the front, just like before, and Aunt Teensie was still smilin' as she carefully held her shoppin' bag in her lap like a newborn baby. She reminded me again about the dancin' lessons, and I said I wouldn't forget. I thought'ta myself, *All in all, this was a pretty good day*. She was still the coolest aunt on earth and still deserved'ta be *Queen for a Day*. I just made sure not'ta rub my arms against hers!

CHAPTER 37

The Unmentionables

I was pullin' clothes in off the line for Grandma Fannie and wonderin' how long it would take before I finally fell outta the kitchen window, crackin' my head open on the cellar door like a coconut fallin' out of a palm tree. The top'a the windowsill pressed right under my belly button just about the place a bikini bottom would be as if I'd ever have the nerve ta'wear one. One day, I'd be stretchin' my arms out just a little too far while pullin' on that frayed and raggedy old rope, losin' time in the perfect rhythm'a my routine. I'd probably be thinkin' about the girls on the TV show *Petticoat Junction*, wonderin' if they hung their unmentionables out on the line and while laughin' out loud ta'myself like the *scimunita* that I was, go down like humpty-dumpty, my scrambled brains splattered all over Grandpa's freshly painted white cellar door.

Still laughin' out loud, I'd be lying there, singin' "Since I Fell for You" by Lenny Welch, thinkin'a myself, *Great job, Mikey. You really did it this time. Then my mother's voice would shake the ground echoing like an earthquake* through the neighborhood. And the leaves on the trees would be shakin' in her aftershock, even in the one-hundred-degree summer stillness.

"Mikey, where was ya'head? What were ya thinkin'?"

"I wasn't thinkin' anythin', Ma. And you can see where my head is! I'm the egg without the yoke. Don't ya recognize me? The Cracker Jack Box without the prize, ya'know, the fortune cookie without the fortune?"

"Don't get smart with me!" she'd yell. "And get up off'a the cellar door before people start talkin'! I hope you weren't daydreamin' about flyin' again?"

Wow! I woulda thought'ta myself while tryin'a scramble'ta my two left feet. *How'd she know about that? I didn't tell her!* I hope I wasn't talkin' or flappin' around in my sleep last night while flyin' across the Atlantic Ocean, lookin' down at the pitch-black water, the crisp midnight air blowin' my imaginary super cape over my face. I hope I wasn't yellin' out loud as I waved to London Bridge, callin' "Cheerio," or when I ducked and weaved over the chocolate peaks'a the Swiss Alps tryin'a sing like Julie Andrews in *The Sound of Music*. I know that I sure as heck didn't spill the beans about my flyin' idea with big mouth Sammy or flaky Phylo! I wasn't that stupid!

All of a sudden, like gettin' smacked in the face with a giant tsunami wave, Grandma Fannie jolted me back into reality.

"Ma stupida! Wake up-a! You sleep-a! No gotta all-a day! Scimunita!"

She loved callin' me that, and I hadd'a remind myself not'ta take it personally even though some people might get self-conscious hearin' somebody call'em the Sicilian version'a dumbbell all the time. I knew she loved me. Then the fisherman (or fisher girl) in my head, reelin' in the biggest catch of a lifetime, would hit dry land faster than you could say, "Ahoy, matey!"

The only fish I reeled in that day were Grandma's peach-colored corset or (cor-say), strings flappin' in the breeze like a flag of an unknown country. Comin' in for a close second were Grandpa's sparklin' white Fruit'a the Looms long johns, and don't ask me why he was wearin' those in the middle'a a summer heat wave! I didn't even wanna think about the chafing, but it kinda explained why he walked so funny like he just got off a horse. Anyway, these were the pride and joy'a the neighborhood, at least in Grandma's mind, and she was so proud'a how white she got'em. She had it down to a science from scrubbin'em with brown soap on the washboard to soakin'em in the *biangolina* (bleach) delivered every month by Jimmy, the bleach man. That stuff smelled so strong I thought my eyeballs were gonna fall out! Peelin' onions was nothin' compared ta that, and they probably used it on the soap operas to make the actors cry on cue. Then she washed 'em in blue, which looked like the ink we had on our desks in school. We dipped our fountain pens into the little inkwells—the same one the juvenile delinquent boys use'ta dunk the ponytails'a whatever girl was sittin' in front'a them. How could anythin' so blue turn somethin' so white?

First, Grandma had'da smel'em, givin' a big sniff, then sayin', "*Aahh*!" like the doctor just told her'ta stick out her tongue, or she just took a freshly baked batch'a chocolate chip cookies outta the oven. Then, of course, she'd spray Grandpa's long johns with spray starch then iron'em. Poor Grandpa! His thighs must'a had a bad case'a rug burn on'em! Now most people don't like airin' their dirty laundry and unmentionables on the line for the world ta'see, but not Grandma. She loved havin' her unmentionables mentioned as often as possible, and if she coulda, she woulda blown a trumpet like they did in the army so that everybody would look out their kitchen windows, past all the other clotheslines and see the first-prize winners in the whole borough'a Brooklyn. The whitest, most sparklin' unmentionables in all the land! What an honor! Grandma missed the days when she could pull the clothes in off the line by herself and was sad she couldn't do it anymore on account'a the rheumatism in her shoulder so she made me her *scimunita* sidekick in her little Sicilian laundry service.

CHAPTER 38

The Bird Man

I was pullin' in the last'a Grandma's clothes, Grandpa's brown pants with the cuffs when I started laughin'ta myself, thinkin' about the time I was pullin' in Grandpa's long johns durin' a winter blizzard. Icicles were fallin' off'a them, and they were frozen stiff like an invisible Grandpa was inside'a them or maybe Caspar the Friendly Ghost.

Of course, she caught me and said, "Stupida, ma what I tell-a you 'bouta laugh-a sola-sola? [Alone] You wanna go ou crazy hous-a?"

I said, "Sorry, Grandma, no, I don't wanna go'ta the crazy house. This house is crazy enough for me!"

She gave me her look, and I started'a close the window. Then like a turtle poppin' its head back outta its shell, I stuck my head back out the window and yelled ta'her, "Wow! Do you see that? Look at all those birds! I never saw that before!"

About a hundred pigeons were flyin' over the roof'a the building across the yard, the building where Sally boy in my class, the biggest juvenile delinquent in the whole school, lived! Sister Margaret Rose hung him out on the flagpole one time on account'a he was makin' funn'a her in class cause she stuttered when she got mad. So the madder he made her, the more she stuttered.

So she said, "Yeah this-a the stupida son a Tessie around-a the corner. Poor woman no gotta luck-a. The husband run away with-a some-a putanna [whore] eh she stuck-a two sons-a one more crazy then-a the next-a!"

I said, "You mean Sally-boy in my class?"

She said, "No! I think-a the crazy brother. He keep-a all-a the birds-a on-a the roof-a in the chicken-a coop-a! He no gotta nothing-a better to do! No school-a, no work-a, just-a big-a bum-a! Vagabond-a! Grandpa wanna give-a big-a kick in da ass-a se he catch-a! Birds shit-a all over the yard-a. My snowballs too!" Then she spit on the kitchen floor for emphasis.

Grandma said, "Pleas-a you wanna do me favor, eh clos-a the window? I'm-a gett-a cold-a. You wanna I gett-a pumunia," which meant pneumonia.

"Sorry, Grandma, but how'da'ya know about the brother and the birds? Did'ya see the pigeon coop?"

She said, "Why, you writ-a book-a?"

I said, "No, but I'm just curious about the birds."

"Grandpa go up-a all-a the time-a when they gotta tar the roof-a. This bum-a gotta fool around eh mak-a big-a mess all over, the feathers all over the roof-a. Grandpa wanna get a big-a shot-a gun eh kill whole bunch-a! The birds eh the Scimunitu too! He gotta so many birds-a he open the cag-a, eh they all-a fly away. Eh he wait-a like-a stunada [another word for dumbbell] til-a they come back-a!"

I pictured him lookin' like Burt Lancaster in the *Birdman of Alcatraz* or maybe Saint Francis of Assisi, if he was lucky enough'ta have God on his side cause if Grandpa caught him, he was gonna need a lotta prayers! I kissed her goodbye and ran to leave.

She said, "You no wanna eat-a? I just-a mak-a potatoes and eggs. Grandpa justa buy-a the Italian bread."

I said, "No thanks, Grandma. I'll see'ya later."

My wheels were already turnin' like *I Love Lucy* on her next escapade. Now I'd been on the roof before but knew it was someplace I wasn't supposed'ta be, and that if Grandpa caught me up there, he'd throw me off. Then I'd really have'ta put my flyin' theory to the test. I was sure that my new PF Flyers gave me the superpower a'flyin', but I was still too chicken ta'test it out. The up, up, and away thing was one thing cause I was on the ground and I could only fall a couple'a feet, but the roof was three stories up! Still, I wanted'a see the pigeon coop. I went into the hallway and stared at myself in the big gold mirror on the wall on top'a the mahogany table with the white lace tablecloth and the green glass vase full'a artificial flowers covered in dust and reminded myself ta'find a way ta'tell Grandma that not only was the dust chokin' me, but it was a bit gaudy, even for her.

I stared so deeply into my own eyeballs like a gypsy in a crystal ball that I started goin' cross-eyed. I didn't say "Mirror, mirror on the wall, who's the biggest fool of all," as I figured out how'da get up on the roof without gettin' caught or even expect the mirror ta'talk back ta'me like the magic mirror on *Romper Room*, where Miss Mary talks to all the kids out there in television land, sayin', "I see Kathy and Patty and Johnnie and Joey" cause I knew she sure as heck wasn't gonna say my name. I watched that show every day, and every day I waited for her ta'call my name, but it never happened. I stared myself straight in the eyes sayin', "Are you a man or a mouse?" then thought about the sayin' that said "Curiosity killed the cat" and felt like I was a twin. One good and one evil and wondered who was which.

I laughed imaginin' I was Patty and Cathy, the identical cousins on *The Patty Duke Show*. Cathy was sweet and innocent and she'd never go up on the roof while Patty, the mischievous and daring one, would fly up the steps two at a time, not wastin' time talkin' to an imaginary magic mirror. Then I wished I was Bewitched or I Dream of Jeannie and could snap my fingers or just wiggle my nose and be up there without anybody seein' me.

I heard Ricky Ricardo askin' Lucy for the billionth time, "Lu-cc-eee! What crazy shenanigans goin' on inside that head'a yours now?" and I was tryin'a wipe my foggy breath off the mirror with the heel'a my hand when who comes walkin' in the front door but Bobby from the second floor, whose real name was Roberta, and she really looked a lot like Ethel Mertz with her short platinum-blond hair that she did home permanents on.

She said, "Hi, Mikey! Are you admiring yourself in the mirror?"

I said, "What?" makin' believe I didn't hear or understand her, then said, "No, I just had an eyelash in my eye."

"Well, lucky you," she said, "to have such long dark lashes. Mine are so pale blond I can't even see them!"

Then she giggled like Ethel and said, "How come you're not outside playin' with all the other kids on such a beautiful day?"

I told her that I was helpin' Grandma take the clothes off'a the line, and she said that I was such a good granddaughter, and I thought ta'myself, *Not if you knew what I was planning!*

I just said, "Okay, see ya later," and headed for the front door. I stood on the stoop for a couple'a minutes til the coast was clear then went back inside. I tiptoed into the hallway then scurried like the little rat that I was to the first staircase, makin' a dumb face at myself in the magic mirror. Of course, being the good Catholic girl that I was, I blessed myself then started creepin' up the stairs, my new PF flyers silently tappin' each step, and I was glad that Grandma invested in carpeting on the stairs. I made it up'ta the second-floor landing and took a breath. I didn't know how spies or criminals did it. I definitely didn't see a life'a crime in my future. I knew Bobby was in her house and probably watchin' her soap operas. She'd never hear me cause she wore a hearin' aid and blasted her TV. The fruit man and his wife were at the store, so I was safe til the top floor.

I got'ta the top floor and was in front'a Mr. and Mrs. Cavanaugh's apartment. They were a cute little old couple. She was a hunchback and kinda walked sideways, and he was short with suspenders that brought his pants almost up'ta his chin. Sometimes I went ta'the store for them, so if they came out, I had an excuse ta'ask if they needed anythin' from the store. Their house was so weird with boxes all over like a warehouse and stacks'a old newspapers piled six feet high all over the apartment, and I wondered how they didn't get lost in there like Alice in Wonderland walkin' in a maze. I could hear her callin' him, "John boy [like the Waltons], yoo-hoo! Where are you?" Or they were playin' hide-and-seek, and he'd yell back, "Here I am, darling, all-ee all-ee outs and free!"

In that house, you could seek, but I'm sure you'd never find, and I was scared if one'a them died, it would'a taken the Army and Navy months ta'find'em. And why did they have so many yellow old newspapers from the year'a the flood? It was like they were hidin' from the FBI or the mob (whoever they are), and then I thought that maybe they were counterfeiters and on the lam like Ma and Pa

Barker, and I started lookin' around for shotguns! Why else would they need every newspaper since the Great Depression? Hidin' evidence? Then I wondered if the tip money they gave me for goin'ta the store was even real, and could I get arrested if one day I went into Inkelbrinks to buy myself a Mary Jane handin' over a dollar from Ma and Pa Barker. Mr. Inkelbrink would hold it up'ta the light lookin' at it funny, and then say, "Wait right here a minute, little missy!" The next thing I knew, the authorities (whoever they were) woulda been carting me off'ta the big house! Wow! I stood there lookin' at their door, thinkin' I'd better find a way'ta get outta goin'ta the store for them anymore, just ta'be on the safe side, but maybe I was just imaginin' it and watchin' too much *Twilight Zone*! Hopefully, that was it!

I finally landed in front'a Beverly Hanson's door, who I babysat for sometimes. She was divorced and had five kids, so she sometimes went out with her new boyfriend. Word on the street was that he was a shady character, but what did I know? I was just a dumb kid who couldn't figure out how'ta climb up'ta the roof without gettin' caught, and anyway, on this block, he'd fit right in. Her kids were okay'ta babysit for. All I had'da do was read'em stories and give'em snacks, not like the three brothers I used'ta watch, who literally hung from the chandelier and drank outta the toilet! You couldn't pay me enough ta'watch them again—real or counterfeit money! It wasn't worth a nervous breakdown.

The linoleum on the third floor was so squeaky that I tiptoed like a clumsy ballerina runnin' from the cops. I laughed at myself as I passed the tiny mirror on the third floor, which was a little square of the big one downstairs. It was like Grandma was sayin', "The big-a mirror go by my house-a 'cause I'm-a the La-law! [Landlord] Ha ha!" I started gettin' nervous when I reached the steps ta'the roof. The door was locked, of course, with that heavy iron latch, and I could see sunlight peekin' out through the cracks'a the door. I tippy-toed up, kinda holdin' my breath, and tried'a lift the latch. It was heavy and stuck like an old jar'a honey. After a couple'a tries, I finally got it then pushed the door open with all my might, my body against the wind. Then I heard it pop. Like crackin' a safe, I was in—or about'ta step onto the moon! Make that the sun cause I could already feel the heat. Like sayin' "Open sesame!" the door flew open while I was still hangin' on. It was almost like a new ride just like the Whip and the Rockabye Baby that came down the block. My foot stepped out onto the black tarry roof, and I felt like the first man on the moon. I also wished that I was wearin' sunglasses cause I saw rainbows in front'a my eyes after comin' from the dark hallway. I felt like I was walkin' on melted black licorice and wished I wasn't wearin' my brand new PF Flyers. Hopefully, I could get'em clean and wipe away the evidence. Maybe the Cavanaughs could gimme some tips. They were good at hidin' evidence! I looked around for sunbathers like Cassie's sisters and their friends cause I knew they went up there latherin' themselves with baby oil, but I didn't see anybody, so as they say on *The Hardy Boys*, "The coast is clear!" I looked for the pigeon coops and saw two big black metal cages on the roof across the yard, and they were empty. I started'a take a few steps back, thinkin' maybe I better get outta there before Grandpa saw me and tossed me over the ledge like a fish he caught and decided'a toss back into the lake. Then I heard the other roof door open and saw Sally-boy's brother come out and walk over to the cages. I suddenly wanted'a hide but where could I go unless I jumped and I wasn't desperate enough for that yet!

He yelled over ta'me, "Hey, whad'dya doin' up here?"

I said, "Nothin'," like a real *scimunita* and wished that the sticky tar would swallow me up like quicksand.

I heard the Drifters singin' "Up on the Roof." It musta been comin' from Norman's radio, and I hoped the whole block didn't know I was up there. Then I really wished I could fly and was about ready'ta give my new PF Flyers a try when he asked, "So you like birds?"

"I guess so" was all I could think a'sayin' as I felt my feet sink into a mountain'a Black Jack Gum.

Tryin'a move away, he said, "Where'a ya'goin'? Wait, they're comin' back!"

I couldn't believe that he knew when they were comin' back like it was time for dinner, like my mother callin' me out on the stoop! I hoped he didn't yell like my mother, and I wondered if he named them and could tel'em apart.

All of a sudden, I heard'em comin' in over my head like a jumbo jet takin' off from Idlewild (which became Kennedy Airport). Instead'a flying in the shape of a V, they were goin' in circles like Lisa, the dog, when she chased her own tail. I heard The Shangri-la's singin' Leader of the Pack and wondered if the birds had a leader who said, "Come on, guys, follow me" or "Let's go. Fun time is over. Our master is waitin'!" I thought about the Alfred Hitchcock movie *The Birds* and hoped they wouldn't be evil like them or crap all over my head even though my mother said it was good luck. I'd rather chance my luck without a hundred birds doin' you know what all over my head! I started laughin' ta'myself, imaginin' them all singin' the Frank Sinatra song, "Come Fly with Me," and I'd sing back ta'them, "Fly Me to the Moon!" Haha!

Of course, he caught me laughin'a myself and yelled, "Are ya'enjoyin' the show?"

I said, "Yeah!" and smiled wonderin' if they were gonna start dancin' like Fred Astaire and Ginger Rogers.

Then they swooped over my head, makin' the sound'a baseball cards stuck in the spokes of a bike goin' down the block at fifty miles an hour. Then they flew back to his roof and kept circlin' around him like they were playin' farmer in the dell, and he was the cheese standin' alone. Then he opened the cages and they started slowin' down like they were runnin' outta steam. They circled around him a couple'a more times, slow enough that he could reach out'n tap each one like he was givin'em a high five, sayin', "Thanks for gettin' home on time, guys! Now you can get your rewards." I imagined him tellin'em, "Cause you were all such good birdies, you're gonna get ice-cream sundaes when we watch Ed Sullivan, and maybe Saturday, I'll take you all to the movies to see *The Birds* or *Birdman of Alcatraz*!"

I laughed out loud this time, and so did he. I couldn't believe it! It was amazing how they were like his kids, and I bet my mother woulda liked'ta know his secret cause she'd do anythin' ta'get us'ta listen'a her that way too. I wondered if he gave lessons.

I asked him, "Why do they come back? I mean, they're birds, and aren't they supposed'ta be free and just fly around all day doin' whatever they want? Isn't that the point'a bein' a bird?"

Now I was kinda askin' for myself just in case the bein' able'ta fly thing turned out. He put his hand on his chin, shrugged his shoulders, then smiled at me. Actually, he was kinda cute, cuter than his brother Sally-boy. If his brother was a juvenile delinquent, then he was the opposite cause anybody who could make birds wanna fly into a cage instead'a fly around heaven all day had'da be some kinda guy! No matter what Grandma said. Maybe Tessie had one bad kid who made nuns mad, but she also had one good one who took care'a birds. Maybe that was his superpower. Who knows?

He said, "What could I say? They love me!"

Then I figured, yeah, he definitely was more like St. Francis of Assisi and I had'da tell Grandma without lettin' her know I was on the roof, of course.

"Come back again tomorrow if you want," he said. "They leave around nine in the morning and come back at three."

Wow! I thought. *Like they were goin'a work or school!*

"Where'da they go all day?" I asked him, and he said, "How'da I know? I never asked em. Anyway, they're birds and free, right?"

"Right," I said.

I started'a walk away, thinkin', *I better get the heck outa here before Grandpa comes up here or my mother sends the Army out lookin' for me,* when he said, "Hey! What's your name?"

Then I wondered if I should tell him cause I didn't wanna get in trouble, but I answered, "Mikey."

He said, "Okay, Mikey, see'ya tomorrow."

I said, "I don't know. Maybe," then started'a pull my PF Flyers up and outta the feathery, tarry mess I was standin' in.

Didn't they use tar and feathers back in the old days to torture people? I think so. Anyway, this was definitely evidence, and I had'da figure out how'ta clean my shoes later. I could picture Grandpa tarrin' and featherin' me. He'd be jumpin' up and down the way he always did while pullin' his hair outta his head and cursin' in Sicilian.

He yelled out, "Bye! My name's Joey."

I was gonna say I know but didn't cause that woulda been really doofy. I just said, "Thanks!" then slowly moved my feet off'a the land mine I was standin' on. I opened the roof door and turned around. He was still wavin' at me. Yeah, he was definitely nothin' like his brother. I guess one juvenile delinquent in a family was enough. I suddenly didn't feel so sorry for Tessie.

CHAPTER 39

Dance Lessons

On Saturday after I ate a peanut-butter-and-jelly sandwich on Wonder Bread that my mother cut in half straight down the middle and not in triangles like Cassie's mother did, I went over'ta Aunt Teensie's house ta'start our dance lessons. We had grape jelly that came in a Flintstones jar, where Fred, Wilma, Barney, and Betty all hung out in their car without a bottom as their feet pedaled around Bedrock all day. I wondered if they ever ate peanut-butter-and-jelly sandwiches back then or just brontosaurus burgers. I laughed out loud lookin' at the jelly jar and wondered if they had foot doctors back then cause I'm sure their feet musta been killin' them! Too bad, they couldn't go'ta Grandma's Red Cross Shoe store where she bought my PF Flyers. They really took good care a your feet. I swallowed my milk and started'ta run out when my mother said, "Hey, where's the fire? Can't you put your glass in the sink? Do I look like a maid just like Hazel on TV?"

I said, "Sorry, Ma." I put the glass in the sink and said, "I'm goin' over'ta help Aunt Teensie with dance lessons for Aunt Sally's birthday party next week. She said she's got two left feet."

"That's crazy!" my mother said. "She's Italian and from Brooklyn!"

"That's what I said!" I told my mother.

"Okay," my mother said. "Don't forget it's Saturday, and we gotta go'ta the A&P with Grandma. Be back by three o'clock. Don't make me have'ta call'ya!"

"Okay," I said and realized it didn't gimme too much time. I flew outta the door, and ran down the block, prayin' that I was a great teacher or she was a fast learner. Both woulda been better.

I rang the bell, and Aunt Teensie buzzed me in. When she opened the door, Lisa, the German shepherd, came runnin' out like she always did. She was a good dog, always jumpin' on me but playful, not like *gumada's* Dobermans who thought my feet were lunch.

Lisa was so smart, and I think she could read minds. Guess that was her superpower, like Super Dog, and I could picture her runnin' around wearin' a cape with a big SD on it. I can't explain what she did exactly, but she just knew stuff, like the time I was with Aunt Teensie and we were walkin' her down the block. She started barkin' like crazy, pullin' on her leash so hard, that she dragged Aunt Teensie all the way across the street. As soon as we got to the other side, we heard a loud cracking sound and couldn't believe that the telephone pole came crashing down, the wires and all. We coulda been killed, electrocuted, or both.

I started yellin', "Oh my God! She saved us from becomin' toast! She's a genius!"

Another time when I was takin' my final exams and was so scared that I failed the math part, she just kept climbin' on my lap, whimperin' at me while holdin' her paws up in the air makin' the "it's okay" sign, tryin'a calm me down. Then there was the time that Aunt Teensie's friend Susie was sick with stomach cancer and didn't know it. Lisa kept jumpin' up on her, cryin' and whackin' her in the stomach.

Aunt Teensie was like, "Lisa, stop it. What's wrong with you? Tell Suzie you're sorry!" Lisa wouldn't stop, though. Not til Suzie admitted that she was havin'a lotta stomach pain for a couple'a weeks. Then Lisa started jumpin' up and down and clappin' her paws together like she was sayin', "Yeah! Now you're gettin' it! Boy, you humans are slow!" Suzie ended up goin'ta the doctor, and thank God and Lisa, the doctor caught it in time, and she was okay.

Yeah, Lisa definitely had some kinda superpower, and maybe she was a gypsy dog, if that's even a thing, and then I started wonderin' how come Uncle wasn't takin' Lisa to the track with him if dogs were even allowed in. Maybe he didn't even know about Lisa's powers cause, if he did, I'm sure he woulda been reapin' her rewards and rakin' in the big bucks! He'd be makin' so much money on Lisa he wouldn't even have'ta go'ta the track. Instead a bettin' on horses, all his buddy's down at OTB woulda been bettin' on Lisa. Then she'd be in the newspapers, on TV, and become rich and famous. They mighta ended up movin'ta Beverly Hills just like the Beverly Hillbillies, and Lisa woulda had her own doggy mansion wing, wearin' doggy sunglasses out by the cement pond and signin' autographs all day long for all'a her fans. That's if Uncle and Aunt Teensie didn't end up in the big house (jail). I wouldn't want'em'ta move away even if it meant I coulda visited them at their mansion in Beverly Hills and live like Elly May Clampett.

I laughed out loud picturin' Uncle at the track with Lisa askin' her'ta scratch her paws in the dirt one time for the number one horse, twice for the number two horse all the way up'ta how many horses were runnin'. Poor Lisa would'a been so tired if it was the number thirteen horse. Uncle would'a been wearin' his hat that he wore sideways like a banana just like Ed Norton on *The Honeymooners*, smokin' his little ginny stinker cigar and pacin' back and forth, holdin' his hands together like he was prayin'. He'd be tryin'a stay calm while askin' Lisa, "Did you say two or three? Do it again. Slower this time!" Then he'd blow his gasket all over the track, steam comin' outta his ears, while yellin' at poor Lisa in front'a all the degenerate gamblers!

Yeah, come'ta think of it, I figured I'd better keep my idea about Lisa's superpowers ta'myself—for now, anyway. It might be too dangerous for certain people ta'know. Hopefully, the right people, and the humans smart enough ta'get Lisa's messages would figure it out on their own.

Aunt Teensie was happy as a clam that we had the whole house'ta ourselves, except for Lisa who was entertaining herself in the kitchen with a hambone. My cousins were out "gallivanting" (her word), and my uncle was you know where. I laughed ta'myself again, imagining Lisa at the track wearin' one'a those visor hats collectin' bets from all the old men hidin' from their wives. I brought some'a my 45 records to play on the big Victrola in the livin' room. It was inside a cabinet with the television set and called a console. Aunt Teensie was as excited as a teenager at the senior prom and came runnin' outta the kitchen still wearin' her apron and singin' "You Can't Sit Down" by the Dovells. I started laughin', askin' where she learned that song, and she said on the radio. She loved it cause it reminded her'a how she'd be dancin'ta every song at Aunt Sally's party next week. I started prayin'ta myself, thinkin' from your mouth to God's ears. We put on American Bandstand, which was just startin'. Dick Clark came runnin' out, and all the kids circled around him like an episode'a *Wagon Train* when all the cowboys capture the one lone Indian. Then they all started applauding like trained seals. The boys wore their big pompadour hairdos just like Ricky Nelson on *Ozzie and Harriet*, and I'm sure they musta been in front'a the mirror for at least three hours til they used every drop'a Alberto VO5 or Brylcream that they could find. They'd twist and shape their hair just like grandma rollin' out pizza dough and wouldn't stop til it looked like a stuffed animal was sittin' on top a their heads. The girls wore poodle skirts and their cashmere sweaters were on backwards, so the pearl buttons traveled up and down their spines. Just like Mary on *The Donna Reed Show*. They also wore ugly saddle shoes that were half brown, half white and looked so much like bowlin' shoes, I almost expected them ta'be carryin' bowlin' balls.

If the boys took three hours on their hair, the girls musta taken only three minutes. They all had ponytails and musta run outta the house so they wouldn't miss the show cause they were late waitin' for their stupid boyfriends. The first song they played was "Easier Said than Done" by the Essex, and I hoped they weren't talkin' about me bein' able'ta teach Aunt Teensie how'ta dance. All the kids ran into the middle'a the dance floor and started doin' the jerk.

I yelled out, "Jerk?" askin' a question, and Aunt Teensie answered, sayin', "What, I'm not even dancin' yet!"

I said, "No, not you. The dance. Stupid!"

Then she said, "Now you're callin' me stupid? That's not nice, Mikey. I'm ya aunt, ya know."

I started laughin' and said, "No! They're stupid! Don't look at them. Just follow me. Do what I do! We can do the mashed patāda's to this."

Then, of course, she said, "Oh, good cause you know I make great mashed patāda's with lots'a milk and butter. Uncle loves'em!"

I felt like I was talkin'ta Gracie of George Burns and his wife, Gracie Allen. Now I knew for sure that "Easier Said than Done" was the perfect song ta'start our lesson, and I hoped that it wasn't our theme song. So I started movin' around doin' the mashed patāda's and told her'ta copy what I did. Well, she started flappin' her arms and wigglin' her feet like a baby ostrich tryin'a crack outta its shell.

I said, "No. Like this. Like you're tryin'a stomp out cigarette butts!"

Then she said, "But that's what we have ashtrays for!"

This was gonna be harder than I thought. We tried it again, and this time, she looked like she was killin' cockroaches with her feet and swattin' flies with her hands.

I started thinkin'a myself that maybe she really did have two left feet when I realized the song was over. Now all the kids had'da rate the song, and of course, some stupid girl gave it only a five, sayin' it had a good beat, but she couldn't dance to it.

I yelled out, "Of course, ya can't dance to it, ya moron, ya have two left feet! Crazy!"

Well, Aunt Teensie's eyes started wellin' up like giant pools'a chocolate milk, and she started cryin', "I told ya I had two left feet! I knew I was hopeless!"

I said, "No! Not you! Her!"

Thank God, the song was over, and they started playin' "The Peppermint Twist" by Joey Dee and The Starliters. I grabbed her arm while she was still honkin' her nose and said, "Come on, you could do this. It's the 'Peppermint Twist'!"

So she went runnin' into the kitchen, and Lisa started barkin'.

I said, "Whad'dy'ya doin'?"

She said, "Lookin' for some peppermints. I know there's some in the drawer here!"

"Oh boy!" I told her she didn't need peppermints and ta'just follow me.

She said, "I thought Chubby Checker was the twist?"

I said, "Yeah, but this is a little different. When they say one-two-three-kick, just kick your heel backward. It's easy!"

Well, what could I say? I suddenly knew what a wild bronco looked like kickin' and screamin' its way outta the corral!

By now, Lisa was dancin' with us, and I have'ta say, this dog amazed me with her talents. Lisa was really good at "The Peppermint Twist," especially the one-two-three-kick part. We were laughin' at Lisa when I noticed the clock. It was almost two, and I knew I hadda hurry, or suffer the wrath'a Lucy and Fannie. I reminded myself that I needed'a start spendin' more time with people my own age when "The Locomotion" by Little Eva came on.

I grabbed her hand and said, "Come on, I love this song! It's 'The Locomotion'!"

"Like a train," she said. "But who makes up these crazy dances?"

I told her I didn't know and ta'just follow what Little Eva says. First, jump up, then back. I started'a laugh cause she looked more like the Easter Bunny doin' the bunny hop. On the other hand, Lisa was doing a really good job with the locomotion, hoppin' on her two back paws, her two front ones out in front'a her like she was at the beauty parlor gettin' her nails done.

I almost said, "Do what Lisa's doin'," but stopped myself cause I could hear her sayin', "Now a dog's gotta teach me'ta dance? I guess I'm gonna need four feet before I could dance!" I thought ta'myself, *Don't feel so bad. Lisa has two left feet too. Lucky for her, she also has two rights*! But I had enough sense not'ta say it out loud.

Lisa started clappin' her paws together, and I think I saw her scratch her paws ten times on the carpet, givin' the song a ten rating. I guess she really liked it!

I said, "Let's shut the TV and put a record on."

I put on "Everybody Likes to Cha Cha Cha" by Sam Cooke and told her she could definitely do this one. "I'll lead you."

I grabbed her hands and started countin' out loud, "One, two, cha, cha, cha," movin' my feet back and forth to the music, and a miracle happened! She started doin' it and was really good too like Cyd Charisse! I don't know who was more surprised, her or me. Lisa looked so cute dancin' nex'ta us as she counted, "One, two, cha, cha, cha," in doggy barks and smilin' her big toothy grin at Aunt Teensie, givin' her the okay sign with her right front paw.

Aunt Teensie was so good at the cha-cha that she wanted'a dance'ta another song, so I put on "Foolish Little Girl" by the Shirelles and hoped the Shirelles weren't talkin' about me! Well, she scored another ten, and so did Lisa. I looked at the clock, and it was already two thirty. I told her I hadda leave ta'go shoppin' with Grandma and my mother, or I'd really be a foolish little girl.

She said okay but asked if I could come back that night ta'teach her the polka so she could dance around with Grandma the way I did when we spun around in circles without fallin' down. She said Lawrence Welk was on that night, and he was the polka king. That's all I needed was'ta jump around her livin' room doin' the polka while Lawrence Welk blew his bubbles and twirled his conductor stick in the background! Boy, my life was boring!

I asked, "What about Uncle?"

She said, "Don't worry about him. Dependin' on how he made out at the track today, he's either gonna wanna go'ta bed early cause he's aggravated or go next door'ta his friend Jim's house and get drunk on a bottle'a Grandpa's wine. Either way, he'll be outa my hair!"

Boy! She really knew him! I said okay.

Then she said, "Oh, and don't forget ta'bring 'Runaround Sue' so we could do the Lindy! I know it's your mother's favorite, and I gotta dance to it with her at Sally's party!"

I said, "Okay," wonderin' ta'myself how she knew you could do the Lindy to "Runaround Sue" but didn't wanna get into another George and Gracie conversation.

Now I not only had'da teach her the polka but also the Lindy and knew I'd be sayin' a lotta Hail Marys while on line at the A&P. Hopefully, the cha-cha wasn't the only miracle dance she could do, but I wasn't holdin' my breath. As I walked outta the door, I thought about Lisa and wished we could take her'ta Aunt Sally's party cause she'd be the life'a the party like it was her sweet sixteen! Everybody would be in shock cause not only could this dog read minds, save lives, and win at the track but could dance the cha-cha and the locomotion too! Who knew what other talents she had that I didn't even discover yet, and I'm sure she'd be in the *Guinness World Book'a Records*. I reminded myself ta'work on that as soon as I got some free time.

I knew that Lisa needed her own TV variety show like *Red Skelton Show* or *Carol Burnett Show*, and I laughed out loud just thinkin' about it! As I walked outta the door, Aunt Teensie yelled, "I'm so excited and can't wait for tonight! I'll make Jiffy Pop popcorn!" I guess Lisa was excited too cause she was doin' the polka all around the coffee table.

I ran down the block, thinkin'a myself, *Wow! That dog really is a genius and smarter than most people I know*! Then I realized that I really didn't have'ta come back ta'give Aunt Teensie dance lessons at all. She could learn any dance she wanted from Lisa! I wouldn't'a said that ta'her, though. It woulda been too mean, and anyway, I liked spendin' time with Aunt Teensie, and I think she liked spendin' time with me. It's what they called bondin' time! Who knew?

CHAPTER 40

Foffil's Mother

Aunt Sally's birthday party was a blast, and if it was the Fourth'a July, Aunt Teensie would'a been the cherry bomb on top'a the cake. She was a bigger hit than Gumba Gaspano's accordion and even better than Aunt Sally's acrobatic act. She turned heads with her cha-cha, even doin' the extra side steps where you turn your partner in and out like openin' and closin' an imaginary door. I had the honor a'bein' her partner but wished that it coulda been Lisa. That woulda snapped all their heads right off'a their tracks! Aunt Teensie did the polka with Grandma, and they spun round and round like a merry-go-round or the bettin' wheel at the feast when the guy went "Round and round she goes. Where she stops nobody knows!" She didn't trip, fall, or even throw up. She even kept up with my mother doin' the Lindy to "Runaround Sue." I never saw her so happy, not even the day she cashed in her billion-plaid stamps for her ceramic Christmas tree. She was like a kid on Christmas morning all right. I'm not sure who Santa Claus was, but I was sure glad that he finally showed up for her! All in all, it was a great night. Nobody got drunk—well, not drunk enough for the cops to show up, and that mighta been a first for my family, especially when wine was involved—Grandpa's homemade wine ta'be exact.

My mother's birthday party was another story! It always landed on the same weekend as our annual block party, the first weekend in August. Well, as if it wasn't enough that we were in the middle'a one'a the biggest heat waves since forever, we got hit with a major blackout!

So now not only were people droppin' like flies, but 'ya couldn't even find the bodies under the eggs ya' just fried on the sidewalk. Panic set in, which wasn't hard for the motley crew on my block. Everybody spent the night on the stoop or sleepin' on the fire escape while tryin'a figure out what ta'do with the mountain'a assorted meats in all our freezers. So our block party, besides bein' my mother's birthday party, turned out'ta be the biggest barbecue known'ta man. There were charcoal grills up and down the middle'a the street, and people were comin' from as far away as Ozone Park and Cypress Hills ta'see and smell who or what was bein' burned at the stake. It was like the whole world was followin' their nose or doggy snout ta'eat the biggest steak'a their lives! The neighborhood reeked'a burnin' flesh, and it was startin'a make me nauseous. It felt like ancient Rome and I was lookin' around for the Colosseum, hopin' I didn't find any vomitoriums! Yuck! I thought'a Joan of Arc and people in the electric chair, and imagined what that must'a smelled like. I reminded myself ta'become a vegetarian after this was all over.

There was a smorgasbord'a meats. Of course, we had the usual Italian stuff like sausage and peppers on the grill, and my mother's famous meatballs, but Grandma was emptyin' her freezer and pullin' out pig's feet and tripe! That's when I really wanted'a barf! Meanwhile, the Irish people had hot dogs and hamburgers, but the O'Flannagans had leftover corned beef from St. Patrick's Day and a rabbit from Christmas. Now I couldn't imagine them havin' any kinda leftovers of any kind with all the kids in their house and was surprised that they had any meat at all. We broke out the wine, and of course, they broke out the beer. The Lithuanians were grillin' kielbasa, which I liked, but was on the lookout for anythin' with eyeballs in it! Of course, they broke out the vodka and Krupnikas!

Meanwhile, Sandy Matone's father, the butcher, had a cornucopia of every meat known'ta man! When I saw him puttin' a deer on the grill that he caught while huntin' last winter, I started screamin', "Oh my God! He's cookin' Bambi!" Bambi and Buggs Bunny all in one night! I looked across the street, and Lena Sorento was sittin' in front'a her house. She set up a small card table in the street, and I didn't see any food cookin' but saw plenty'a Rheingold beer cans piled up in the shape of a pyramid, and kids were playin' kick the can. She was settin' up a little gamblin' ring where she took bets on which kid could knock down all her empty beer cans and I heard Linda Scott singin' "Don't Bet Money Honey". Nancy and Josie were on line, and so was Angela Turso's grandfather who smoked the ginny stinker cigars. Whenever he passed by, I heard Peter Paul and Mary singin' "Puff the Magic Dragon." I don't know how much she was chargin', but she was sittin' there laughin' like a hyena, throwin' money into a shopping bag. It looked like she had a pretty little racket goin' on, and I wondered why Uncle wasn't there. He was too busy throwin' another mountain'a neck bones on the grill.

I needed'a go for a walk, and of course, the johnny pump was open down the block. Everybody and their grandmother (literally) was dunkin' themselves under our little Niagara Falls just'ta cool off and keep from passin' out. Charlie was drownin' his brother Nicky as Norman's radio played "You Really Got a Hold on Me" by Smokey Robinson, and even in one-hundred-degree heat, Sandy Matone and her faithful Hula-Hoop twirled themselves into a frenzy. I passed by crazy Charlie who had poor Nicky in a headlock, screamin', "Do'ya give up?" when Norman's radio started playin' "He's a Rebel" by the Crystals.

All of a sudden, Dylan Connor started screamin', "Hey, everybody, they're givin' away ice cream in the ice-cream parlor!"

So just like when all the kids ran for Winston's latest snack, every kid was runnin' to the ice-cream parlor. Angela Turso was runnin' past me with Clare O'Flannagan, so I kicked up my PF Flyers, and they ate my dust. I was imaginin' a river'a rainbow-colored milk shootin' outta the ice-cream parlor like an oil well, but the only thing I saw was a long line'a sweaty, thirsty kids. Guess it was all the salty meat. Now Clare and Angela were standin' nex'ta me, and Clare was sayin', "I hope they still have chocolate," and I was thinkin', *Yeah, more like chocolate milk!*

Angela said, "I want tutti-frutti," and I thought, *Of course, ya do cause you're so fruity!* I looked behind me, and it was Norman. I asked him if he liked ice cream, which was a really stupid question, and he said, "Oh yeah! My favorite is pistachio! Do they have pistachio?"

I said, "I hope so, Norman, cause that's my favorite too!"

Then Norman's radio, which luckily had batteries in it, started givin' the weather report.

"Sorry, folks. No relief in sight. Try'ta stay cool. Go under the johnny pump and eat some ice cream before it all melts. Hope the power comes back on soon!"

I looked at Norman and said, "We all knew that already."

He said, "I know. Sometimes this radio is useless."

Now I wondered if he knew it had magical powers too. They finally started lettin' kids in, and of course, Charlie was up ahead like a dirty water rat tryin'a push his way'ta the front. Norman's radio started playin' "Another Saturday Night" by Sam Cooke, and I thought, *If this is just another Saturday night, I'll eat my hat (if I had one)!*

All of a sudden, I heard Clare yell out'ta Angela, "Look, it's Foffil's mother!"

Before I could say, "Who's Foffil's mother?" I felt her onion breath on my neck. *Uh-oh*, I thought. This had a strange resemblance to Rock and Roll, and so did Foffil's mother, except she was bigger and scarier, if ya'could imagine that. As I was tryin'a figure out what was goin' on, I heard Gus, the owner, say'ta Charlie, "Hurry up and make up ya'mind already! I don't have all night. I'm standin' in a river'a strawberry ice cream here! There's a million kids behind'ya. Stop doin' eeny-meeny-miny-moe, or I'll throw'ya ass'ta the curb!"

Charlie, Charlie, Charlie! Always causin' a problem! Meanwhile, Norman's radio sang "Tell Him" by the Exciters.

Gettin back'ta my big dilemma, Foffil's mother yelled out, "I know what you did to my son!" And of course, she was breathin' down my neck while wimpy Clare and Angela tried'a back up into the crowd—figures. I was the innocent one in whatever crime they committed, and I was the one takin' all the heat! And it was smokin' hot! Again, she yelled in my face, "I know what you did to my son!" And before I could mouth the words, "Lady [and she was no lady], I don't even know your son!" I felt myself two feet off'a the ground, and noticed for the first time the beautiful octagon-patterned tiles on the ice-cream parlor floor. If I got outta this alive, I'd have'ta compliment Gus on it. I didn't have the time or guts ta'scream "Help," and was outside on the sidewalk before I knew it. I heard Norman ask for pistachio while the two traitors who crawled outta the woodwork yelled out, "We'll go get help!"

Thanks a lot, I thought. *It's the least' ya could do*!

Well, if Rock and Roll was six feet tall, she had'da be at least seven. And she was big like a bear or a football player with real bushy gray hair and a wild look in her eyes, kinda like Rock and Roll. I wondered if they were related. This wasn't the time ta'ask. She grabbed me by the collar'a my white tank top, which didn't have a collar, and I was wigglin' around like a lobster, tryin' not'ta get dropped into the big pot'a boilin' water. I was starin' up at that big scary face with my mouth and eyeballs wide open as I flapped my arms like I was doin' the doggy paddle in Uncle Bob's beautiful pool;—I wish.

All of a sudden, I heard Trini Lopez singin' "If I Had a Hammer" as Norman's voice echoed in my ear. "Leave my friend alone. Let go of her now!" I said.

Foffil didn't loosen her grip and hung onto me like I was her catch'a the day—her first prize, blue-ribbon winner in whatever crazy game she played in her mind. Maybe I was the only pair'a size 16 sneakers in the bottom'a Cheap John's treasure chest'a shoes. Either way, I was hers, and she wasn't lettin' go! Then I felt Norman grab my arm to pull me away and realized my blouse was practically hangin' off! Finally, I saw her look over at Norman like she just realized he was there and somethin' changed. She turned that ugly head'a hers and crinkled her eyebrows as if ta'say, "Can you actually be stronger than me?" And thank God that Norman was. He let out a yell almost like a lion's roar, screamin', "Let her go, you beast!"

All of a sudden, my feet were on the ground again, and I was pullin' my tank top back up. Norman screamed, "You better run as fast as your big fat feet will take you! Stay away from my friend!" Then Norman's radio started blastin' "Runaway" by Del Shannon. I heard her thunderin' paws echoin' down the block before I saw that enormous body fleein' like the last dinosaur on earth. Then Norman, my newfound friend, superhero, and protector, just like Clark Kent turnin' into Superman, patted my arm as we both steadied ourselves in her aftershock.

CHAPTER 41

The Italian Olympics

I was still standin' there with Norman, who was covered in melted pistachio ice cream, when Clare and Angela, the two rats, came runnin' across the street with my father. The story goes that when they ran over to the stoop and told my father what happened, he dropped his glass'a wine like a hot pa'ta'da, spillin' Grandpa's nectar'a the gods all over the stoop. Then he sprinted like he was in the Italian Olympics, first stretchin' his fingers to his toes, then yellin' out "Hup!" like an Italian soldier runnin' from the Nazis. Then he jumped up, and like lightning, flew down the block towards Liberty Avenue. I guess I got it from him.

The Crystals were singin' "Then He Kissed Me" on Norman's radio when my father ran up'ta me, and instead'a listenin' ta'the song, didn't kiss me but gave me a slap in the face! Between the three of us, I don't know who was more surprised. I think he shocked himself, and I was like, "Whad'dy'ya hittin' me for?" This was the first and only time my father ever slapped me, and he was basically a big wimp. He'd make believe he was whackin' me in the butt, like with Rock and Roll, but it was mostly just for show so he wouldn't look like a wimp in front'a my mother. She was the one who really let us have it. Like she always said, "I'll fix your wagon!" which I never understood.

So my father just said, in his Ricky Ricardo accent, who was Cuban but kinda sounded like my father, "When somebody hit-a you, ma you gotta hit-a back-a! Capeesha?"

I almost answered him back in his accent but figured this wasn't the right time'ta make fun'a him. I just said, "But, Daddy, did'ya see what she looked like?"

Then all of a sudden, he started motioning like he was boxin', shufflin' his feet, circlin' around Norman in an imaginary boxin' ring. He was tryin'a take a swing at Norman, the gentle giant panda bear, and he looked like Barney Fife from *The Andy Griffith Show*. I asked him what he was doin', and he started wavin' his pointer finger in Norman's face, callin' him all kinds'a crazy Napolitano curse words that I know he was makin' up on the spot. There was one about he should eat a dog, which sounded a lot scarier in Napolitan-ish. Now I was hopin' that he wasn't puttin' a *malocchio* on Norman, but I didn't think so cause he wasn't Sicilian, and I never saw him do it before. Poor, sweet Norman just stood there, lickin' his sticky green fingers and smilin' his big innocent grin as he tapped his feet to "One Fine Day" by the Chiffons. Boy, his radio played great music, but I think maybe it was time for a battery change cause it was startin'a get mixed up. If this was "One Fine Day," I was still waitin' for the fine part.

I said, "Daddy, Norman didn't do anythin' wrong. He's the one who got the monster off'a me!"

Then Norman said, "You're my friend, right?"

And I answered, "Yes, Norman, I'm your friend." And I meant it. Who knew? So as the smoke stopped shootin' outta my father's ears like Vesuvius erupting, he started slowin' down his fancy footwork and the Napolitano curse words stopped flyin' outta his mouth at a hundred miles an hour! So he said in his special way, "Ma-he help-a you?"

And I said, "Yeah, Dad, he help-a me." I couldn't help it, and he didn't even notice I was makin' fun'na him.

So my father started blessin' himself, prayin' to the Madonna, and knelt on the sidewalk, tryin'a kiss Norman's hands! He didn't even care that they were all sticky with melted pistachio ice cream. Norman just grinned from ear'ta'ear as I said, "Daddy, whad'dy'ya doin'? He's not the pope!"

Then we all started laughin' and walkin' back up the block to my mother's birthday party/block party/BBQ in a black out/heat wave, which was already in progress and, from the sound'a things, was in full swing. My father asked if we both wanted ice cream from the ice cream parlor, and I said no, that it was all melted by now.

He said, "No worry. After this-a black-out-a finish-a, we go Vesuvius Restaurant-a, eh I buy-a you Spumoni eh Tortoni Italiana ice-a cream-a. The good-a stuff-a you like-a, okay?"

Then he did that thing he always did when he swiped his right thumb across my cheek like a windshield wiper. Maybe he was tryin'a wipe the slap away. As we walked down the block, we saw and heard that the blackout barbecue, my mother's birthday party, was turnin' into a big bordello wild and crazy party. It was very appropriate that Norman's radio was playin' "Norman" by Sue Thompson in his honor. He sure deserved it, and he was so happy'ta be invited ta'my mother's birthday party. Let's see how that goes! I had enough excitement for one night already!

CHAPTER 42

The Bordello

The air smelled sour like a mixture'a onions, sweat, and exhaustion. Every piece'a meat was cooked, burned'ta a crisp, and every belly swelled'ta the rim. The streets and sidewalks were wet like a scene from *Dancing in the Rain* as the johnny pump spit out its final performance'a the night. Everything was cooler, below the hundred-degree mark, and I wondered how long I was gone. It was like the whole Foffil adventure aged me somehow. All the kids were runnin' up'ta me askin' what happened and tryin'a get the scoop, but I just wasn't in the mood for their amateur news reportin'. I walked towards my house with my father and faithful newfound sidekick Norman, the three of us like the Three Musketeers, returnin' from a victorious battle.

The streets were pitch black, except for the orange glow'a the charcoals that did a hard day's work and a thousand lightning bugs puttin' on a show like the northern lights. It was amazing! They formed a blanket in the sky just above our heads, flickerin' ta'the music for my mother's birthday party! They didn't bite or fly in your ear, except'ta whisper that you were playin' their favorite song. The Night has a 1000 Eyes by Bobby Vee. They were just the light show!

My mother, on the other hand, was puttin' on quite a floor show'a her own. It wasn't disgusting like Vicky and Lilly's but scary just the same. I don't know how much'a Grandpa's wine she drank, but I never saw her like that before. Maybe she was too busy cookin' and didn't eat, or maybe he just concocted another crazy batch, but she was drunk as a skunk. Aunt Sally brought her transistor radio, and my mother was singin' and dancin' to "It's My Party" by Leslie Gore. When she got'ta the "I'll cry if I want to" part, she started fake cryin' like a baby then crackin' herself up the way she always did when she thought she told a funny joke. Well, nobody was laughin' this time either, especially not my father when he caught wind and whiff'a her. I kinda felt sorry for him. I just put him through one fiasco and now he had'da deal with my mother's shenanigans. I couldn't believe it was just like Phylo, except instead'a whiskey and the Supremes, my mother chose wine and Leslie Gore. Now I knew that my family liked'ta sing, dance, and party, but I hoped this didn't mean they were alcoholics (whatever that was). I'd have'ta keep a lookout.

My aunt Teensie made my mother's favorite cake, pineapple upside down, and they waited for me'ta return from battle ta'start the festivities, but I couldn't imagine her blowin' out the candles right now and was sure that she had so much alcohol in her the cake would explode. So my father started cursin' in Napolitano again while my grandmother screamed to anybody listenin' ta'start makin' black coffee, but I didn't think there was enough black coffee in the world to make her stop singin' "It's My Party!" Leslie Gore would'a been so proud!

Meanwhile, poor Norman, our honored guest in this crazy fiasco, kept askin' me when we were gonna have the cake and if it was his favorite, chocolate. It looked like Aunt Sally had quite a few sips'a Grandpa's nectar herself, and like they said (whoever they were), she was feelin' no pain and I heard Norman's radio playin' "Sally Go Round The Roses" by The Jaynetts. So she started singin' and dancin' to her old standby, "I Know You Don't Love Me No More" by Barbara George. No music accompaniment necessary in her one-woman show! She had her signature dance moves too, kinda like the pony but in reverse, more like the swim. In our family's crazy cast'a characters, she was definitely the most colorful and always a party all by herself! She started wavin' her arms up and over her head, goin' in a backward motion like Esther Williams doin' the backstroke, lettin' loose with her signature phrase of "I don't care if I never die!" as if she was in full control'a the matter. We all, of course, believed every word she said. She was, after all, larger than life. Then she made her crazy face, like Sammy blowin' the biggest Bazooka bubblegum bubble of all time. So Aunt Sally, who always dressed in stark white from head'ta toe, like she was dipped in a gallon'a Grandma's special *biangolina* (bleach), started screamin', "Gimme' room! Get outta my way!" Mr. Clean, the white tornado, was comin' through. She was five feet nothin' but a powerhouse from the tip'a her sparklin' white headband to the tips'a her scuffed-up white sandals. It was time for her tricks and the main event.

So Sammy, for once, made himself useful and yelled out, "Clear the streets!" as he blew the whistle he always wore around his neck and probably stole from one'a the nuns. I hope he confessed it. Like Moses partin' the Red Sea (no way am I callin' Sammy Moses), everybody moved ta'the sides and gave Aunt Sally a clear path for her destruction (I meant show)! Lookin' like George, the ice cream man, or Willy, the milkman, in her white costume, she started by gettin' in position. Boy, my family was so dramatic! With one arm above her head and the other hangin' at her side, she quickly switched positions like a pair'a blinds openin' and closin', and she was off like a light switch. She started flippin' through the air like a giant spool'a white thread, rollin' up and down the middle'a the street, and weavin' her tapestry at the speed'a light. Now everybody was yellin', even Norman, who finally stopped askin' for cake and started clappin' like crazy while his radio played "Dancing in the Street" by Martha and the Vandellas. It was like a three-ring circus. My grandmother was pourin' black coffee down my mother's throat like she was spoon-feedin' a starvin' baby while Grandpa, who hid what was left'a the wine, started pullin' the few strands'a hair he had left outta his head. He did his crazy Sicilian jig while screamin', "Dam-a crazy family-damag-a all-a bunch-a!"

In ring two, Aunt Teensie was havin' a ball, showin' off her newfound dancin' skills as she danced the mashed pa'ta'das with Lisa, the dog, who came for the meat but stayed for the floor show. Of course, everybody clapped and cheered for Lisa as Aunt Sally continued to turn herself into a human spinnin' top.

The other neighbors were havin' a ball too, and I wondered how many'a them had Grandpa's wine. Honey Dew stopped cryin' over spilled milk, and the husband who hadn't returned from the store in five years and was dancin' with Aunt Teensie instead. All of a sudden, Aunt Teensie, with her newfound confidence, went from student to dance instructor in a week, and Honey Dew asked Lisa if she could cut in on "The Mashed Pa'ta'das" by Dee Dee Sharp. Lisa just gave her the okay sign with her right front paw and started'a dance with Norman, who was so happy he saved my life cause now he was one'a us. Then Norman's radio started playin' "Heat Wave" by Martha and the Vandellas as Honey Dew tried'ta follow Aunt Teensie in the jerk, but she really couldn't dance at all and looked like she was havin'a epileptic fit. She started trippin' all over herself, and Aunt Teensie started laughin', lookin' over at me and winkin', sayin', "She really has two left feet!"

Of course, I looked down at her feet, and they looked normal ta'me, but she still kept trippin' all over herself and fallin' into Aunt Teensie who told her not'ta worry about it.

She said, "Two weeks ago, I had two left feet too and didn't think I could ever dance, and look at me now!"

Wow! She really had confidence in herself and was like a whole new Aunt Teensie. All the good stuff about her was still there, but now there was somethin' extra added in that was missin' before. It was like makin' a big pot'a sauce and forgettin' the fresh basil. Her confidence was her basil. Now I hoped that my dance lessons helped ta'get her confidence, but I think just like Dorothy in *The Wizard of Oz*, she had what she needed all along. Weird!

Then I thought about the two left feet thing and realized that it really didn't have anythin' ta'do with sneakers at all. Sometimes we all had two left feet in one way or another, dependin' on what day it was. One day, we'd be clumsy, trippin' all over ourselves, and then the next day feel like we had superpowers. It was up'ta us ta'find the courage in ourselves, just like the Cowardly Lion. Of course, it didn't hurt'ta have friends like Dorothy, the Tin Man, and the Scarecrow, who always had ya'back and gave'ya the confidence'ta believe in yourself! Wow! I couldn't believe I just thought'a all that! Maybe I wasn't such a dumbbell or *scimunita* after all. Maybe I was changin'. Maybe I was growin' up! Who knew?

Anyway, back at the circus, the Lithuanians next door were dancin' in a circle, holdin' hands and doin' their traditional folk dance, the Klumpakojis, while Princess Leja spun around in the middle, her long and thick Vermont Maid braids, like heavy ropes, slappin' everybody in the face. Then Speedy got in the middle, handin' over the bottle of vodka to Mr. Apamadis who was hangin' on'ta his own stash'a Krupnikas for safekeeping while yellin', I sveikata linksmai (meaning, to health)! Speedy started dancin' ta'the Lithuanian music, doin' what they called a Cossack kick. With his arms firmly crossed against his chest, like a two-year-old takin' a tantrum, and screamin' "No!" he started bendin' down ta'the ground, kickin' his feet straight out like a grasshopper as the others danced around him. All eyes were on Speedy who was squattin' and kickin' like a marine in basic training; the same Speedy who took an hour'ta walk down the block with his tree stump holdin' him up. What was in their vodka? Was it magic like Grandpa's wine or maybe their Krupnikas was handed down from one'a their grandfathers?

Still, Aunt Sally flipped like a beached whale. My mother was finally soberin' up, and my father was makin' her walk the curb ta'pass his inspection. Meanwhile, I found out that Grandma Fannie ate some'a my mother's world-famous meatballs cause she said she was old and didn't wanna die without ever eatin' one again. Well, I guess she was makin' up for lost time cause I heard that she was poppin' em in her mouth like popcorn in a movie theater.

We were watchin' Grandma like a lab experiment about'ta go wrong, waitin' for her'ta explode. Grandma Fannie swore'ta Michelina on her deathbed that she'd name my mother after her, or she'd never eat another meatball again. Well, of course, my mother was named Lucy cause Grandpa's mother was conjuring up her own *malocchio* if my mother wasn't named after her. This was my mother's forty-first birthday, and it was that many years since Grandma Fannie's last meatball. It was a couple'a hours since she swallowed her last meatball, and she didn't gag, throw up, turn green, or even grow warts all over her face, so we figured she was okay and that maybe Michelina's curse had finally ended for good.

So my father, who always sang at parties and feasts, got up on the stoop like it was his own private little stage and started singin' all his Napolitano songs acapella. He opened with "Mala Femmina" dedicating it ta'my mother by rollin' his eyes at her, and then shakin' his hands in the air like he was the Pope givin' a blessin' in Rome. He was about'ta start "O Sole Mio" when Grandma got up from her chair, balancin' herself by holdin' on'ta the table, then lettin' out an operatic high C note that pierced the air like an icicle. All of a sudden, everythin' else went quiet as all eyes and ears were on her. Grandpa's wine glass shattered in his hand, his bloodred wine drippin' down his white undershirt, and he just stood there in shock like a soldier gettin' hit by a sniper. It was the only time I didn't see him get mad and start yellin' in his Sicilianish. Lisa stopped dancin', and her ears stood straight up like antenna. So Grandma, in her dramatic way, sauntered over to my father's makeshift stage, and his solo performance became a duet. Now Grandma, who couldn't sing'ta save her life, and sounded like the cats she tried'ta drown with the hose in the backyard, climbed up the stoop steps, pink flowered handkerchief in hand, lookin' like Billy Holiday at the Apollo Theater. All eyes were on her, and even Grandpa, still in shock, had'da sit down. Even my father's eyes were poppin' out. Then she whispered somethin' in my father's ear and turned ta'face her amazed audience. I was waitin' for her ta'say "Maestro, please!" but the maestro wasn't there. He musta had the night off with her ten-piece band!

All of a sudden, she belted out her favorite Italian song of all time, "Arrividerci Roma," and she was amazin'—like nobody I ever heard before! My father, in between blessin' himself, sang backup harmony in all the right places just like they were rehearsin' for weeks. I could tell what was goin' through his head. "Just like Sammy!" Sammy sang like a canary with Grandpa's wine, and it looked like Lucy's meatballs turned Grandma Fannie into a Sicilian songbird. Well, the audience cheered, yelled encore, and of course, the two hams obliged, goin' through my father's repertoire, and Fannie's own bag'a tricks. My father was already plannin' how'ta take the show on the road, even if Grandma had'da be wheeled across the country! Well, my father was sayin' the rosary, thankin' the Madonna for his luck, strikin' gold twice in one lifetime!. Whoever said opportunity never knocks twice was wrong or just standin' behind the wrong door!

Well, my father and Grandma never did take the show on the road, and they never made it to the Copa either, but they were still a big hit at the block party that landed on my mother's birthday in the middle'a a heat wave and a blackout. They had plenty'a encores, nobody threw tomatoes at'em, and everybody clapped like crazy. Even Lisa, the German shepherd, who danced the night away, provin' that two left feet were a good thing, especially if you also had two rights.

Grandma still ate my mother's meatballs every Sunday, and she always gave a little solo performance after we ate. The roof didn't cave in, but she did crack the dinin' room mirror once. We tried puttin' away anythin' breakable and started duckin' for cover just like the air raid drills back in school. So it looked like Michelina's curse was finally over. Grandma could not only eat my mothers' meatballs without gaggin', but even sing like the female Caruso.

All in all, it was a great block party, and everybody started cleanin' up and goin' in. Nobody killed each other, and the cops didn't come. They couldn't'a gotten down the block even if they tried. So I was bringin' stuff into Grandma's house, and as I passed the big gold mirror in the hallway, I heard Norman's radio from outside singin' "Hello Stranger" by Barbara Lewis. The mirror was singin' to me? Wow! I didn't even drink any wine! I shook my head and went into her bathroom. Now her toilet was always runnin' like Niagara Falls and loud too, like a wild ragin' river. And as soon as I walked into the bathroom, it made a loud foghorn noise like it was sayin', "Hi! Come on in and have a seat!" Crazy! Talkin' mirrors and toilet bowls! Guess the curse'a Michelina, my namesake, was focused on me now! Great! Like my life wasn't crazy enough already! So I went back outside, and was almost scared'ta look at the hallway mirror, but then, just as I was passin' right in front of it, it started singin' "It's Up to You" by Ricky Nelson! Now, of course, the music must'a been comin' from outside, Norman's magic radio, but it really sounded like the mirror was singin'ta me! Funny! All those years watching *Romper Room* and Miss Mary's magic mirror called every other kid's name in the world but me, and now I had my own private mirror concert.

I heard a loud commotion, even louder than what was already goin'on before. Grandma was cryin', and Grandpa was yellin'.

"What happened?" I asked my mother.

"Somebody just ran down the block and stole Grandma's pocketbook from under the table!"

"What?" I asked. "Who? Where? When?"

Then I saw him runnin' away. This was it. I was up at bat, and I smelled a home run!

CHAPTER 43

Feet Do Your Stuff

(The End)

I ran onto the stoop and saw him two doors down in front'a Mrs. Maynor's house. He had Grandma's pocketbook under his arm like a football player runnin'ta make his goal. I jumped down the five steps in one giant leap without sayin' "May I?" my bloodred PF Flyers landin' firmly on the sidewalk. I didn't sprint like my father in the Italian Olympics—I just took off like a rocket into space! My mind was kinda in a fog, focusing on my criminal target up ahead but still hearing and seeing all the craziness goin' on around me like Honey Dew huggin' her long-lost husband who returned after all with gallons'a milk that he pulled along in a Radio Flyer red wagon. She jumped up and down for joy as Norman's radio blasted "He's Sure the Boy I Love" by the Crystals. I was gainin' on him and could almost see the hairs on the back'a his neck shootin' up in the air like a flag'a surrender. From the side'a my eye, I saw my hero, Norman, dancin' with the girl from around the corner, the one we use ta call monster. They were slow dancin'ta "If You Wanna Be Happy" by Jimmy Soul. The next part'a the song went "For the rest'a your life never make a pretty woman your wife," and I was happy that Norman was in love. He deserved it. I heard his magic radio follow up with "Then He Kissed Me" by the Crystals.

I was only about a yardstick behind him when I got' ta Cassie's house. Mrs. Minghe was in the street, liftin' her dress ta'show everybody the rash on her thigh, and Cassie looked like she was gonna barf up all the knockwurst and sauerbraten she ate on account'a her mother bein' German. Her cousin, Superhero Alice, was there, her long red hair braided like Vienna sausages on top'a her head as she entertained 'em all with her yodelin'. They all drank German beer and Rhine wine, except for Cassie's father who stuck with his Rheingold. Well, at least it still had a Rhein in it. I was almost up'ta the corner, and Mrs. Maluchi, as usual, was screamin' for everybody to shut up and to get "avay from her vindow" in that crazy accent'a hers. My PF Flyers were workin' hard for me now as Jackie Wilson sang "Baby Work Out", and I knew that they were worth every penny Grandma spent on 'em. I turned the corner, and he turned his head'ta look at me, fear in his eyes like a chicken about'ta get its head chopped off. *He'd better be scared*, I thought. *Nobody steals my grandmother's pocketbook and gets away with it, or my name isn't Michelina, the namesake of the one and only Sicilian* strega! I ran past Bo Peep, the glassy blue-and-green eyes'a the silent children in the window followin' me along with the horse out front. I could almost hear'em cheerin' me on, sayin' "Go, Mikey, go!" I saw him sweatin' like a pig, his blue T-shirt soaked, and I yelled out, "I'm gonna get you, ya'dirty rat!" and I felt like James Cagney. I could still hear Norman's radio blastin' "So Much In Love" by The Tymes.

I was two feet behind him when I passed Red Cross Shoes, home'a my beautiful PF Flyers, and gave'em a silent nod a'thanks. I looked across the street in front'a Cheap John's home'a my two left feet Keds, and who did I see also runnin' but the girl from the apartment house, the one with the PF Flyers. She smiled a great big doofy smile at me, then pointed down'ta her sneakers just like mine but in opposite colors. Then she gave me a great big thumbs-up sign, noddin' in a yes motion like we were both in on a secret that only we shared.

I stretched my arms out in front'a me, like a giraffe grabbin' a leaf from a tree, and I almost touched his greasy black hair. I took a giant leap upward and grabbed the back'a his shirt.

With all the superhuman strength I could muster, I jumped on him, tacklin' Grandma's pocketbook outta his slimy arms, and jumped back up without skippin' a beat. Now I was really runnin' faster than I ever had before. Doofy girl across the street was cheerin' me on as I ran across the street. This was it. I heard Elvis Presley singin' "It's Now or Never." Now or never! I yelled out as loud as I could, "Up, up, and away!" and took a giant leap up into the air as a hot breeze lifted me upward. Wow! Cheap John's roof was covered in pigeon crap! I knew it! Haha! The streets echoed with Frank Sinatra singin' "Fly Me to the Moon!"

The End

ACKNOWLEDGMENTS

This book references 1962 and 1964, but the bulk of its content and main theme takes place during the summer of 1963. I've tried to acknowledge some of the major events of the day, but none more so than the great music of 1963.

I'd like to thank all the great artists who recorded the soundtrack of my life as this book would not have been possible without them. Just like any great movie, the story comes alive with a great soundtrack behind it.

This book is mostly written in the Regional Dialect of Brooklyn, with non-standard spelling, and narrated by an eleven year old girl from Brooklyn.

ABOUT THE AUTHOR

Tomasina Decrescenzo resides in Queens, New York, and is a retired operating room nurse, as well as a single parent and grandparent. She has written poetry and short stories over the years, but this is her first full-length novel. She has spent many years enjoying painting, as well as performing in theater and comedy venues.